CAMBODIAN DANCERS
ANCIENT & MODERN

Cambodian Dancers
Ancient & Modern
George GROSLIER

Based on his original work:
Danseuses Cambodgiennes
Anciennes et Modernes

Edited by **Kent DAVIS**

Translated by **Pedro RODRÍGUEZ**

Featuring:
Le Khmérophile:
The Art and Life of George Groslier

Kent DAVIS

DatASIA
MMXII

About the Cover

"Danseuse dorée (Rôle religieux)" - "Golden Dancer (Religious Role)" by George Groslier

George Groslier (1887-1945) devoted his life to the art and culture of his birth country: Cambodia. In 1912 he assembled the magnificent graphic tribute to Cambodian dance presented in this book. His painting shows royal dancer Ratt Poss performing under a full moon, the indispensible witness of all important Cambodian festivals. See Appendix I for details.

DatASIA Press
www.CambodianDancers.com

Production Credits

With gratitude to **Nicole Rea Groslier** for her generosity,
guidance and inspiration in reissuing her father's work.

With special thanks to the extended Groslier family:
Margaret Squires, Patrick Rea; Brigitte Lequeux-Groslier and
the sons of **Gilbert Groslier: Thierry, Sylvain, Antoine, Martin, Guillaume** and **Thomas**.

Edited by **Kent Davis**

Translated by **Pedro Rodríguez**

Cultural Consultant: **Ravynn Karet-Coxen**

Cover, text and graphic design: **Kristen Tuttle**

Appendices, Bibliography and Index: **Kent Davis**

Archival assistance Cambodia: **Khlot Vibolla** and **Jade Furness**,
Bibliothèque Nationale de Phnom Penh

Archival assistance United States: **Erin Cartwright** and **Melanie Hensey**,
Manatee County Florida Interlibrary Loan Department

Additional blessings to **Paul Cravath, Sophaphan Davis, Meng Dy, Jon Dobbs,
Tom Kramer, Darryl Collins, Sam Ghazi, Colin Grafton, Denise Tranchand,
Roger Warner** and **Duffy Rutledge** for their special contributions and encouragement.

ISBN 978-1-934431-12-2 (paperback)

Copyright collective work: © 2012 DatASIA, Inc. Holmes Beach, Florida
Copyright text: © 2012 DatASIA, Inc. Holmes Beach, Florida
© 2012 Copyright all illustrations and photos (except as noted):
Nicole Rea-Groslier and all recorded heirs of George Groslier.
All rights reserved. No part of this book may be reproduced, stored in a retrieval system, or transmitted, in any form, without prior permission in writing from the publisher.

Published simultaneously in the United States and Great Britain

*Dedicated to Sacred Dancers,
past, present and future,
whose devotion preserves
the Khmer legacy.*

George Groslier
February 4, 1887 — June 18, 1945

In his home study, on December 5, 1922 George works below a bust he sculpted of his daughter Nicole. Today the bust is in her home in Sarasota, Florida.

TABLE OF CONTENTS

Preface by H.R.H. Princess Buppha Devi..IX
Foreword by Paul Cravath...XI

CAMBODIAN DANCERS - Ancient and Modern

Endorsement of His Majesty Sisowath..4
Preface by Charles Gravelle..6
The Dance Hall and the Audience..9
Education of the Royal Dancers..19
Gestures and Poses..35
Costumes and Jewels...55
Preparation and Make-Up of the Dancers..75
Their Organization..83
Their Life..91
Their History...109
Author's Note...159

APPENDIX I - Biographical Materials

Le Khmérophile: The Art and Life of George Groslier...163
Charles Gravelle - Friend of Groslier and Patron of Cambodia......................................281
Timeline: Groslier Contemporaries in Khmer studies..292
Groslier Family Voyages...295
Works by George Groslier..298

APPENDIX II - Related Articles

1913 - Cambodian Dancers in France by George Bois..303
1914 - Review of *Danseuse Cambodgiennes* by Henri Parmentier....................................322
1929 - Cambodian Theater by George Groslier..329
The Ouled Nail Dancers...348

APPENDIX III - The Future of Cambodian Dance

2010 - Dr. Paul Cravath Interviews H.R.H. Princess Buppha Devi...................................351

Bibliography..362
Index...370

Her Royal Highness Princess Buppha Devi
Prima Ballerina - The Royal Cambodian Ballet - 1962

H. R. H. Samdech Reach Botrei Preah Norodom Buppha Devi

It is my pleasure to introduce new generations of readers to this classic account of Cambodia's royal dance tradition by artist and historian, George Groslier.

Born in Phnom Penh in 1887, Groslier infused his love for the Khmer people and their culture in all of his work. In 1913, he published *Danseuses Cambodgiennes - Anciennes et Modernes*, presenting his study of classical Cambodian dance to King Norodom Sisowath, to the Cambodian people, and to the world.

Now, nearly a century later, editor and co-translator Kent Davis reintroduces this artistic work in English for the first time, including a personal glimpse of the author himself through the eyes of his daughter, Nicole Groslier.

With this book, George Groslier became the first Western scholar to document Cambodia's dance tradition. Recently, Dr. Paul Cravath affirmed and expanded this record with his award-winning work, *Earth in Flower - The Divine Mystery of the Cambodian Dance Drama*.

Both books come at an auspicious time in our history because there is now a reawakening of sacred dance in Cambodia.

My August Grandmother, Her Majesty Queen Kossamak Nearireath, entrusted me with the responsibility of perpetuating the spiritual legacy of Cambodia's Royal Ballet tradition. In 2006, I granted my first Royal Patronage to the *NKFC Conservatoire Preah Ream Buppha Devi* within the Angkor Heritage Site of our forefathers at Banteay Srey. Established by Ravynn Karet-Coxen and the Nginn Karet Foundation, this rural school is again recreating and perpetuating the sacred dance rituals of our ancestors.

George Groslier's historical account is especially joyful to read anew, knowing that our sacred Khmer heritage of dance is again blossoming through the children of Angkor at the *Conservatoire*.

May the pure dance of these children bring blessings to our King, harmony to the governance of our land and prosperity to our people.

H.R.H. Samdech Reach Botrei Preah Ream
Norodom Buppha Devi

Earth in Flower
The Divine Mystery of the
Cambodian Dance Drama

Paul Cravath

FOREWORD

The significance of George Groslier's 1913 text and the primary justification for this auspicious translation into English lies in the fact that it is the first commentary in any language—Asian or European—on one of the world's most refined performing arts whose roots stretch to antiquity.

As a court- and temple-based tradition, Cambodian dance can be traced to the seventh century and by the thirteenth had achieved the zenith of its refulgence in the Angkorean kingdom. By the early twentieth century when Groslier experienced Cambodian dance, control of the royal troupe (consisting of some 70 dancers) remained one of the few prerogatives available to an aging king in a small land beset by the demands of a European colonial overlord.

In the early 20th century, as in previous eras, the royal dancers could rarely be viewed by anyone and then only at the king's invitation. Groslier composed this work based on seeing just three evening performances (for the king's birthday) and three short "supplications" performed in the throne room. Fortunately he was able to consult with palace officials and a former dance teacher as well as spend considerable time sketching dance students in rehearsal and at rest. As a young, 25 year-old French painter with a passion for the dance, Groslier remained a palace outsider, but his book received the imprimatur of King Sisowath and the approbation of high French officials.

Why? Because *Danseuses Cambodgiennes* was an impressive achievement. In addition to its many wonderful drawings, the text drew upon the documentation of late 19th century scholarship and early 20th century epigraphic translations. His eight chapters delineate the major topics deserving scrutiny and into them he poured a myriad of detail.

Today some may question certain theories Groslier accepted or even espoused, but the specific details that he noted with a keen eye remain invaluable to our understanding of what the dance has been and how we perceive its meaning. For example, Groslier described the use of wires to suspend dancers mid-air during one of the palace performances he viewed. Today if one proposed suspending Cambodian *apsaras* or other characters mid-air on wires, any modern dance teacher would be more than skeptical. Moreover, any dancer who had never read *Danseuses Cambodgiennes* would certainly deny that flying on wires was ever a component of Khmer dance drama. Still, Groslier saw it in the palace and this recounting is merely one instance of the extraordinary value of his text as history. Today all scholarship concerning the performing arts in Cambodia begins with Groslier.

In the 1970s when I began my study that culminated in *Earth in Flower: the Divine Mystery of the Cambodian Dance Drama*, Groslier's 6-month project served as my foundation. This was inevitable because few French colonial scholars before Groslier even mentioned dance in their analyses of Cambodian culture or history. After his 1913 publication no one in any language wrote comprehensively on the subject, with the most detailed work being Sappho Marchal's 1926 illustrated booklet *Danses Cambodgiennes* (which was expanded to 95 pages when it was republished for the 1931 Colonial Exhibition). This dearth of information inspired my 10-year effort to make *Earth in Flower* a more comprehensive analysis of this sacred art.

Today I am pleased to note that Cambodian dance scholarship has continued to evolve with great depth and perception, and modern works increasingly address the profound dimensions discernible in this ancient but vital art form.

Until the present translation, *Danseuses Cambodgiennes* remained an extremely rare text, nearly impossible to procure except by loan from one of the few libraries possessing a copy. In 1975 I was able to borrow the book from the National Library in Phnom Penh which I then had photocopied onto the stiff paper used in that era. The original was the only copy of the text I ever heard about in Cambodia. Groslier's frontispiece recorded 30 copies printed; an electronic search of libraries today indicates only 46 copies available. The present translation fortuitously expands the accessibility of Groslier's work and makes it available in the English-speaking world for the first time.

Cambodian Dancers was written and illustrated by a painter who, apart from short articles more than a decade later, never wrote at length on the dance again. But we twenty-first century writers who share his reverence for Khmer dance and are sensitive to its near miraculous survival over the centuries, are as profoundly grateful to George Groslier for the informative and imaginative foundation his work provides, as we are for this English translation.

Publication of *Cambodian Dancers* opens a window into the scholarship, belief structures, colonial conflicts, dance practices, and court realities of Cambodia a hundred years ago. For its re-appearance in the twenty-first century may we all be, not only grateful, but…celebratory!

Paul Cravath
Honolulu, Hawai'i

Cambodian Dancers

ANCIENT & MODERN

Text and Drawings by
George GROSLIER
Painter

Original preface by **Charles GRAVELLE**
Translated by **Pedro RODRÍGUEZ**
Edited by **Kent DAVIS**

Originally published in French by Augustin Challamel
Paris, 1913

This work, published under the High Patronage
of His Majesty Sisowath, King of Cambodia,
of the Minister of Colonies,
of Mr. Outrey, Superior Resident of Cambodia,
is honored by a Subscription from the Minister of Colonies.

Original copies printed
5 proofs, numbered 1 through 5, on Imperial Japanese paper
25 proofs, number 6 through 30, on vellum in the style of the Papeteries du Marais

I dedicate this book,
with profound gratitude,
to the memory of my dear teacher
Albert Maignan.

                                              G.G.

NOUS

Préa Bat Samdach Préa SISOWATH Chamchakrapong

Préa Chau Crung Campuchéa Thippedey,

ROI DU CAMBODGE,

donnons bien volontiers, Notre approbation et Notre patronage à l'ouvrage que M. GROSLIER a consacré aux danseuses Royales.

Nous savons combien M. GROSLIER a travaillé pour réunir tous les dessins et tous les renseignements exacts qui font de son travail un précieux document pour le Royaume.

Fait en Notre Royal à Phnom-Penh, le 2 Août 1912.

ទំរង់ព្រះរាជបញ្ញត្តិនេះ យើងខ្ញុំព្រះករុណា បានយកមកទូលគាល់ថ្វាយប៉ុស្តេចំពោះ
និងអស់ម៉ឺនលោកក្រមព្រឹទ្ធ ហើយហាក្រុមនេះបានវែងឆ្លងបច្ចុប្បន្នព្រះទ័យ។
ព្រះរាជកុមារ្យ ត្រេកព្រះហឫទ័យយល់ព្រមតាមប្រការទាំងឡាយនេះហើយ។

រាជធានីភ្នំពេញ ថ្ងៃទី... ខែ... ឆ្នាំ ១៩៥២។

×

Présentée à la signature de Sa Majesté par Nous,
Oknha Véang,Ministre du Palais Royal,des Finances
et des Beaux Arts.

Preface

I saw this work come to life. I love the author and his subject. This is my sole — sole but quite good! — excuse for writing this preface.

Born in Phnom Penh twenty-five years ago, and thenceforth always far removed from our exotic land, you returned here as if marked by destiny. A Buddhist, or rather Brahmanic, providence had made you the most restless artist we had ever encountered to devote himself to Cambodian dancers and their secrets, their present and their past. And had they not already posed their delightful problem to the illustrious sculptor Rodin?

Their dances are secular rites, plays, with all human sentiments expressed in immutable gestures, by disconcerting anatomy. It is the glint of jewels, fabrics, and tinsel, the artifice of make-up and masks. It is a noisy and sonorous music, whose origins and transformations need uncovering. It is an entire people become, or born, contemplative, sweet, and smiling; a people who place before their good King the many-colored tableau of their *sampots* and scarves, and surround the apotheosis with it. It is the pure, star-studded moonlit night, showing through the background....

All this, you felt deeply, with the fervor of a believer, a fervor nurtured in you by your teachers Édouard Toudouze and Albert Maignan, as well as by your friends, from times already lost or slipping away.

All that springs from your brushes or pencils is thus more than an homage to the craft and virtuosity that they were able to transmit to their best disciple. It is a little of their souls and methods you have brought to us from France, as you led us into the midst of the wonders of Angkor.

Angkor! Its past so very remote, a past to which we hardly dare assign a date, yet a past so near in terms of our choreography! Did you not rediscover there, omnipresent on the flowered panels of the galleries and sanctuaries, the elder sisters of our *lokhon*, though devoted as they were to purely religious dances? You took note of their features, more Indian at Angkor Thom, already Khmer at Angkor Vat. And there you show us, evidence in hand, the absolute differences in costumes and intentions, though the gestures remain the same.

These officiating creatures embodying ritual invocations in their prayers have, over the centuries, been replaced by mimes, by well-proportioned actresses evoking legends or scenes of the Ramayana, playing persecuted princes, giants, kidnapping *garuda*, monkeys white and black, bird-women, smitten women radiant with gems….

But these performances, whose flexibility and grace still enchant those who know how to appreciate them, deserve the melancholy attention we pay to things that we sense are slipping away, that will soon cease to exist and be lost.

At least the memory will remain, thanks to you, thanks to the long and patient studies that have made you the greatest authority on Cambodian choreography.

Without always being of much help otherwise, I kept track of the worries, delays, difficulties, and disappointments that your complex task caused you. Together we once again confirmed that in Asia — and particularly in Cambodia — you had better have time on your hands. Those gracious enough to help did not immediately understand our efforts. Our prior results gradually persuaded them.

You gained confidences on intimate matters from various sources, comparing them for clearer understanding. There were long sessions of hurried sketching during the three-night festival for the King's birthday, sessions that revealed the instantaneous aspect of the poses and positions to you. To these were added two timely evenings dedicated to Mr. and Mrs. Sarraut, to the Prince and Princess of Sweden, and three short but charming prayer scenes in the illuminated Throne Room.

But these were the culmination, the vision expressed. Details had to be checked. Palace dancers are not loaned out, and what you needed was to consult an authority on the art. That authority turned out to be Siamese. No longer onstage, because of her age, she had become a ballet mistress, and was imbued with all the traditions. It was she who gave you the movements, all the essential profiles.

Later you had the fabrics in your possession. Finally, the royal treasures were opened up for you. *Mokot* tiaras, *panntiereth* crowns, bracelets, broaches, chains, and rings all surrendered their archaic goldwork to your pen. In your seemingly unquenchable thirst for knowledge, you not only recorded the accounts of dancers but also spoke with senior Cambodian officials.

Without such opportunities, without your will and patience — and especially without that double or triple distension of time in the Far East — your book would have been impossible, and I, witness to its creation, would not have dared say what I now assert with joy: that it is sincere, complete, and definitive.

You have delivered to us your seven months' harvest. For that, many lovers of Beauty may be grateful, and may thank you, as I thank you now myself, as a friend to Angkor, with great affection.

CHARLES GRAVELLE

Chapter I

The Dance Hall
and the Audience

Wall of the palace enclosure.

Today the long, spacious dance hall does not remain empty, as is usually the case, after the departure of the mendicant monks who gather there daily to receive their food.

The palace servants have come, laden with leafy garlands. Around the base of each tall red column they have placed, in alternation with floor lamps, two earthenware pedestals bearing graceful plants.[1]

High above, in the roof trusses, they have checked the rudimentary machinery that will suspend the King of the Skies and the Nymph he pursues.[2] They have reinforced the cardboard clouds, covered the uneven floor with rugs, and spread out mats for musicians, the women of the chorus, and the time-beaters. Finally, they have placed two broad, low, rug-covered tables, one at each end of the room, to represent a bed or a throne. The King, Hero, Spirit, or Princess will recline there or assume the ritual poses of the legends to be played out onstage, for tonight there is a dance.

Though it is still broad daylight, and though dances only take place when the full moon — that queen of Cambodian festivities — adds her cold illumination to the palace lights, admiring spectators have already gathered, happy and content to watch the preparations.

A spectator.

Peaceful, speaking softly, they mill around smoking, without a care in the world. They have left their huts open and quiet under the areca palms. Their oxen are asleep, and their canoes lie on the riverbank. The men wear tight white jackets and bright *sampots*.[3] The women have carefully pomaded their short hair. They have wrapped their torsos in their most beautiful scarves, orange like the sunset, red like persimmon, or pale blue like the evening sky. And they arrive, one following the other according to age and status, as is proper.

---

1. These quite old, and now electric, lamps are made of copper and consist of a cup and an elevated stand. In the past they would burn several wicks at once. With French influence in Cambodia, petroleum replaced oil, and electricity was installed at the end of the reign of H. M. Norodom. Large, dazzling chandeliers imported from Europe were the final ingredient in the palace dance hall's current, very intense lighting.

2. Translator's Note: Here, and on pages 62 and 152, Groslier makes specific reference to special equipment that actually suspended dancers in the air. Pages 44–45 describe its use in the context of a scene. The opening of the 2008 Beijing Olympics revisited this concept with flying *Apsaras*, a dramatic stage effect that innovative Cambodians had used one hundred years earlier.

3. The *sampot* is the Siamese national costume, long adopted by the Cambodians. It is a rectangular piece of fabric, rolled around the waist and tucked from the front to the back between the legs.

A spectator.

Evening falls at last... The trees from which the flowers were plucked turn silver. Flocks of ravens perch on the elephant trunks carved at the roof corners. The crowd pours in through every gate of the palace and packs itself tight around the edge of the wall-less hall. It is brilliant, vivid, and splashed with innumerable colors, but very calm, very patient, and very gentle.

There are a thousand varied fabrics, bare shoulders and arms, heads with short, black hair. There are wrinkled old women with shaved heads, their collarbones standing out like cords, their curved backs lean and girded with white scarves. There are opulent matrons decked out in little jackets and chewing betel like ruminating cattle; women with round, soft figures, with naked children riding astride their hips; young girls dressed in *sampots* shiny and brittle like oil-cloth; servants carrying betel boxes; and children with long braids seemingly attached to their shaved heads in small circular patches.

You can still see some Annamite women in their tight black bodices, gold pearls around their necks, and some opulently coiffured Malayans. They have settled on the mats, squatting, lying down, propped on an elbow. The men stand together in the back, having climbed onto the steps as best they could. A few royal guardsmen walk around. The crowd is a deep, multicolored wave, washing in from the night all along the sides of the hall and breaking in the light![4]

---

[4]. Palace dances are held for the birthday of H. M., for his coronation, for the marriage or ceremonial hair-cutting of a great princess, and, lastly, for when a high-ranking personage arrives in or passes through Cambodia.

The Dance Hall and the Audience 13

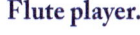

The time beaters mark the tempo of each measure by clapping their wooden time-keeping sticks together.

Flute player.

Music collected by Mr. Tricon, in Phnom Penh.

Musician.

The musicians sit at the center of a circle of small gongs, which they strike with two felt mallets; before large kettledrums, held at an incline on crossed wooden mounts; and in front of xylophones shaped like junk boats, curved and gracious on their square stands; all occupying an entire side of the long dance hall.

In front of them, near one of the ceremonial divans for high officials, the orchestra leader and then the Chief of Protocol sit in dignity, with a large copper spittoon between them.

The instruments are of great beauty, made of precious wood and inlaid with ivory carved in graceful shapes. The tom-tom, the tiny viol, and the flute alone are Cambodian, and too trebly to be heard throughout the hall. Other instruments, imported from Siam, are thus necessary. Marking the tempo, their foreign sonorities dominate and hammer out the musical theme.

The sound is like that of a fast carillon, now merry, now serious. Rapid phrases suddenly break into slow tones, change pitch, and repeating the original movement. The nasal flute hoots a short recitative, the other instruments fall silent as if to listen, and the music takes up again in remarkably precise rhythm, dragging or rushing madly ahead, before breaking up again.[5]

Annamite spectator.

---

5. Cambodian music is not notated. Melodies always have two parts: a call and a response. They are played on the xylophones and the 18 small circular gongs. The remaining instruments improvise in support of the melody, and the tom-toms intone the rhythm.

Dancer wearing "*panntiereth*" crown.

Such is the background against which the Cambodian dancers will perform. The hall is nothing but a light roof supported by high columns decorated with garlands. The moonlit night, the beautiful Cambodian night, gentle, scented, and translucent, is the only wall, and it is from the ineffable night that they emerge, the gold-helmeted actresses, as if stepping out of a dream or some mysterious past, as if arriving from some remote country, the imagined home of their most beautiful illusions.

The people gathered here will see the beloved and dreaded genies appear and watch as the legends passed down by their fathers unfold. Soon the most beautiful of the imaginary women — the fairy, the goddess, the mermaid will appear, to hope, weep, and love before them. They can imagine nothing more beautiful than what is about to occur before their marveling eyes. All of their riches, their art, their highest and purest aspirations will be expressed. The dazzling heritage of bygone kings, of dead civilizations — all of these things they, the poor Cambodian people, will possess!

They wear ordinary *sampots* and white jackets. They have no throne, no guard, no diamonds, no harem. They have left bamboo houses built by their own hands and constituting their entire fortune. They have left behind for the evening the calm and voluntary solitude that is their peace and happiness. Like their monarch, Son of Rama, they have come to attend the show, that representation of their dreams and of supreme joys.

Happy are the people who, at a glance, effortlessly, without coercion, and in the serenity of a single night, can watch as their every ideal is realized!

The time-keepers.

Time-keeper.

The King is expected. His royal box juts out, dominating the room. Inside, his divan, its cushion embroidered with gold, awaits him under a white canopy with scintillating pendants. On a round table covered with a beautiful rug lies a large golden salver. On the salver are arranged some of the king's favorite objects: a red box decorated with a grimacing monster, a betel box decorated with diamonds and rubies, a wick holder, and a spittoon. Already the pages have, with due respect, placed near the divan the royal sword, that the women have decorated with a loop of jasmine flowers; an engraved halberd; and an old revolver of unknown origin, dreadful and ridiculous among all these pure, ancient treasures.

The King arrives, under his seven-stage white parasol. He takes small steps, his back round, his neck thrust forward. A diamond buckle gleams on his belt among the folds of his silk *sampot*. From the constellation of ornaments on his white jacket, glints of moonbeams mix with torchlight. Ministers, those "pillars of the kingdom," and guests follow the king as the palace guard salutes.

The King has arrived. He has greeted the crowd with a debonair smile, through the smoke of his perpetual cigar. The bowing backs straighten. White and gold *pankas* begin their slow beat. The chorus stirs. Other lamps light up. Servants run about, brushing the ground with their knees. An old woman, on all fours, attaches small ritual candles to the instruments. The Vice Minister of the Palace transmits an order to the Chief of Protocol, who transmits it in turn to the conductor and the directress of the chorus. One after another, the time-beaters begin clacking their wooden sticks. The orchestra strikes up the prelude in the illuminated hall, in the heart of night. The percussive, sonorous, joyous music takes flight, races out through the crowd, brushes the tree tops, and is lost towards the moon.

Ah! The moment is filled with promise….

All eyes are fixed on a door, veiled by a curtain, facing the orchestra. When the curtain finally parts a mysterious sparkling — distant, like the gleam that mermaids must make amid somber waves — becomes visible in the darkness beyond. There are furtive flashes, evanescent and incomprehensible rays, fine golden points, a shimmering, and sometimes a face stands out, round and white, like a tiny moon.

The dancers have arrived, behind the frail curtain that no one can penetrate! There they are, with all their accoutrements, their partners, their attendants, and their costumers. They are ready! Before appearing in the light, they seem to acquire yet a bit more mystery and receive supreme guidance from invisible divinities, to be all the more exquisite, flexible, and worthy of adoration.

Chapter II

EDUCATION OF THE ROYAL DANCERS

Prince Inao.

The Education of the Royal Dancers

The dancers, all members of the harem, are offered to the King by his people. Their parents bring them to him, as early as the age of six years.[6]

The first phase of sadness.

They were the most beautiful, the whitest, of their villages; and their fathers were convinced that in offering their daughters to the King they were inviting the benevolence of the Spirits and bringing supreme protection on themselves and their families.

So one day they had made their offerings to Buddha. Monks had read brilliant destinies in the lines of the girls' tiny hands. They had piled into ox carts, and the future royal women had been taken to meet their brilliant destinies.

Each with her lock of well-combed hair and her crown of jasmine, the girls had understood very little. They had felt a vague fear on penetrating the massive white walls of the palace, hardly suspecting that they would never again leave.

6. This custom is disappearing.

Type of Cambodian.

And shortly thereafter they found themselves all alone, among forty young girls of their age, well dressed, and already displaying sophisticated manners. They had wept on seeing their mothers disappear. When their big eyes were dry, however, when they saw beautiful gardens, flowers, pretty houses, and merchants with fried cakes, they had found their consolation.

Parents would receive 20 to 500 piastres, in accordance with their daughter's beauty, her age, and royal generosity. They would leave a few *sampots* and silk scarves to the child, and then they would go away.

And they would never see their daughter again, in the shade of their thatch hut, playing with heliconia flowers, crunching kernels of ripe corn between her teeth....

One phase of the grand salute.

The royal dancers never again leave the palace, unless they are expelled from it. On this point H. M. Norodom was unrelenting. A dancer asking his permission to go into town and see her parents would have it granted only once per year. She would leave at daybreak, would have to be back before nightfall, and would be accompanied by an imposing guard of matrons and children.

Under the more tolerant H. M. Sisowath things are more easygoing. He even grants leaves of several days. But a thousand hardened eyes of jealousy and intrigue dog any woman who ventures outside the palace. Gossips train a keen, relentless ear on the traveler, especially if they cannot account for some half-hour of her journey. In this small world of grace and charm, the reward for a tip-off is the protection of a minister or a favorite. You spy, and you watch your step. Dancers remaining in the palace dispatch emissaries to town, to spy on the girl granted leave! Who approaches her? Whom does she speak with? Who is that man? Is it truly her brother? Everything is known, everything is told.

There is thus no need for eunuchs at the palace. No man can enter, and the Cambodian dancer is inaccessible.

Moreover, would engaging in an intrigue with one of them not tarnish the King's prestige since, after all, she belongs to the King?

Apart from extremely rare exceptions, due to the will of the all-powerful, seeking to please some high-ranking personage, the tales of good fortune that we hear so often are just boasting or malicious lies. Dancers roam the streets of Cambodia, certainly, but dancers expelled from the Palace, as well as low-class girls who claim to be dancers, even *premières danseuses*! These, then, are the dancers in question, not the venerated little goddesses whom one sees take up ritual poses under the eye of the King.[7]

No, the Palace dancers truly are the virginal idols of a chaste and gentle people. These ballerinas with faces as white as a milk drop, after taking off their tiaras of pure gold, would not want to compromise or sell themselves. They will sleep in peace on their mats, and continue in their slumber the dreams they have given us. The spectator gone home, whether to a hut or a palace, can exclaim, "My heart is serene! I have seen the Gods dance!" And he will be filled with no vile passions for having seen women dance.

---

7. Formerly there were traveling troupes of dancers. Great mandarins also had their *corps de ballet*. But new ideas and needs drove these expensive troupes to extinction. Not one remains today. The last surviving actresses were those of His Excellency the Minister of Justice, who died in 1911.

The Education of the Royal Dancers

One phase of the grand salute.

At the age of eight, the *lokhon* start to work. Every day for at least a year, from eight to eleven o'clock in the morning, and from two to five o'clock in the afternoon, they practice under the direction of female instructors, themselves former dancers.

It is a long and painful apprenticeship for these poor little girls. The rehearsal room is gloomy and often stifling. Sitting on the ground, they twist and rotate from the pelvis up. Or else, seated in pairs, facing each other; they pull each other's fingers toward the back of the hand until all the knuckles crack. Finally, still in pairs, one takes the other's arm and bends it back over her knee, as if snapping a thick branch!

It is necessary to eliminate the articulation of the elbow joint for the forearm to break the line with the upper arm. Thanks to this hyperextension, so astonishing for Europeans, a bare arm, floating on the musical waves emanating from the orchestra, can undulate from the shoulder to the extreme flourishes of the upturned hand, like the body of a *Naga* on the waves of the Ocean of Milk.

With these successive exercises, the anterior protuberance of the olecranon of the ulna digs itself a deeper cavity in the young and tender bone. It also dulls itself. The ligaments and opposing tendons stretch, making it possible for the joint to achieve those disconcerting angles.

The greatest angle that I saw on a former dancer, a palace instructor of about forty years of age, measured 40 degrees to the posterior face of the arm, coinciding with the protuberance of the olecranon.

Limbering exercises.

This hyperextension exists somewhat naturally in the women and especially the children of the yellow race.

Siamese and Annamite women can often be seen propping themselves up on an arm bent backwards at the elbow. These two sketches of a woman made in Moï country, well before my studies in Cambodia, bear comparison with those of the Cambodian dancer at rest. To have possessed the same arm as the latter, the former would have needed only a little practice during her childhood, when her arm was more flexible.

Twisting the torso on the hips and bending the arm.

Natural arm bend of a Moï native.

The difficulty of Khmer dances lies not just in the elbow. Hyperextension must be possible between the hand and forearm, between the metacarpus and the carpus, between the second and first knuckles of the finger; from the third knuckle to the second. Equivalent hyperextensions are required of the legs. Moreover, these hyperextensions must be possible simultaneously, as certain dance figures show.

But none of these movements provoke the same queasiness as the dislocations of acrobats, or the ignoble writhing of the Ouled-Nail dancers (see Appendix II, p. 348). The Cambodian movements melt and fold into one another. There is a deep undulation of the dancer's entire being, a gliding. The gesture doesn't stop. It slips away, melts into the air. One thinks it is finished, yet it goes on. It does not stop at the hard edge of a joint's expected limit. It changes character and becomes immaterial. No longer restricted by a coarse skeleton, the charming body of the actress falls, as it were, out of existence. It fluidifies. The angles, the very flexions, disappear. All that remain are soft curves, wave profiles, an airy undulation and moments of unimagined grace.

Exaggerated arm bend of a dancer at rest.

If she aims to attain such perfection and realize such an esthetic ideal, if she hopes to charm the King and make him desire her, if she wants applause, a dancer must work obstinately. When her body has been sufficiently kneaded, when she can quickly unfold her arm and crack it into an uncommon backbend, only then will the little dancer learn her roles.

Nymph taking flight.

The Education of the Royal Dancers

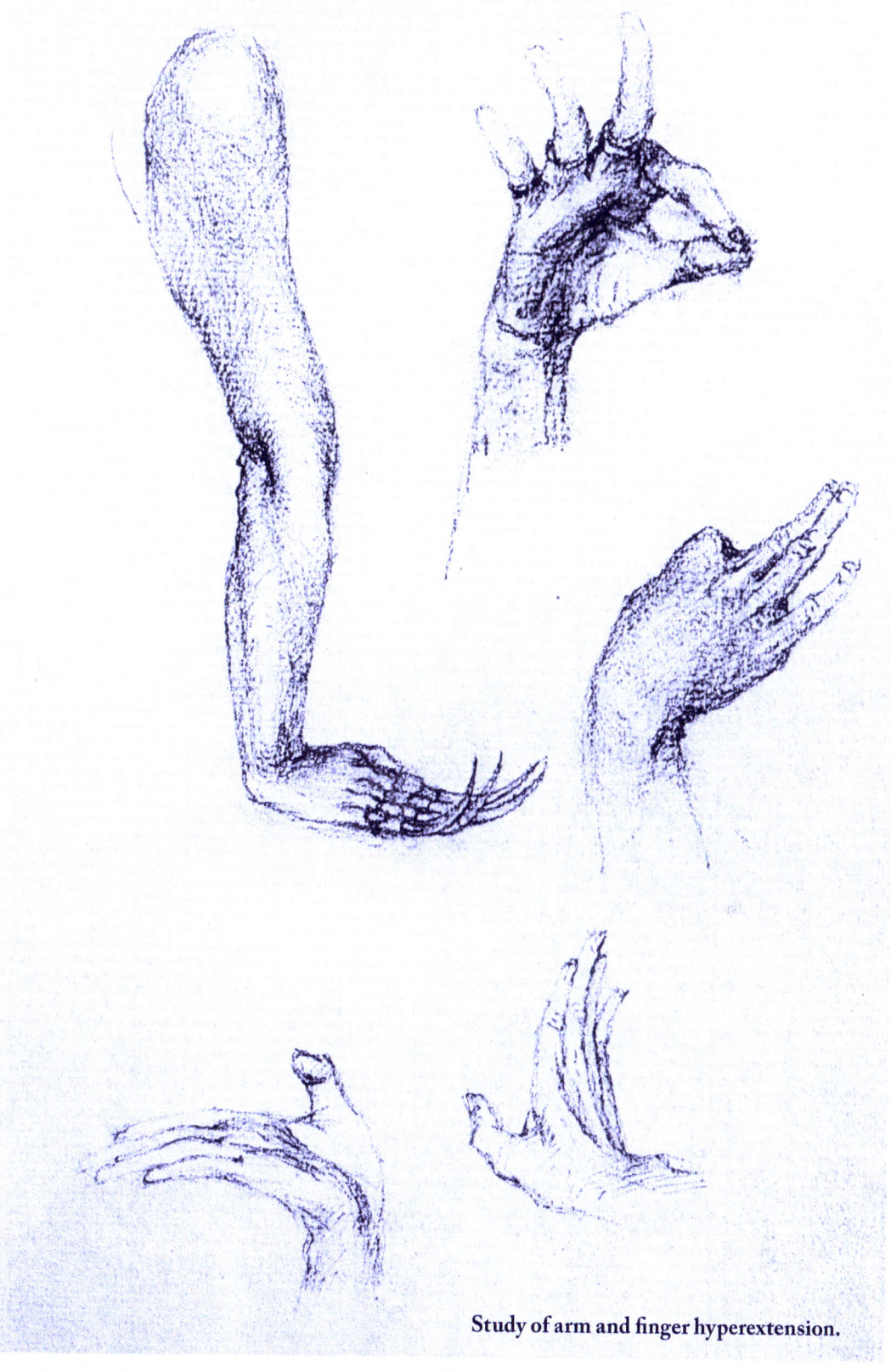

Study of arm and finger hyperextension.

Cambodian Dancers

A phase of the grand salute.

A Malayan warrior.

"Her hand dries the imaginary tear."

The Khmer dancer is an actress, a mime. She plays a legendary character. She expresses the emotions and portrays the actions chanted by the chorus of women, seated along the sides of the hall.

Each phrase of the singers calls forth a gesture or determines a pose for the always silent dancer. The gestures and poses are ritual, unique, and transmitted from generation to generation, without the help of a precise, written didactic model.

Take, for example, the grieving of the heroine Bosseba over Enao's departure. Whenever she expresses her pain as a poor little princess, her head bends forward. Then her hand opens and, like the caressing wing of a dove, dries an imaginary tear at the inside corner of her eye. Should her heartache increase and make her forehead ache, the same expressive hand will pass over her brow to help it contain the torment.

These gestures are regulated by more than the development and sequence of the ideas they express. There is also an absolute synchronism. If at a certain moment the right hand is at the belt, palm forward, then the left hand must be at another place, precisely determined by an all-powerful and formal tradition stretching back into time immemorial.

Reversing the hands.

These are subtle correlations. Even Cambodia's metal founders do not know what they are, and the gestures of nearly all of the small dancer statuettes that they cast are wrong. Any dancer who served as my model would immediately point out the errors in my overly hasty sketches.

These gestures generally culminate in a specific pose, which is held for a beat, whether the rhythm is slow or fast. A pose taken up at one clap of the chorus's time-keeping sticks is abandoned at the next, having existed just long enough to be perceived, admired, and subsequently missed.

The clap of the time-keeping sticks not only emphasizes the chorus's words and the gestures of the actresses but also marks the first beat of musical measures. It is thus easy to imagine the perfect cadence with which notes are struck, words are uttered, and actresses move.

A few absolute principles, of which the instructors and dancers are not aware, can be inferred:

- Whatever their direction of motion, the arms oscillate around a point on the sternum.
- Whatever the overall movement, this point traces a noticeably horizontal and uniform line.
- Head movements are independent of body movements.
- No pose is struck and held with the legs outstretched.
- In walking, the foot is always thrust forward and turned out, with the toes flexed up.

All these slow, precise poses, which dissolve and emerge in keeping with the meaning and cadence of poetic words, are thus studied and learned one by one, as soon as an actress's limbs can execute them. Such is the second logical phase of the school of Khmer dance. Long practice and natural taste refine the lines to perfection. And the beauty of the celebrant actress—her charm, her jewels, the sparkling costumes—all cast their inexpressible, infinitely disconcerting spells.

Scenes are learned to the sound of the tom-tom. Severe and attentive, fifteen mistresses presently supervise rehearsals. They are of various rank and earn from three to fifteen piastres per month accordingly.

The hand that offers the flower.

They are former dancers and *premières danseuses* whom age has driven from the stage. Some live in the Palace and constitute a relentless guard watching over the dancers. With stinging blows from a rattan cane they punish their pupil for mistakes, inattention, or bad behavior. On festival days they are assisted by a great number of dressers, four prompters, five singers, and twenty-one time-beaters. These come from the outside and earn from three to five piastres per month.

Her education complete, a dancer attends rehearsals less and less. Under the strict King Norodom, they regularly attended three sessions per week. Even the *premières danseuses* were present. But now that everything is slipping away, dancers work less and less, and no longer maintain their demanding flexibility. It is now considered rigorous if there are a few serious rehearsals, exempting no actress, before the festivals. For these the orchestra is in full force and a few chanters are present. All these rehearsals take place without special costumes. The *sampots* are held in place with a belt and a simple Siamese jacket.

Rehearsals take place in sampot and petite jacket.

Chapter III

GESTURES AND POSES

The curtain behind which the *lokhon* wait opens at last. There emerges San-Krinh, the exquisite current *première danseuse*, with her rounded forehead and delicate smile. This evening she is Princess Bosseba, one of the Khmer theatre's many beloved heroines.

It is a marvelous apparition, occurring as it does among women chanting on the ground, opening wide their betel-blackened mouths. She wears a tall red-gold tiara of two triple stages, keen as a sword and built like a tower. To one side of it dangles a pendant of jasmine and *champa*. The dancer's face is round and white, like a milk drop. Her eyes, staring out under penciled-in eyebrows, look at nothing and no one yet seem to be following something, as if the invisible pattern determining her complicated poses were suspended before them. Mouth serious and closed, head motionless on her upright torso, scarf sparkling, arms bare, the legendary Princess advances. The clap of wooden sticks sets her steps, and the music carries her along.

Encircling her flexible wrists are ten ritual bracelets and two large rings of flowers. Sapphires, emeralds, rubies, and diamonds gleam on her slender fingers. A *sautoir*[8] with thirty rows of gold chains, each link chiseled on its own, passes over her left shoulder. Her bent legs create great folds of shadow and light in her sparkling, gold-embroidered silk skirt.

Yes, it is an extraordinary apparition! She moves slowly and serenely before the multicolored backdrop of the crowd. Her willowing arms sway like stems, jointless, and offer up hands that bloom like flowers. A diamond plate on her breast sparkles like a star. Light ripples in streams along the long scarf. It is reflected by each sequin, flows over round hips and flowery gold silk, and fades away, after this magic illumination, on the thick carpet, where flowers have fallen.

8. Editor's Note: When referring to Khmer dance costumes, the French term indicates a sash, chains or jewelry bands crossing the chest from one or both shoulders. This cover illustration from Roland Meyer's 1919 book, *Saramani*, shows chains crossing the chest from the left shoulder as well as the regular sash. A similar accoutrement is first seen on special *devata* (sacred women) whose images fill King Suryavarman II's temple of Angkor Wat. Later, King Jayavarman VII included the *sautoir* on many *devata* featured in his temples, including the Bayon, Preah Khan, Banteay Kdai and Banteay Chhmar.

The grand salute.

The Cambodian actress, princess of the pose, walks proudly erect and charming toward her King. She is a precious slave, a serene celebrant, enigmatic, impenetrable, entirely graceful and entirely splendid. Ringed with gold, her bare feet brush the floor.

Sitting on her heels with knees tightly clasped, so slender, she seems to gush forth from the shining *sampot* opening around her like a corolla. Three times she bends forward at the waist and straightens, raising her joined hands toward the Supreme Divinity, the King, and the people.

Her fingers, bent backwards, give her joined hands the form of a delicate cup. In this warm, white vessel she seems to be offering up her veneration, the soul of an innocent little artist, her thoughts, her humility, all the poems planted in her by generations past. And the diamonds of her diadem, mounted on small springs, twinkle like stars!

This deep salute recurs often during the ballet. Behind the Princess, six attendants, also kneeling, perform it in unison and then remain respectfully seated, propped up by their arms.

"Waiting."

Gestures and Poses 39

First and second phase of the grand salute.

Next, Bosseba strolls in the gardens of a marvelous palace, by the banks of sacred pools. These figurative strolls are the only danced parts in Cambodian theatre. They are, in other words, the only moments when the actress's gestures have no particular meaning. Her only concern is to be beautiful, harmonious, and supple.

At this point, every now and then, she stops and something extraordinary occurs. Her legs folded, her torso slowly undulates with a movement seeming to originate in one of her upturned hands. This undulation glides and winds softly along her arm, passing from one shoulder to the other, lifting the scarf. Passing over the heat of her heart, it is rekindled, creeping along her twisting arm and through her other hand, which floats lightly like a white wing, to expire in the air....

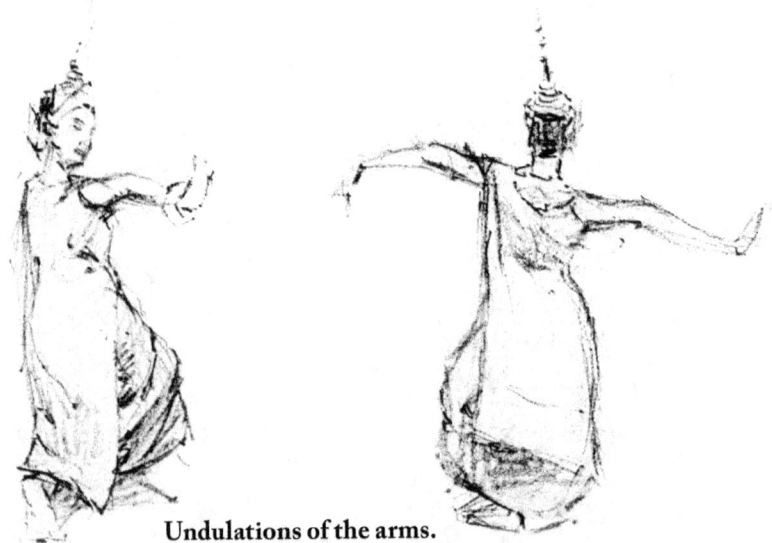

Undulations of the arms.

That very instant, the sorceress arches her body at the waist. Her belly hollows out under the torrent of heavy folds spreading out upon her knees in lustrous sparks of metal and silk. Behind her, the gold fringes of her scarf continue trembling from the interruption of her forward progress. From the enigmatic white face, beneath rising eyelids, stare brilliant pupils moist and black as sapodilla seeds. They flash darkly and disappear!

Grace, charm, youth — in no other country of the world could they be more strange, hieratic, rare, or unforgettable.

All human emotions are expressed by Cambodian actresses with remarkable veracity, precision, and malleable simplicity. Though her face remains serious and impassive, the mime's entire flexible and trained body, her hands set in place or soaring in rhythm, externalizes and materializes the troubles, emotions, sadness, and joys of her heart, all the things that make up the singers' marvelous words.

There is no pretension in her gestures. They are naïve, like the gestures of children. But rhythm stylizes them, the suffering and joy of past generations regulate them, and they are the expression of a secular experience, of a vanished art, of a deep psychology or remote philosophy. And the Cambodian people of today would be incapable of conceiving or creating the least beautiful among them.

Look closely: the lover pleads and begs and promises his beloved a happy life over yonder, in faraway regions.

"In love one begs."

He wants to sprit her away in his chariot, which awaits nearby. "Come, O adored princess!"

"He wants to take her in his chariot."

Heartlessly, she refuses, pushes him away. She turns her eyes askance. Beneath that scarf lies a heart of ice. "Go away! I don't want to leave…"

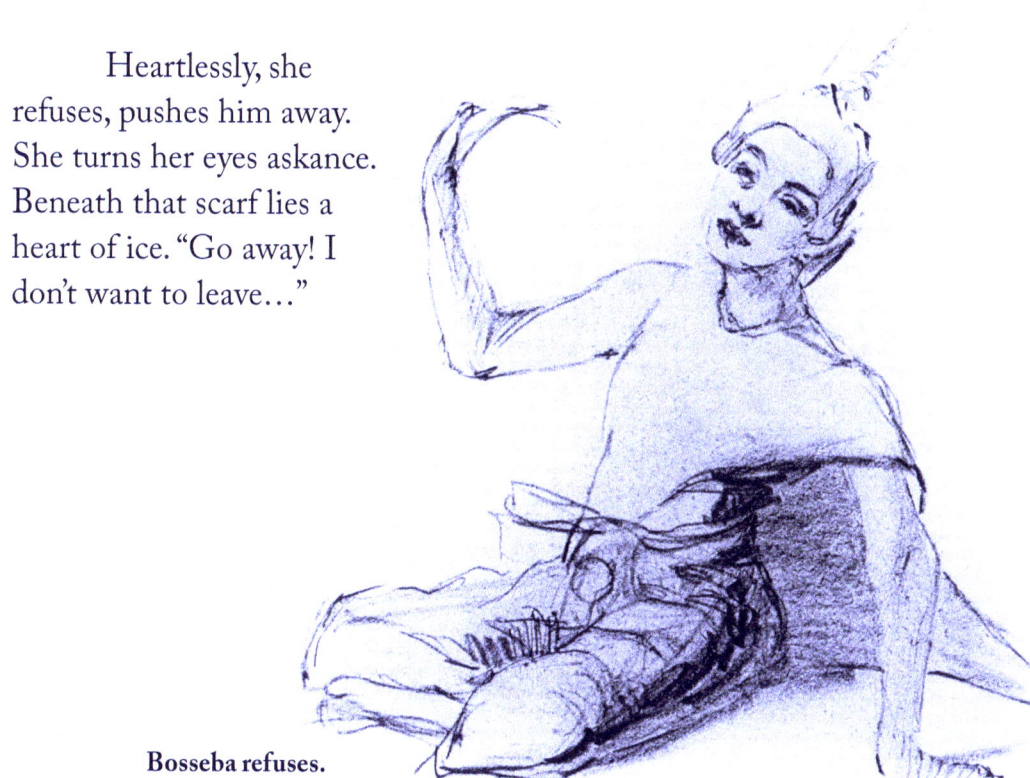

Bosseba refuses.

He tries to grab her, but she wriggles free. Rising anger bends her body and quickens her gestures. She strikes the ground with her hand. "Go away! Go away!" she says, filling the hapless wretch with the aforementioned despair. He weeps. There is nothing for him but to die….

Anger. "Go away! Go away!"

Imploring.

But wait! Is the cruelty of the Princess abating? Oh joy! Oh tenderness! Behold his love reflected back! They chastely embrace and offer each other flowers in a scene turned charming.

And then — it was destiny — they run away, in flight ethereal....

The escape takes place, lightly.

Tired, they fall asleep in a propitious place. Then from the sky, in the dazzling glare of his magic wand, appears Garuda the kidnapper. He takes extreme precautions. He first conveys his surprise, then his covetousness, next his resolution, and the sleeping Princess is carried away a second time!

Pity the lover upon his awakening! His pantomime is heartrending. He flies to his father, King of the Giants,[9] and recounts his misfortunes. The King goes into a fury. The wretched child receives weapons: a magic bow whose arrows never misses their mark, an axe whose blows produce thunder. One can well imagine that thus equipped our young lover finds and reclaims his poor little sweetheart. She is a blur of tears, bound up with a scarf, held prisoner by an exceedingly evil "ugly man," and we watch with pleasure as he is quickly blasted away.

Garuda flying.

9. Editor's Note: Groslier's conclusion of this play lacks continuity in both the scenes and character names. It is difficult to determine if this is due to errors in typesetting, in the author's notes or in the way the action was described to him by his Cambodian translators.

The Indonesian legend of Inao and Bosseba is ancient and complex, stretching back to the Srivijaya Empire (Shailendra dynasty, in Java), circa 778-864 AD. A millennium later, the Thai King Rama II (who reigned from 1809-1824) hosted many poets in his court, including the renowned Sunthorn Pu. Both men spun tales based on the Inao legend. One hundred years later in Phnom Penh, Groslier apparently witnessed a variation of this legend portrayed by Cambodian dancers, but his account is garbled.

On this page "the lover" (who is never identified as a Prince or as Inao) goes to his father, the "King of the Giants," to secure weapons to free Bosseba. Next we find the "*lokhon*" in a sampan on a river as "the army of King Kayakat" searches for "the beautiful Séla." In the next paragraph, we have "Rulachak, the King of the Giants" entering, furious "at the kidnapping of his daughter, the delicate Butsomali." Is the King of the Giants also Bosseba's father? Are Séla and Butsomali other names for Bosseba? What happened to "the lover" and why didn't he use the magic weapons his father, "the King of the Giants" gave him? On page 52 we have "a new character, the Prince" entering the scene...with no more explanation of this curious series of events. If any scholars can shed light on this situation the publisher would be pleased to add an appendix with clarifications to future editions.

The *lokhon* is in a light sampan, on the river. With every step her arms plunge an imaginary oar into an imaginary wave.

Dancer in sampan: she rows.

The army of King Kayakat searches frantically for the beautiful Sela. Charming soldiers march in tight formation with haughty stride, invisible weapons gripped in their fists.

The adorable soldier marches with a proud pace.

Are they cavalrymen? Then their hands will grip reins and wield riding crops. They will move out with a sharp kick to the floor with their heels, like fiery steeds champing at the bit.

Dancer on horseback.

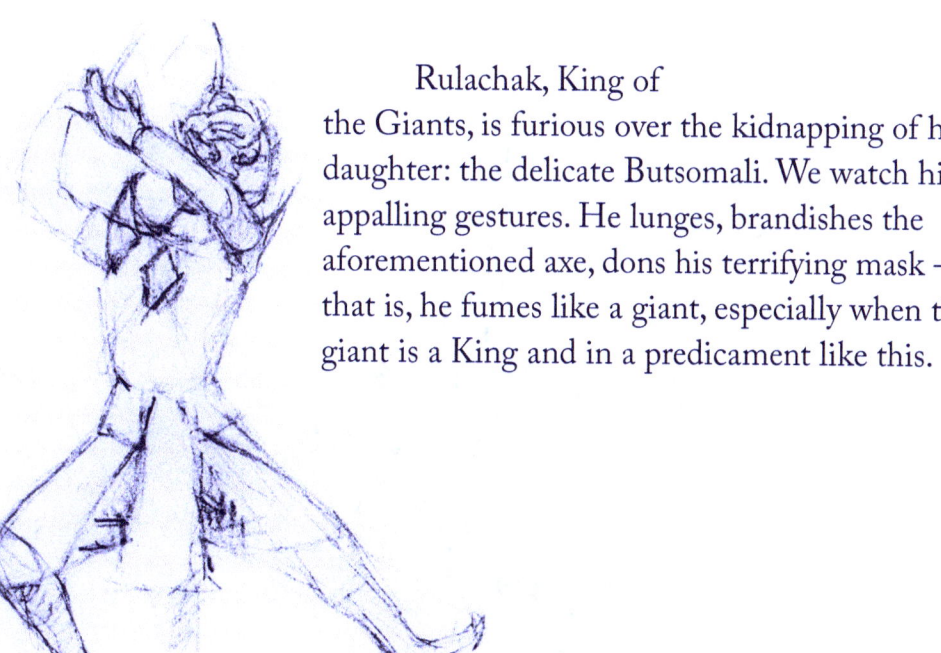

Rulachak, King of the Giants, is furious over the kidnapping of his daughter: the delicate Butsomali. We watch his appalling gestures. He lunges, brandishes the aforementioned axe, dons his terrifying mask — that is, he fumes like a giant, especially when that giant is a King and in a predicament like this.

Fury of the King of the Giants.

If the dancer wishes to create the illusion that she is flying, fleeing into space, she seeks out the least earthbound, the most tenuous, of poses: one knee to the ground, the heel raised high, arms out like wings. Alternatively, she quickly turns in her nimble hand a long magic wand encrusted with small, sparkling mirrors, thereby seeming to envelop herself in a cloud of ether and rays.

Meanwhile, Garuda, the extraordinary bird-man, whose character requires not grace but force, takes flight with a body tensed up like a wrestler's, arms open and quivering, hands rigid like talons.

The nymph takes flight.

Protestation.

These, then, are what the harried traveler and the inattentive colonist dismiss as obscure and monotonous gestures. Ah, but if they would stop for a moment, if they would reflect upon this foreign art, which perhaps defies immediate understanding but whose forms and meaning are in fact quite accessible... Let the pedagogue who considers these gestures ugly find, if he can, some other system of grace more perfect and more complete.

I, who have studied the gestures tenaciously and at length — without adapting them to established theories, which are of no use in places like this, so far from our native land and the Greek temples — I say that the gestures of these white ballerinas are a gentle joy to the eye for those who want to look and see.... Yes, I say that the gestures of the Khmer dancers do not merely present themselves to the curiosity of these observers as the materialized words of mystical sentences, or the notes of some harmony, or the rhythm of some strange music of the eyes, but also as caresses!

Monotonous, are they? Look at the rapt audience! Look at them, perched uncomfortably on a plank for the past two hours, missing not a single sign, not a single glint of a jewel! Smoking their cigarettes or chewing their betel, they sit in silence and contemplation all night long. They marvel innocently, like children.

They do not always understand, however. If they do not hear the chanted phrase mimed by the actress, they are incapable of grasping the pure expression of their forefather's genius. Our psychological analysis is not for them. Yet there they remain, filled with wonder! They recall that their wives, by custom, had also been dressed like little princesses on the day of their wedding, that they had crouched in the same manner, while the yellow monks chanted prayers, behind their fans.

To be happy, do these naïve people need explanations, spiritual depth, a mysterious past, or poems recounting their origins? Their dancers are beautiful in and of themselves. They shine. They are white and supple. They are venerated. They have flowers. There are lights and music; and that's everything.

And they remain attentive the entire night, like devotees and worshippers. Swaying jasmine infuses the air with its essence. The night is magnificent. Both Poetry, which has neither country nor dialects nor customs, and Harmony, which defies definition, are present for the occasion. They are gently rocked by the ballerina's caress and exclaim:

"O Sister, that gesture is of us!"

Only a few old women fall asleep on their elbows, and a few little children, stretched out on their backs, their hands on their foreheads, their bellies in the air....

Yes, it really is a goddess appearing before our eyes. The tiny laughing doll with the black teeth disappears beneath snow-white make-up. In every country in the world, to be very white is to be very beautiful, and what is true now was true eight centuries ago. Chinese envoys spoke of the King's women as always keeping out of the sun, so as not to tarnish the whiteness of their skin.

In accordance with the rites, an actress might be entirely coated in white, to make her more inhuman, more impenetrable, to be as if made of infinitely pure matter, to become a sacred vessel, a small virginal wave in that milky sea where legend begat her. She is white because white is the color of the invisible, the divine, the immaculate, the immaterial, the serene. It is the color of the royal parasol, the robe of the Brahmins, the sacred lotus, the astrologer's *sampot*, the moon, and the elephant that protects the kingdom.

She is white because, as an ideal Princess, no trace of anything personal about her, of what she was before the dance, a simple woman, must remain. She must retain nothing of the humanity that she has shed, and from which rituals and sacred rules temporarily separate her. She must be rid of all that is commonplace. Desires, sensuality, and jealousies must expire on contact with this marble mask and its hermetically sealed lips.

This celebrant is no longer a woman but a divine statuette, gradually animated by Art, beliefs, the past of a people who admire and venerate in her their most beautiful imaginings and the most perfect expression of their religion and life.

The ballet unfolds.

The six attendants set out for a walk with their Princess. White feet rise in unison and come down, turned out, in front of their little counterparts. Arms turn and twist up in time with the walk. Then the troupe stops in two rows and a strange undulation passes from arm to arm. It is like an ocean swell gliding from dancer to dancer, the floating of a soft scarf, an invisible something that passes from one to the next, dissipating and regenerating. All hands rise together, with fingers splayed like the fragile ribs of an ivory fan. And suddenly, joined two by two, the dancers slip together into a light run, legs bent, feet brushing the carpet, scarves aflutter.

Then our imagination carries off the seven ballerinas, who take flight and alight in the magic gardens where the scene unfolds, and where legend has situated every sort of bliss. Perfumes that assuage all pain filter in through the trees, which spread their sweet, sweet shadows and loom in harmonious silhouettes, reflected in the basins. Fronds tumble from the sky. In the distance, the palace's towers of gold and coral shoot into the air like the flames at the heart of an opal. Birds more beautiful than precious gems take flight, and Bosseba, at the bend of a vine shrouded path, meets her true love.

Enter a new character, the Prince, played like every other great role by a *première danseuse*. As Prince, he too is crowned with a pointed miter.

The slave before the Prince.

Gestures and Poses 53

Inao and Bosseba.

He wears a tight-fitting ruby vest trimmed and braided with silver. Sleeves of saffron velvet extend beyond other shorter sleeves, and end under his bracelets.

On his shoulders rise two golden horns, like the gables of a pagoda. He has a diamond-studded breastplate, a double band of red gold, and a collar of precious metal with large cabochons. His red and gold *sampot* is drawn up between his legs and sewn in place behind. Saffron pantaloons with a silver lining reach down to his knees.

A flame of crimson and gold sparkling with gems, the Prince expresses his tenderness. Bosseba, listening, lies on one of the low tables. Her attendants are gathered at her feet. He comes near. And he is allowed to hope that soon, chastely, they will consummate their mad love.

But there is never, even in scenes of the most burning passion, anything immodest or suggestive. Hermetically sealed in a sewn-on costume, armored with gold ornaments, no character will ever strike a vulgar pose.

In chaste supplication, the Prince will chastely put an arm around the object of his tenderness. Thus, at these most decisive moments, and amid the most opportune shadows, the two lovers merely walk together, in characteristic rhythmic flexibility. Nothing dubious, no unveiled or glimpsed feminine beauty, destroys the harmonious candor.

Yet the sweet little sniffle that is the Cambodian kiss would not be immodest! The heads of two charming young women touching at moments of great passion, amid their fragrant headdress flowers, the points of their two tiaras in great proximity, even crossing, would upset neither the senses nor the most unforgiving virtue. Only hearts…

No! Not even hearts, for gods cannot love like men.

"Protestation."

Chapter IV

Costumes and Jewels

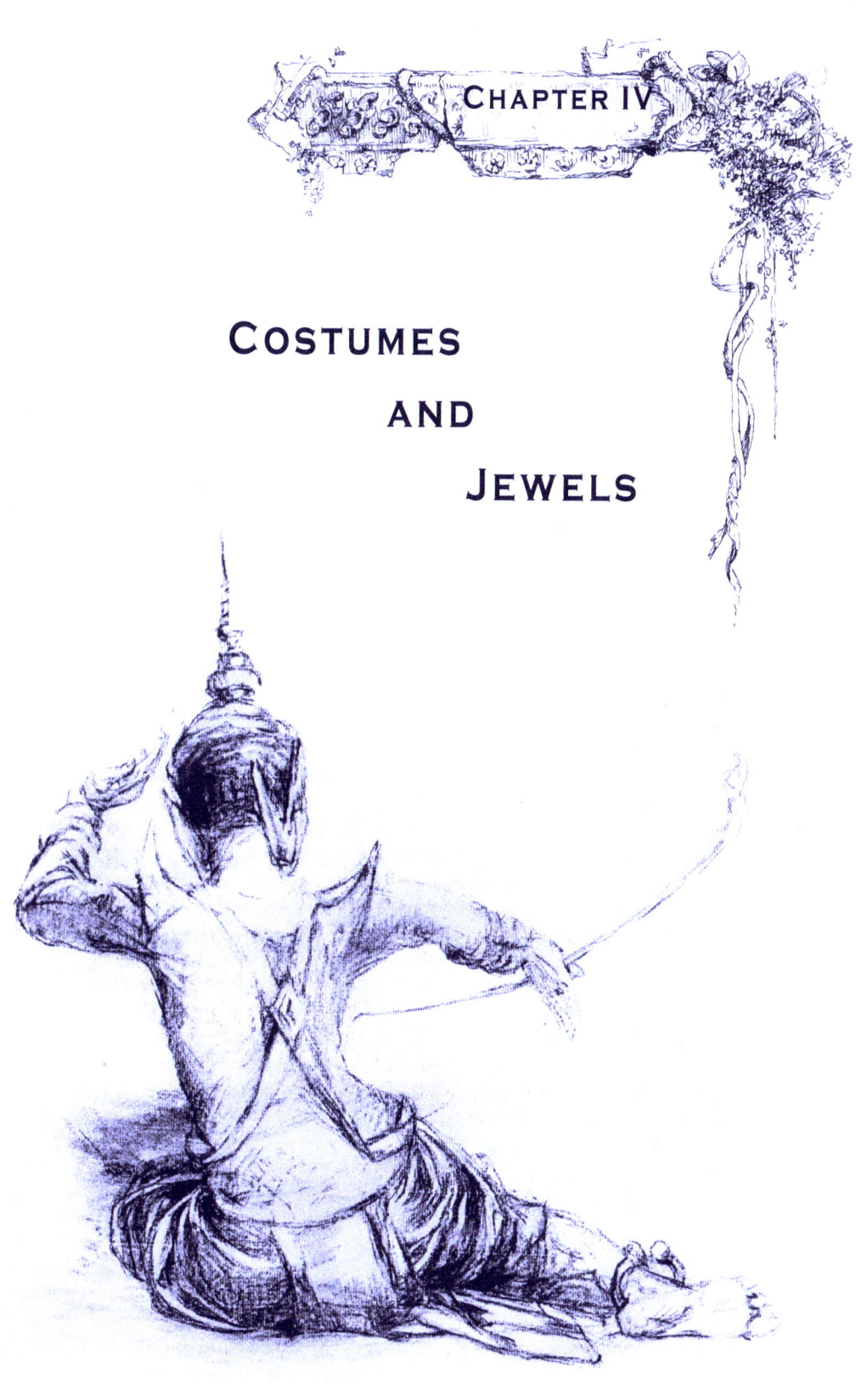

Arm bracelet.

The prince costumes resemble those worn by the King at his coronation. The princess costumes resemble those worn in everyday life, by young girls at their tonsure (hair cutting) ceremony and by brides. Otherwise, the characters of the great Khmer mythology have their own particular costumes.

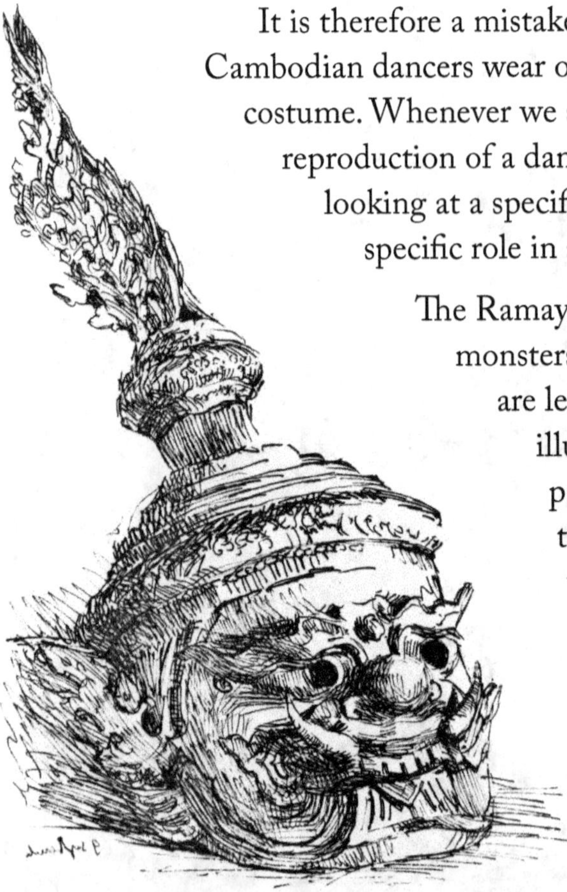

It is therefore a mistake to believe that Cambodian dancers wear one distinctive dance costume. Whenever we see a dancer, or the reproduction of a dancer's image, we are looking at a specific actress playing a specific role in a specific play.

The Ramayana is a poem in which monsters, Spirits, and Gods are legion. To complete the illusion, brightly painted paperboard masks hide the dancers' cute heads, which really would not be appropriate on the bodies of Giants or monkey warriors.

Mask of the King of the Giants.

Frightening or grotesque, the heavy masks have two eye holes. Each dancer holds her mask in place with a cord gripped between her teeth. The mask covers her head completely. Because of the weight, it rests atop her head, on a small handkerchief.

The grimacing head of the King of Giants sports two boar tusks and red eyebrows. The prodigious *garuda*, celestial bird and steed of Vishnu, holds in his beak a magic ball that renders him invisible.[10]

Garuda.

Hanuman, the Monkey King, appears with a white countenance; the divine Rama, with a green face; Ngo, a physically ugly man who possesses all moral qualities, with a black head. To these we add masks for animals and fantastic monsters.

10. This *garuda* mask is an exact replica of the *garuda* head that figures among the bas-reliefs of Angkor. It can be found, among other places, on the eastern face of the Terrace of the Elephants in Angkor Thom.

The Princess on her bed.

We should note that the women remain graceful. The Cambodian aesthetic has not seen fit to provide masks for heroines. They always appear in their snow-white makeup, just as they are and just as they're relished.

Wearing these paperboard heads is near-torture. They are very difficult to keep on. An actress is all but smothered inside and can barely see. She can move only by extending her neck, and all her movements are checked.

As the action demands, all the characters move about simultaneously or alternately. They fight, chase one another, cast their evil spells, and woo at the center of the dance hall, facing the King. They have the utmost respect for local tradition and strive to push the illusion to its limits.

In attendance.

Costumes and Jewels

A General.

The bird-woman affixes two rigid wings to her hips. Behind her, attached to her waist and jagged like a flame, rises a bird's tail. Unlike the Princess, she has no scarf, but a sort of flame-colored leotard instead. Cupped over her breasts are two small engraved gold shields. A short skirt is puffed out over her *sampot*, and feathers cover her legs.

The mermaid has a fish tail on which disks shine like scales. Generals, military officers, and crafty emissaries wear a light, charming crown. A golden half-moon adorns each shoulder. As circumstances dictate, they carry a sword or a dagger. The favorite attendant wears small wings on her headdress. Slaves wear a scarf over both shoulders, and the warriors of Javanese Prince Inao wear a scarlet turban.

Apart from two jesters, who very rarely take part in royal ballets, no man is ever onstage simultaneously with the actresses. Any masculine presence would destroy the charming and gracious harmony.

Moreover, in Cambodia as in every other country in the world, it's better not to let wolves in among the sheep.[11]

---

11. There are about sixty male dancers throughout Cambodia. If necessary, they can be summoned to the palace. They simulate the epic battles of the Ramayana. Their chief is both Deputy Minister of the Palace and keeper of the costumes, which are styled after those of the royal dancers.

Costumes and Jewels

Kinnari: the bird-woman.

Several childish things, like carnival floats drawn by jesters wearing horse heads and shadow theaters with heroes chasing heroines for entertainment, have survived to the present day.

Sometimes the actresses dine as if at Antoine's (*chez Antoine*),[12] and it's an ugly sight. Seated on rickety chairs at a cloth-covered table of turned wood, wielding dubious utensils, these divinities quickly fall from the mystical heights where we love to see them.

To turn the action up a notch, certain poor little dancers are suspended from the ceiling. With cords fastened under their arms, they stroll among the chandeliers, bumping into them on occasion, and freezing in their nearly impossible poses without any support at all.

Such are the naïveté and the errors to which Cambodian theatre subjects our actresses. Need we dwell on them any further?

Phase of walking on the knees.

12. Editor's Note: This unusual reference remains obscure. At 17 Rue de la Fontaine in Paris an establishment founded in 1911 called Café Antoine is still in operation. But whether its rickety furniture and "dubious utensils" warranted recognition half a world away is unknown. Certainly Groslier must have thought his readers would understand this reference, but after a century the connection has faded.

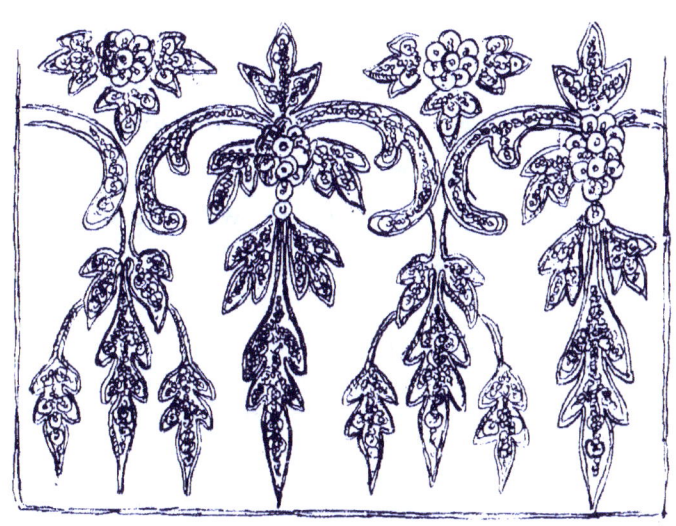

The embroidery of the grand scarf.

The costumes of the *corps de ballet* are kept in a stockroom under the responsibility of a male and female guardian. They are folded and stored in series and in armoires. Each is marked with the name of the dancer who wears it and to whom it was fitted. *Sampots* aside, the costumes are cut, assembled, and embroidered by expert seamstresses at the palace, under the direction of a *grande première danseuse*: at present, Princess Réa-Srey-Yaolac.

When an evening dance is scheduled, each *lokhon* goes during the day to fetch the right costume for the role she is going to play. She returns it at the end of the ballet. It should be in good condition and carefully folded, lest she be fined or given a few lashes with the rattan. The jewels are withdrawn from the dancers immediately after each performance and stored in coffers. Under no circumstances are they left with the dancers.

Malayan warrior.

As we can see, an actress's splendor is quite fleeting. She profits very little from the glory that she worked so hard to achieve. But to preserve her illusions, if she has any, it is much better this way, because the splendid costumes enveloping her under the stage lights are by daylight often nothing more than flashy rags.

A *première danseuse* will don her costume only about ten times. It is then worn by ordinary dancers for about thirty performances, for its tarnished gold and threadbare silk go unnoticed within the *corps de ballet*. Next it is re-cut to fit a small girl. And finally, when it is but a foul, sordid thing, soaked through with sweat and soiled with everyone's makeup, it is burned.

The *sampots* of the *premières danseuses* are a piece of silk embroidered with flowers in gold thread. They used to come from India. They were supple, thick, and superb, and cost from 70 to 100 piastres. Now — dare I say so? — they come from Lyon and cost hardly half that!

A *première danseuse* costume — minus jewels, of course — currently costs from 200 to 300 piastres.

The large velvet scarves are light green, daffodil yellow, crimson, or white. Under H. M. Norodom, they were made from fabrics in gold thread.

Two officers.

Costumes and Jewels

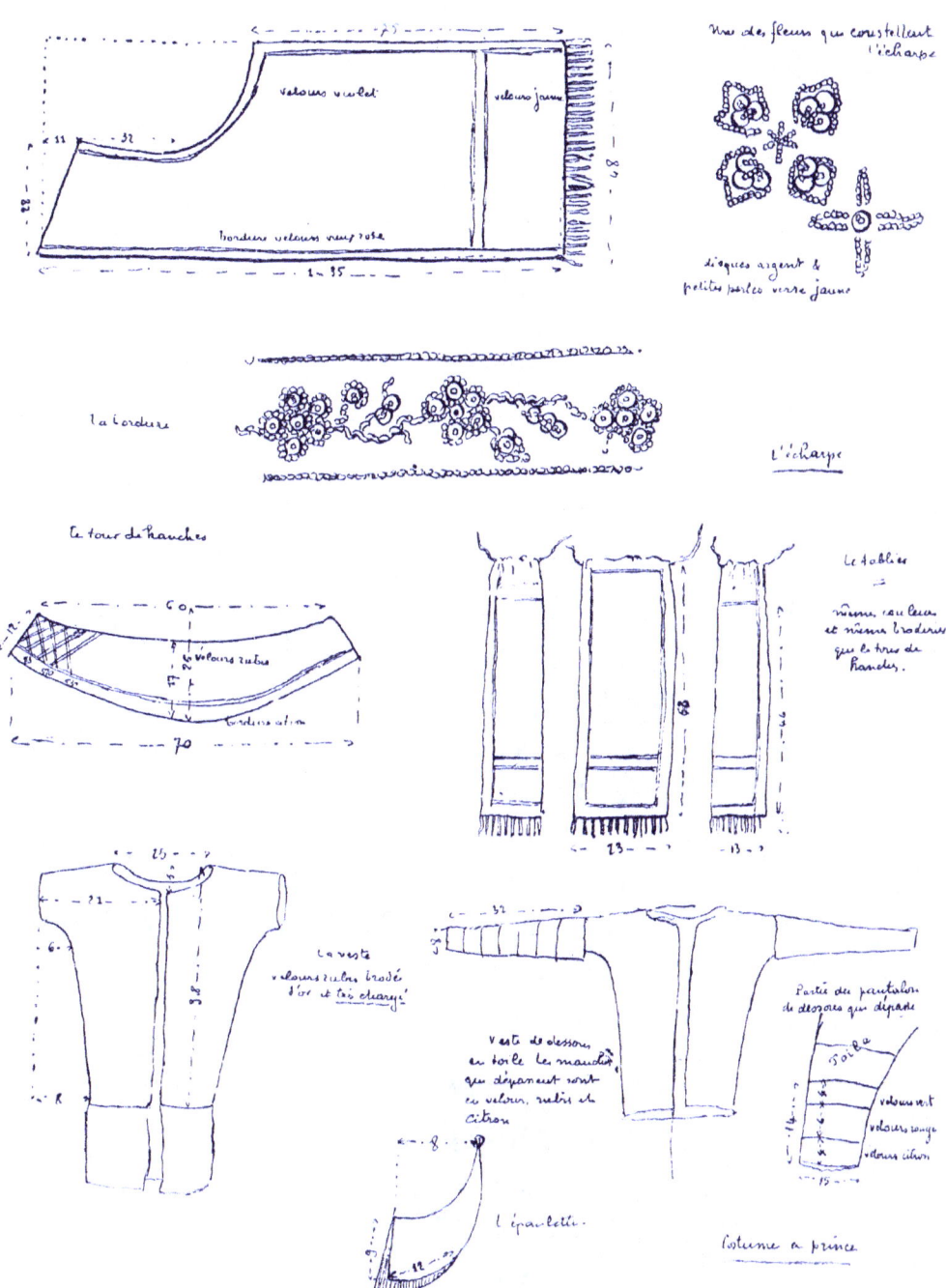

Costume patterns and their average measurements.

The scarves are entirely embroidered with pearls and small disks of gold, silver, or metal. The favorite embroidery consists of a regular lattice pattern with a flower gleaming in the center of each square.

The jacket, embroidered like the scarf, is of satinet or silk.

The three flaps of the apron that hang over the thighs of princes and officers are also made of velvet. The wings of the bird-women, meanwhile, are stiffened with a framework of metal wire covered with embroidered fabrics.

All of these costumes are heavy, stiff, and hot. They have no fasteners and are sewn onto the dancer for each performance. The scarf is attached under the arms; the jacket, in front and along the seam of the sleeves; the man's *sampot*, over the *derrière*.

Under her scarf, the dancer wears a sort of silk undershirt of yellow, rose, or blue, just visible on the left side. Before slipping into her Princess *sampot*, she puts on very short cotton underpants, in order to not be entirely nude. I should add, finally, that very young ballerinas whose breasts don't fill out the heavy scarf or the jacket to their liking make up for their insufficiencies with a ruse, padding their costume with deftly folded little handkerchiefs.

Costumes and Jewels 67

The *mokot*.

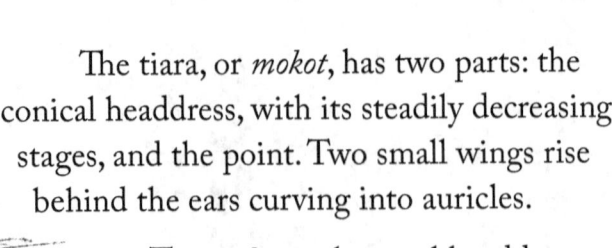

The headgear of attendants.

The tiara, or *mokot*, has two parts: the conical headdress, with its steadily decreasing stages, and the point. Two small wings rise behind the ears curving into auricles.

The *mokot* is the royal headdress. *Mokots* worn by dancers playing kings, princes, or divinities are exact replicas. They are mounted on a framework of leather or cardboard, covered in gold-leaf, and set with gems.

Tiaras worn by men differ a bit from those worn by women. They are generally higher and lack the frontal crescent, which encircles the top of the face and rises slightly in front of the ears.

Small diamond rosettes, arranged in rings a few stages from the point, tremble perpetually on tiny springs. Dangling from other stages and swaying at the slightest movement are lightweight triangular mirrors.

That, in sum, is the unusual headdress, light and slender, crafted like a jewel in a lovely style. A head ornament blending more elegance with more majesty can hardly be imagined.

The dancer often readjusts it on her forehead with a familiar gesture. The slightest movement sets the diamonds aquiver and the triangles sparkling. The gem at the top sometimes casts its rays in all directions, like a small astral body or the flame of a distant beacon.

In fact, it is to keep the *mokot* in its precarious balance that the actress's troubled forehead retains that quasi-immobility and rejects participation in the movements of the rest of her body. The actress never angles the distinguished and lofty ornament toward the ground.

The *panntiereth* is the light crown of the officers. It is less imposing than the *mokot* but is no less gracious an ornament. A tight knot seems to close it at the back. All around it hang delicate garlands, from which the dancer hangs a strand of pearls, as a light covering for her nape.

The *panntiereth*.

Yet to be described are the headdresses for favorite attendants: a truncated cone topped by a circle of tiny wings pointing skyward. Young girls wear a light, crescent-shaped diadem, which hides the small chignon on top of their head. So ends the list of headdresses for Khmer actresses.

A gold *mokot* is worth from 500 to 600 piastres; a *mokot* of gilded paperboard, 20 piastres. Ordinary dancers wear the latter, which is much lighter. The gold *panntiereth* costs 200 piastres; the one made from paperboard, 10. Any *panntiereth* encircling the much-admired head of a favorite is decorated in front with a bird of diamonds.

The smallest gem's detachment from the sacred headdresses or masks during the dance is a sure sign of misfortune. The *lokhon* is overcome with fear and finds no peace until she has made liturgical sacrifices to Buddha.

The fantastic heads of Giants and Gods, like everything drawn and brought to life from the mythological epics, are objects of the same religion. Are these sacred accessories not haunted by their individual spirits and guardians?

These beliefs are so powerful and deeply held that sick dancers ask for their *mokot* or mask to be brought to them. They have it placed at their bedside, burn thin wax candles before it, and speak to it of their ills and devotion.

How can the occult powers haunting the object not be touched by such naïve confidences? How could they tarry in restoring the health of their faithful celebrants?

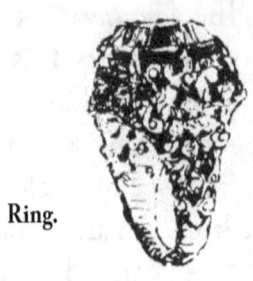
Ring.

Finally, we reach the jewels.

Gold abounds. Thirty or forty rows of gold chains, each different, all with engraved links, wrap around the bust of the *première danseuse*, from shoulder to side. The belt is a ribbon, three fingers wide, of gold mesh. Its engraved, elliptical buckle is convex, like a shield, and set with approximately one hundred and eighty diamonds and roses.

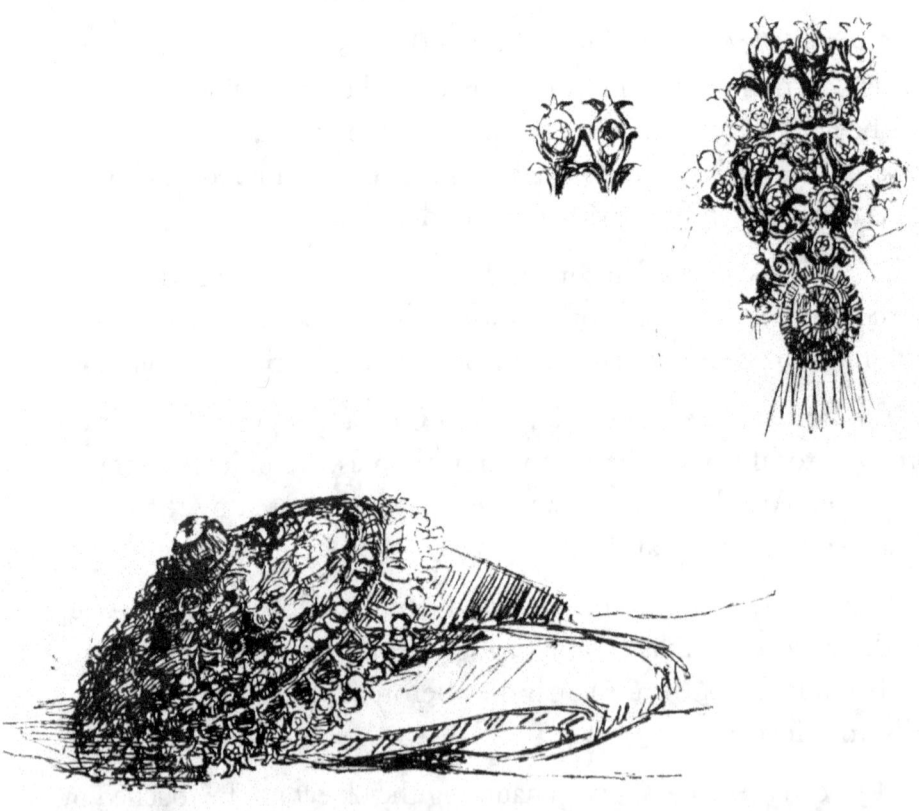

The belt buckle and detail.

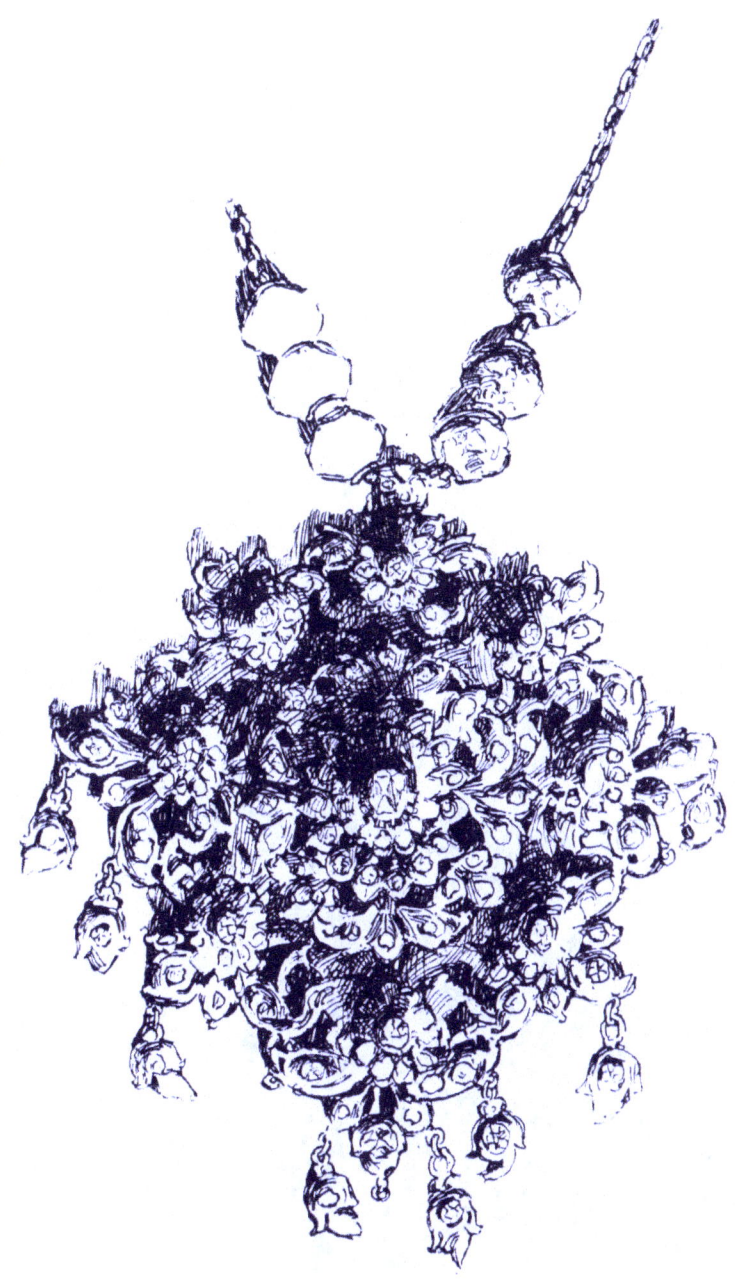

The chest pendant.

On a chain, against the *lokhon*'s chest and between her breasts, hangs a pendent as large as a hand. It resembles the belt buckle but is decorated with still more diamonds.

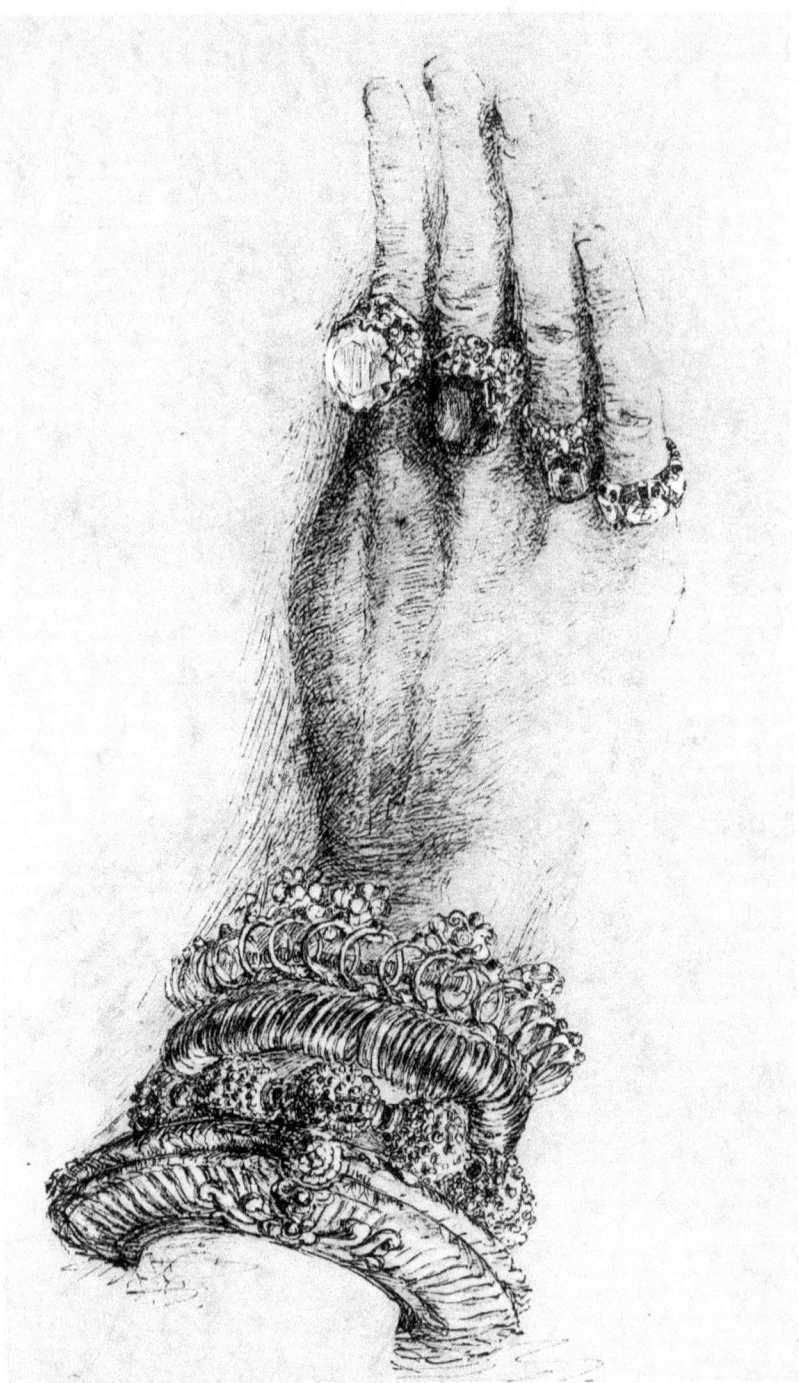

Her hand is one great jewel. Every finger but the thumb carries an emerald, a sapphire, a ruby. On her little finger shines a small engraved ring with three large diamonds.

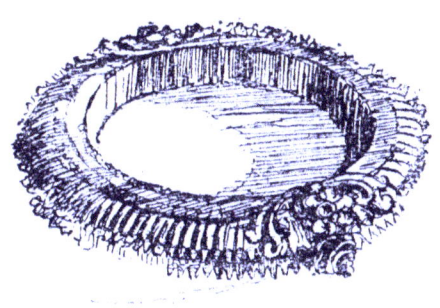 

The first and fifth bracelet.

Five kinds of bracelets, in unchanging order, weigh down her flexible wrist. For the first, we have gemmed ornaments separated with wound gold; for the second, small rings attached with a cotton string; for the third, a large, flexible, cylindrical spring in gold; for the fourth, eight or ten large filigree pearls; and for the fifth, an exact replica, engraved in gold, of a bracelet that Cambodian experts make by pressing peculiar flowers.

There are two ball-tipped anklets for the feet. And I almost forgot the long spiral earrings, made in the image of a floweret whose every petal is a diamond; and the sheaths of gold bent into half-crescents, which the dancers use to extend their fingers and exaggerate the upturning of their hands.[13]

Earrings and ankle band.

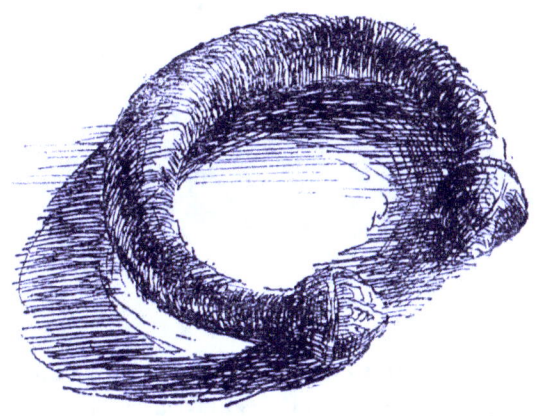

13. These sheaths are no longer used.

Such is the often priceless finery of a lead actress. The finery for secondary roles is of gilded silver and glasswork, but it nevertheless shines with a few pure jewels and constitutes a veritable fortune.[14]

14. I weighed all the jewels of a lead dancer — minus the *mokot*, which alone weighs 870 grams — and found the fantastic weight of 2 kilos, 770 grams of gold, diamonds and gems.

Chapter V

COSTUMES
and Make-up

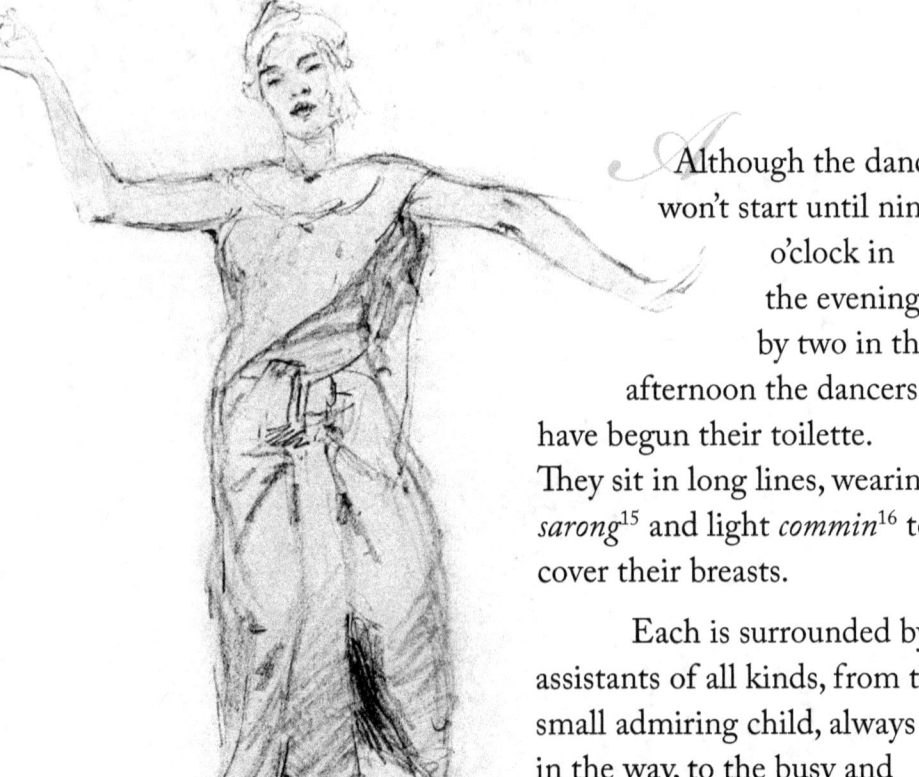

Undulation of the body.

Although the dances won't start until nine o'clock in the evening, by two in the afternoon the dancers have begun their toilette. They sit in long lines, wearing *sarong*[15] and light *commin*[16] to cover their breasts.

Each is surrounded by assistants of all kinds, from the small admiring child, always in the way, to the busy and meticulous *baya* (old woman). One of the expert dressers mixes in her hand a pinch of saffron and coconut oil. Slowly, carefully, she rubs this rich paste onto the dancer's face, neck, and arms, all of which turn gold. Anyone at rest is chewing a quid of betel.

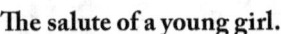

The salute of a young girl.

---

15. *Sarong*: a piece of cloth wrapped around the lower back and tied in the front.
16. *Commin*: a long scarf.

The white is mixed in turn, but in water, which is used to warm it up. If the dancer is to play a male role, a hint of saffron is added. Otherwise, it remains pure.

This white substance, sold by the Chinese, is crumbly and cool. The small lumps are crushed into an impalpable, soft powder, like the finest rice powder. Later, we will see that its use dates back to ancient times. It is applied in the same way as the saffron, in a long and delicate operation. Then, finally, the *lokhon* emerges, white as a Pierrot. The make-up completely changes her face, immobilizing her features, enlarging them a bit. It is as if a ridge of snow at the edge of her eyelids had melted in the glare of her glance, become even darker and more scintillating.[17]

The *baya* captures on a saucer the smoke of a lit candle, dabs the end of an oiled bamboo stick in the soot, and carefully draws with it the slender arc of the dancer's eyebrows. A bit of red Chinese paper gives a little blood, artificial and delicate, to her lips. So ends the ritualistic and subtle make-up session, the same ritual undergone by young girls for the celebration of their puberty and by brides on their wedding day.

Humble attitude.

17. **This make-up is made of pure white lead. It is difficult to say how injurious it is to the skin. After the dance, it is removed by intense washing with soapy water and lemon juice.**

Putting on the *sampot*.

Then attendants sew on the scarf or jacket, affix the graceful epaulets, and roll or pleat the *sampot*. It is only six o'clock in the evening, but our dancer is ready. At the last moment they will add yet a little more white, but this time it will be a powder applied with a small sachet.

Preparation and Make-up of the Dancers

It's only six o'clock!

…The dancer should scarcely move if she is to preserve the expert order of her costume. The bracelets are heavy on her arms. Still three hours to go … but how beautiful she is!

One stitches the scarf.

In the morning, after rehearsal, the dancers made their flower pendants and bracelets.

They patiently threaded fresh jasmine flowers stripped from their stalks; then affixed long *champa* petals, as fringes to the pompoms.

They hang the pendants from one side of their gold headdresses. To the other they attach small bouquets bound in cornets made with pieces of banana leaves.

The dancers spent the rest of their time before the costuming session making large rolls of pressed flowers — jasmine once again — and soaking them in fresh water. In full costume these will encircle their wrists above the ritual bracelets.

The solemn moment approaches. The King, the ministers, the people await. The orchestra strikes up the prelude. The regular clap of wooden time-keeping sticks penetrates backstage, through the curtains.

The two phases of the march.

Saluting the *mokot*.

Respectfully, an assistant brings in the sparkling tiara. It is the royal headdress, the insignia of power, the sacred summit of Mount Meru, on which all worlds rest.

Before receiving this final, delicate ornament, to beautify her further and make her divine, the *lokhon* suddenly turns serious and salutes with joined hands.

Afterwards, she pads it with a scented handkerchief, cautiously accepts it, and balances it on her snow-white brow. Attendants set the two small side wings behind the ears and tie the ribbon chin-strap.

Quickly they apply still a bit more white powder. She takes a last gulp of tea. Suddenly, in bursts an agitated old woman, exclaiming frantically. She has come to fetch our dancer, who is at last ready.

Go, Charming Princess! Go and step into the blazing light. Charm the Gods, your King, the People, and your admirers!

Chapter VI

Their Organization

The *corps de ballet* is under the direction of the Princess, first wife of the King. She is its absolute mistress, ordering punishments, establishing discipline, supervising rehearsals, paying salaries, and ensuring regular service for His Majesty.

Under Norodom, there were five hundred *lokhon* divided into three troupes. The most beautiful, most stylish, and most richly adorned troupe was under the orders of his first wife, Princess Khoun Tanh. Then came the second troupe, a bit less prestigious, directed by his second wife, Khoun Préa Nieth. The third, comprising apprentices, had Princess Man Soun at its head.

A leader like Princess Khoun Tanh would reign with an iron fist. The women's quarters, visited daily by Her Majesty, were kept rigorously clean. In the gardens, there were large bathing pools of finished masonry.

The current *corps de ballet*, under His Majesty Sisowath, comprises eight *premières danseuses*, sixty-six to seventy dancers, and about forty young female students.

A *première danseuse* earns thirty-five piastres per month; an ordinary dancer, from ten to fifteen piastres, depending on her role. Young girls, meanwhile, earn from three to six piastres.

Each actress has four piastres deducted from her salary for her food. When there is a dance performance, she gets a bonus. The *première danseuse* gets one piastre. Dancers playing arduous roles, the mask bearers, get fifty to ninety cents. Twenty-five cents go to those playing ordinary roles and twenty to young girls.

Those are the figures, and such modest ones at that! But by the end of the year, when you add in the costumes, this little world of musicians, chorus women, and dressers drains some thirty to thirty-five thousand piastres from the royal coffers.

The daily service of attending the King is divided into four quarter-day shifts. There are in sum twenty dancers — the troupe's most beautiful — and a few musicians. The service and the selection are the entire responsibility of the first wife.

A large flowery green curtain separates the royal bed from the rest of the room. It is mounted on a raised platform of precious wood. The gold-embroidered fabric covering the mattress matches that day's color.[18]

Sunday - red

Monday - bright yellow

Tuesday - green

Wednesday - purple

Thursday - dark blue

Friday - light blue

Saturday - black

---

18. At court, the color of costumes and *sampots* changes daily in accordance with the chart above, which also regulates the color of the actresses' *sampots* for ballets.

    The King is perpetually surrounded by his wives and his dancers. Day and night, there are always two crouching at the foot of his bed. One works a light feathered fan at the end of a long handle. The other holds at the ready a fly-whisk of frayed silk. Off the platform and arrayed throughout the room, sitting on mats, bright as flowers and merry as children, is the rest of the harem, keeping the Master company.

    They smoke, chew betel, and take turns with the fan or the fly-whisk. His Majesty speaks to them from the bed, his eye caressing their faces with its glance. To please him, they wear pleated *sampots*, scented with *champa* flowers. Their vibrant scarves are infused with sandalwood. They sing in chorus, accompanied by the musicians. If the King is content and not busy, he keeps time by clapping his hands, and everyone is very happy.

    Night swiftly invades the room through great bay windows opening out onto the gardens. Lamps are lit, and cigarette smoke swirls around them. In the hands of an attentive dancer, the fan beats faster to cool the King's brow, for the evenings here are sultry. Then the orchestra suddenly stops. Voices die away, one by one. Soon nothing breaks the silence but the discrete sounds of bumped betel boxes, scarcely perceptible whispers, perhaps the distant bell of a Chinese peddler, the caw of a raven … The King has fallen asleep.

Though always in their company, the King never makes his dancers dance for him alone. If he is sad, he has them sing, or has the musicians play. It was the same in Norodom's time, and there was music every evening. But it was necessary to set the scene, to describe a normal day for our dancers, to show that they are present at every level.

Moreover, the King has a favorite. She has seduced him with her special grace. Brimming with tenderness, forgetting that he is King and God, he has her sit at his side and speaks to her gently.

When this happens all the other women rise and leave. The fan-bearer stops beating her fan, draws the large curtain, isolating the royal bed in the scented night, and withdraws, sandals in hand.

And it is only now that I too, with respect for proprieties and prestige, take my leave, along with the little service dancer. I draw the curtain and depart.

Première danseuse Nou-Namh.

And so the dancer effectively becomes the King's wife.

She has just turned fifteen years old. She is every bit a woman. She has the large, soft, melancholic eyes of her race, the broad, bridgeless nose, the rounded forehead, and the somewhat pronounced, merry lips. Her cropped hair, pulled up over the forehead, has a pronounced wave. The exposed nape of her neck is that of a boy.

From her royal husband she has received an emerald, a necklace, or earrings in the shape of flowers. This earns her great respect and great envy — human nature is everywhere the same.

From now on the King's glances will linger on her hieratic gestures whenever she dances. She will have claim to new favors. She will no longer need to wear imitation jewelry in ballets, and will be able to demand a slight raise in her salary.

But one day, sewing the princess's scarf on, the old *baya* dresser will realize that she can no longer make the ends meet, and the secret will spread like wildfire.

A young girl.

The young mother will leave the troupe. The King, moved, will shower her with jewels and give her a small house of her own within the palace walls. There, respectfully waited on, enjoying the shade and peace of the large trees, she will await the arrival of the royal child. Then she will raise it, watch it grow. Once the child has grown up and no longer needs her maternal care, she will no doubt dream of past splendors, and of the admiration that no longer strokes her female vanity. She will perhaps succumb to nostalgia and wish to reclaim her place atop the Khmer Olympus. But her hand will no longer be able to bloom like a flower. Her joints will be flexible no more.

I cannot say whether melancholy and regret will thenceforth be her housemates, as she awaits the sad moment when she will begin girding herself in the white scarf of an old woman, having shed the triumphal scarf that had gone so well with her beauty.

Anger. The dancer strikes the ground.

Chapter VII

THEIR LIFE

Each dancer has her own dwelling, a compartment in a long, yellow, smoky house. Each compartment is divided into two sections. In one, she eats and does her toilette. The other is a bedroom.

The furniture is sparse: a wooden bed covered with a mattress and a mat, some chairs, a trunk, and a small armoire with shelves inside and a glass door.

This armoire is the piece our dancer takes the most care with. She places it near her bed. On the top shelf, she neatly stores her bottles of coconut and sandalwood oil, her white powder, and her saffron, in glass vials. On the shelf below are her cloth or silk jackets, straight-cut Cambodian blouses, or fitted Siamese blouses with wide lace collars, and, finally, scarves of every color, folded small, rolled, perfumed by the dried flowers inside. In the trunk she stores her *sampots*, her small velvet sandals, embroidered with gold and tiny objects.

This is her entire fortune, the full contents of her hope chest. She also has paper fans, a square mirror, floor mats, and a teapot with Annamite cups. If she is frugal, she might one day be able to afford fabric drapes in her window or a rug to cover the bad planks in her floor, or she might make herself a silk mattress. Such things would be her greatest luxuries.

Even nowadays you can still occasionally come across a blurry, yellowing photograph of the King or a princess hanging on the wall, or some fragrant jasmines in bloom on the low armoire in front of the mirror.

All along the compartments runs a common, sloping roof, which forms a veranda — the preferred gathering spot, weather permitting, for chit-chat and meals.

This, then, is where the dancers live. They may receive only women. Apart from the Minister of the Palace, no man may pass through the guard-flanked gates and penetrate the high walls of this closed quarter.

Favorites and *premières danseuses* have isolated houses, of wood or masonry. There they live surrounded by as many maidservants as their salaries can keep.

His Majesty King Sisowath never enters this gynaeceum, this women's quarter, but his predecessor King Norodom took walks there daily, and demanded that it be kept meticulously clean. Now the barracks are aging, have been soiled by hearth fumes and the rains, and make a rather morose impression. But they still hum with activity.

At ten o'clock in the morning and six o'clock in the evening, matrons or little boys arrive with meals for the dancers. The *lokhon* who don't cook for themselves can thus purchase their food for four piastres a month from women outside the palace or have it sent in by their own parents.

These meals arrive cold, on copper plates, and lack variety. Steamed rice, grilled fish cooked in Chinese sauce, vegetables with *nuoc-mam* (fish sauce), curry, pork, large fried grasshoppers, shrimp — such is the everyday menu.

From morning to evening, female peddlers of all kinds make their rounds in the dancers' quarter, shouting or ringing tiny bells. At seven o'clock in the morning they begin selling rice cooked in coconut milk and duck-egg cakes. Their baskets are loaded with mangos, bananas dried in the sun and flavored with vanilla, roasted watermelon seeds and water lilies, guava jam served in sugar flowers, all neatly laid out on banana leaves.

Everything is so appetizing, and so cheap, that idle dancers cannot help but indulge themselves. They snack all day and have little appetite left at mealtime.

With their thick foliage, the mango trees of the big gardens spread a gentle shade. Their branches, heavy with flowers, hide the walls. The lanes of brown earth are well maintained. The red and gray, creamy-fleshed sapodillas, the tangerines, and the lychee ripen not for the birds and the King alone.

Under the preceding reign, there were, as I've mentioned, large pools of finished masonry covered with flowering lotus. A water-lifting machine would pour fresh, clear water into them every morning. At the hottest time of the day, the dancers, half-naked in light sarongs tied above their breasts, would cavort there in safety. They would play together in the limpid water, chasing one another and laughing uproariously.

The light of day, scattered by the pearly splashes of young, frolicking bodies, would glisten on their brown shoulders. The fabric would cling to their round shapes, and the sky would reflect on their breasts....

Having finished their bath, the dancers would return to their rooms, lotus flowers in hand, leaving on the red ground wet footprints, quickly stolen away by the sun.

Under His Majesty Sisowath, these basins were maintained less fastidiously, the water wasn't changed regularly, and the dancers stopped going there. They were eventually filled in. The culprit here, the Minister of the Palace, never suspected the poetry, the charms, and the traditions that he was burying.

The dancers must have been so pretty and happy in that water, in the fragrant shade cast by those trees, with the blossoms tumbling all around! Taking part in a truly ancient act, they must have formed a truly rare tableau, whose echoes and reflections the artist and poet, though kept at a distance, must have perceived.

The winds and the odors, the mysterious wings of imagination, the subtle insights for which only a word suffices — all now serve no purpose. The hour has struck for the last custom of the ancient *devadasi*[19] to die.

They have evaporated. The clear waves are gone. The happy water sprites frolic no more. Dainty bare feet no longer brush the bed of pebbles at the bottom.

When not engaged in royal service or rehearsals, the Cambodian actress is entirely free.

Now when she rises in the morning she takes a shower, since the pools are gone, and performs the toilette of a simple woman. If her pay, or savings, permit, she buys fabric and sews, hems her scarves and *sampots*, makes herself jackets.

19. *Devadasi* - **In ancient Hindu practices, these were young female temple servants who were "married" and dedicated to a deity (deva or devi). In addition to maintaining the temple and performing rituals, they studied the classical Indian arts of dance and music and originally they enjoyed high social status.**

A phase of grief.

Promenade.

In her compartment she receives her neighbor, or neighbors. It goes without saying that they gab. They talk about other people. They slander and criticize. They tell marvelous stories. They discuss the gossip brought in from the city by maidservants and cooks. They speak of French women, and also of French men. They drink tea. They eat Chinese soups with the water-lily fruit. They chew areca and red lime rolled in acidic betel leaves. They smoke tobacco flavored with orange rinds.

The frightening walk of a Giant.

When evening approaches, when the setting sun seems to dangle from the branches of the big trees like a big red lantern, when the scent of *champa* and frangipani, which no breeze carries away, wafts down to the violet ground, the dancers don their beautiful *sampots*, wrap their softest scarves around their breasts, shoe their bare feet in gold-embroidered sandals, and stroll in groups, arm in arm, a flower over the ear, infinitely cheerful, singing softly, penetrating the mysteries of twilight without understanding them....

Night falls. The red light has reached the summit of the Mast of Honor of His Majesty's palace. The black horns of the Silver Pagoda, crowned by a covey of ravens, are silhouetted for a few moments more against the day's last opalescent band, then they too vanish.

Then, when silence reigns at last in the sleeping palace, the *lokhon* skulk. Trembling with fear, making no sound to attract the guard or make the dogs bark, they slip into the King's garden, to steal roses!!!

The King's insufficient love, the tender stories they play out onstage, the forces of nature in this equatorial region where they live, and their own young senses cannot help but trouble the poor little dancers, separated as they are from the rest of the world.

Marriage is their obsession. Innocent, friendly relations lead to the formation of couples. One plays husband, the other wife. They explore naïvely through play acting, and gradually come to understand. Desires of the flesh, demanding satisfaction, take root in their developing breasts, and the scene between Bosseba and Inao leaves behind but a memory.

Behind the closed door of her compartment, the poor solitary princess thinks of how good it would be to have a husband at her side; but a husband without ritual white, without jewels or golden headdress, one of those beautiful children of the Mekong, an elephant driver, a fisherman, a sower of rice.

Cambodian dancers may not be approached, but to study their psychology it suffices to observe country women and add to their native vanity the large dose of new vanity that goes along with entry into the palace.

Admittedly, the Khmer woman is puerile, lively, authoritarian, and anxious over her status, but the actress is even more so. Talent, favors, and titles are the cause of great envy, secret plots, and stubborn intrigues.

Seduction.

But in general she has a wonderful heart. She is weak and indecisive. She is unable to resist the old peddler women who surround and exploit her. She can be a tender and devoted mother. She is more child than woman and entertains an utterly unreasonable passion for jewels. She is capable of deep feelings and great thoughtfulness. Her heart brims with tenderness and is often charmingly sensitive. This is all relative, of course, and has to do with her race and her instincts, which are those of a simple creature. But it is carried to an extreme degree.

To prove these claims, let us transcribe a few passages from Cambodian songs. After all, aren't song and popular poetry the most reliable gauge of changes among the people, of their feelings and concerns?

> "Deprive me of the points of your breasts,
> and regret will wash over me...."

> "O my love! O my darling!
> Sleep, for it is late.
> I kiss and caress the body of my love,
> on the pretty gilded bed."

"In the quiet of the night, the birds call and respond.
Listen, my darling, to the birds…
What harmony, what tenderness! Could they be speaking?
It is like a distant music, distant and soft…"

"I kiss her velvety body, her cool cheeks, soft and clear.

"I must venerate my sweetheart, and place her on an altar.…
She walks remarkably, harmonious and soft, undulating.

"I beg to kiss her body, her flesh, her substance, and her breasts,
Let us get drunk on caresses!"

"Paired with you, my little one! My sweet, my exquisite darling,
let us enter the quiet and remote forest, to unite!"

"Your body is fragrant, your waist harmonious.
There is no other like you — like you, my darling.

"O my dear, discreet little Kangor,
You come from Bassac, and you put
your hair in a bun
without a fuss!"[20]

How could a people of such tender words have girls incapable of understanding and deserving them?

And why would the most beautiful of these girls suddenly lose their hearts on accepting the superb tiara? Why would they no longer be the "soft and exquisite darlings" celebrated in the boatmen's love songs?

20. Translation of passages drawn from the popular songs of Cambodia, collected by Mr. Tricon, Public Prosecutor in Phnom Penh.

Sougriva.

I have shown the Cambodian actress growing up, working, preparing for the dance, and emerging into the dazzle of a royal festival. I will now complete her biography.

Bound tight and suffocating in her carapace of precious stones, the Cambodian actress streams with sweat. Her throat is so dry that it is sometimes necessary to bring her some tea during the actual performance. Her arms are exhausted. It is past midnight, and she has appeared onstage six times amid the deafening music, the smoke, and the crowd. Under her dark, blinding mask, her teeth grip the cord, she struggles to breathe, and the rough edge of the crown nearly draws blood as it etches a line into her forehead.

Malay Vizier.

She is spent, broken. Soon, when the ballet is finished, and her assistants have stripped off her costume, she will tumble to her mattress like an inert mass, lacking the strength to remove her make-up.

As you have seen, she lies there like a pauper, in her wretched state of grace, having for a few moments possessed all riches and all powers. The make-up damages her skin, ageing her prematurely. She lives in isolation from the world and from life. Then, tired and faded, she will quit dancing.

She could have left the palace, but now it is too late. Her parents are dead and her friends divided by intrigues. Old and withered as she is, who would take her for a wife? Who would take this girl who has wished her whole life for a husband? Her King has let fade the deep velvet of her wide eyes and the amber of her forehead. Her useless youth has died in the prison where she grew up.

"Quiet! She sleeps."

She is, then, destined to become one of those hideous old women who abound in the palace, one of those crones at the root of every scheme and steering all the traffic in jewels. They are the dressers, the teachers, the maidservants, the time beaters, all the peddlers of toiletries!

Tell me, please. Does she really deserve a destiny like that? She falls sick. They take her out of the palace on a stretcher, because no one may die on the palace grounds, and transport her to an open-air *sala*.

So ends this marvelous and miserable existence, with all its contradictions, all its beauties and miseries. The body will be burnt, and no one will bother to collect her ashes. These are deposited in a cinerary urn shaped like an airy bell, as befits her meager estate. In her misery, she had long ago sold off her personal jewels, symbols of meager favors bestowed, as well as the *sampots* of her young womanhood and the small-folded scarves that shone in joyous colors against the blue shadows of the gardens....

Sequential gesture of the grand salute.

The new salute.

But everything here that has withstood time, wars, and religions has now succumbed to civilization. The Cambodian dancers are in agony. I had the distinct impression, during the seven months that I spent studying them, that a little more of their way of life was slipping away with every passing day, that they needed some moral support, and that underneath the make-up their skin was already white, with the pallor of death. In fact, it was more than an impression. I worked daily at their side and am, alas, quite sure of their fate. I should have joined them in driving all things Western out from every last corner of the place. Scurrying after them with no time to lose, lest they die out before my chronicle was done—I should have put the verbs of this chronicle in the past tense.

We have already noted that the people and the mandarins no longer understand their own theatre. The aged King, now nearly blind, is absorbed in all sorts of worries. He has new expenses and two cars in the garage. His successors, raised in France and dressed in European style, will fail to remember when they are crowned that they are the Sons of Indra, and that they owe a debt of love and protection to the descendants of the hospitable dancer who so warmly welcomed their divine father.

The people are gradually detaching themselves from their monks and their gods. Their concerns are now with the material. And if, on rare festival evenings, they still come to gaze at their ideal, it is because they are a race of children. Their soul is all in the eyes. They come as spectators, passive, unaware that they are witnessing its death.

They are in agony, the Khmer dancers! They are mere shadows now. They are wearing out their last costumes. The princesses are selling their jewels, or pawning them. Sculptors are increasingly rare. Royal painters want to learn perspective and the use of oils. And the women in huts shaded by the banana trees no longer weave the beautiful *sampots* of days past.

When there are no more *sampots*, what will the poor bride dress herself in for her wedding day? In a touching tradition, the palace still loans out an embroidered dancer's scarf for the ceremony, but soon that scarf will no longer exist. Soon no bride will dress up as a legendary princess. There will be no more festivals, nothing of the sort. It is quite a sad prospect.

They're dying! The charming traditions and poetry of yesteryear are dying! Our steamships and automobiles generate a smoke in which *champa* flowers wither. Soon, mysterious actresses, we will no longer see you gather the ancient poems and lost beauties floating thick in the air of festival nights. All the wandering harmonies of earlier times, beauties that only you have the power to retrieve and express anew, will be lost in the chaos....

What will artists and poets do tomorrow in this chosen land?

They will be told that, only yesterday, there still remained one hundred twenty Vestals in whom the entire past and all its rituals were preserved; that these Vestals could sometimes be seen emerging from their mystery and dancing slowly in splendid costumes with graceful harmony, under streaming lights; that in a few corners of the earth colors, eurhythmics, enchantments, and dreams persisted... but that now it is gone!

Caveat

The reader should consider what follows as the result of a number of investigations, not as a series of assertions. Except on artistic matters, I claim no right to draw any conclusions.

With respect to the term *devata*, for which I have traced an origin different from the commonly accepted one, I am but an ignorant intermediary between the people of the country where I found it and my readers. The two legends underpinning my explanation are well known in the land of the Tamil people. Anyone can look into them. I have always been careful to restrict myself to the hypotheses of experts, who alone are qualified to venture into the field of pure history, and I have in every instance named them.

On this subject, I sincerely thank Messrs. Foucher and Finot for their excellent advice.

In this uncertain journey into the past, however, the artist's role is clearly laid out. A naturally subtle observer, because of his profession, the artist must act as the historian's helper in the exploration of past artistic performances, for the artist is their most direct heir.

I thus concluded that my duty was to pursue my study of this art as far as possible and to report everything that could be learned about it. From this traveler's harvest, the reader, snug in his armchair, need only make his selection.

G.G.

Chapter VIII

Their History

***Devata*, Angkor Wat.**

How is it that the Cambodian actress, on donning one of her traditional costumes, achieves her strange gravity? What charm, what mystery transforms her? Into what sacred order does she believe herself initiated? This dancer seemingly become Vestal, what sacred fire does she keep? She has no responsibilities, possesses no profound secrets, and takes part in no fearsome act! She learned her trade as a little girl, without understanding it.

Her life is, dare we say, bourgeois, like that of her sisters in the bush. She is ignorant. None of her activities is rare, ceremonious, or sacred. She does not understand most of the gestures she executes, and when asked the why behind them answers: "It is to look pretty."

Even Mandarins, men of letters, the minister, and the King don't understand the meaning of their actresses' poses unless listening to the chorus chant while they watch. And all of these people, the court, and its monarch attend ceremonies whose rhyme and reason utterly escape them. They are stuck in a darkness from which they cannot and do not care to escape.

Suppose you are tenacious in your observation of the Cambodian dancer. Suppose that you know her country, her habits, and her religion and then try to discover the logic, the normal bonds, that should exist between her and them. You will be shocked to find none.

"Who is this foreigner?" you will exclaim.

No, she's no foreigner. Let us step back, search elsewhere, and we shall witness the rise of a distant poetry.

The gestures of the Cambodian dancers are filled with a nobility and serenity both vague and foreign to their immediate sense. The intensity of their meaning is not proportional to the circumstances: everything is always in the superlative. The salute, for example, does not vary with rank. It is the same for a divinity, the people, or the King. It is always a supreme salute. These gestures seem governed by higher rules that cannot be adapted to arbitrary and informal circumstances. They are a sort of Gregorian chant expressing ordinary feelings, the affairs told of in a superior and poetic literature. An attentive look at them reveals that they have two aspects: one plain and simple, and the other, to be studied below, metaphysical.

This last aspect concerns all that is raised up in purity, with fervor; all that is offered disinterestedly, selflessly; all that comes from the soul, from the bottom of the heart; all, finally, that is done in celebration of powers or abstract beauties.

The *lokhon*'s hand is always offering an invisible flower. It is not logic or the needs of plot that oblige her to perform this haunting gesture. Why does she constantly offer, with such affectation, a flower that seems never to wither, like a Christian who constantly raises his eyes to heaven? And to whom is she supposed to be offering it if not to someone or something superior, invisible, and superhuman, but unknown to her?

The offering is the most effective ceremony in Eastern religions, in which all divinities are feared and must be pleased and appeased. Peasants offer bunches of bananas. The King offers heaps of gold. Down at Angkor, how surprised should we be to see carved into the stones a thousand strange women with hands arranged like those of modern dancers, and whose upturned fingers offer invisible flowers?

These women whose effigies smile at the threshold of a remote past, they were the dancers of the immense temples. And it was they, with their mad love for their toppled Gods, aware of their imminent death, who passed on to their descendants this immortal flower, once offered by them and now still offered by others!

Devata, **Angkor Wat.**

Devata, Angkor Wat.

This peculiar gesture, characteristic and precise, is the most indisputable vestige of the mystical Khmer past. Without exception, each of the thousand female dancers at Angkor, whom passionate, skillful artists carved on the temple walls, always in a dance pose, holds her hand in such a way that it seems to contain an invisible flower.

There is an absolute resemblance between these hands of stone and the white, warm hands of the modern dancers. The thumb and index finger are joined and the other fingers open. This pose is nearly the only one that Khmer artists have, as it were, set in stone, clearly indicating its frequent performance in ancient dances and their obsession with it. And just as they found it the most attractive and the most essential of gestures, the humble modern artist discerns it and ranks it among the most beautiful gestures of present times.

The pose the *lokhon* assumes in front of the Buddha in modern ballets — the one for which she supports herself on one arm, leaning forward and sitting on her heels — is the same as that of all the figures of Angkor who worship before a divinity.

Finally, the grand salute, with its joined hands and prayer pose, began or concluded prayers in ancient times, and is exactly the same in our time. Eminently beautiful and devout, it is the pose that has the *lokhon* raise her joined hands three times.

We thus find similar poses surviving into the modern dances: the gesture of offering, the gesture of prayer, the gesture of veneration — i.e., the three essential acts in the practice of all religions.

After all, is the sacred dancer not the symbol of the prostrated crowd? Is she not the crowd's prayer become woman, magnified and taking action at the foot of the altar? What gestures could she make that would be more pleasing to the divinity than those of offering and veneration?

Because she must remain intangible, of course, the woman cannot offer the people's bananas, the King's piles of gold, or the priest's blood sacrifices. She is a symbol, and thus can offer only another symbol. And since she is a thing most beautiful, most rare, and most sacred, must not the symbol that she offers be the most sacred, the most rare, the most beautiful, and the most fitting for the Gods?

It was the lotus flower, the divine flower adorning the temples, whose towers were made in the image of its buds; the flower upon which

Brahma slept; the flower, Queen and Mother of a new religion, that sprouted from the belly of Vishnu.

And the religions are dead. Buddha drove out Brahma, and will be driven out in his turn. The most famous temples are in ruins. The most powerful past is now only dust. All that remains is a fragile little hand holding a flower.

Both are still in bloom. It is through them that the present remains bound to the past. They are the common ground, the common formula. Truly, for the story that we are telling, how could the present be bound to the past in a more charming and more miraculous way than by this flower in this hand?

Modern *lokhon,* we now understand the abstract cadence given you by the instruments, that cadence to which your King and your people are deaf. We know the origin of the metaphysics of your gestures, guided by an imperishable power, and your automatism.

Poor ignorant creature, you are not merely a prisoner, a slave gymnast whom the instructors made suffer. There is more than an embroidered scarf weighing upon your breast. You have more than your King as master and husband. It is not to him alone that you give the velvet of your eyes and amber of your forehead. You are subject to all that stems from the past, as a frail palm tree bends before winds rushing in from far away. You represent something that is no more, but that is not yet dead.

Yes, now we understand your strange gravity. Indeed you do not know what passes through you. You are overwhelmed. You are enraptured with all the distant poetry that we have just seen arise within you and illuminate your frail silhouette....

Devata, Angkor Wat.

Who exactly are the women carved in bas-relief on the temple walls of Angkor? Those in the niches, crowding the friezes and entablatures as ornaments, are certainly dancers, because they are represented in choreographed poses.

They are nude to the waist. Bracelets ornament their arms and broad necklaces their necks. A double *sautoir* (long band) crosses between their breasts. Their single headdress is in grand style. It is a delicate monument, to all appearances in metal, consisting of a headband topped with three vertical rosettes that extend its form. From them sprout three arrows or points, built in stages or simply fluted.

Their clothing consists of a piece of fabric wrapped around the hips, passing between the legs, and gathered up somehow with a decorated belt. We'll study this costume, as well as the jewels, later on. It is, in any case, imprecisely depicted. The uncertainty of the sculptors' chisel blows clearly suggests a draped garment, the costume common to all primitive races, and particularly to the race that concerns us here.

The other women, ornamenting the door frames and walls of the courtyards and galleries, seem to be strolling. They walk arm in arm in groups of two to five. In their hands they hold mirrors, fans, long lotus stems, and flowers. They are exactly like the dancing women, but their waistcloth, held up by the belt, hangs simply, crossing in front, the ends dangling on either side.

It is hard to say on what basis the author of a certain published work on the monuments of Angkor can claim that some are *devata* and others *apsara*. Nor are the *aigrettes*[21] that he speaks of and that distinguish them anywhere to be found.

---

21. **Editor's Note: An ornamental tuft of plumes or a spray of gems resembling plumes.**

What would *asparas* — celestial courtesans and dancers — be doing there, since the *devatas* were created by Brahmanic legend precisely to be the representation of these *apsaras* on Earth? (De Bellouène)

Let us consider this legend…

> "After the epic battles of the *Devas* and *Asuras*, the victorious *Devas* took possession not only of the elixir of immortality but also of all the *apsaras*, themselves borne of the churning of the Sea of Milk. These captives became the heavenly courtesans and dancers of Indra.
>
> "But one of those goddesses fell in love with a mortal. She had a daughter, who, because of her origins, could not gain entry to heaven. The Brahmins raised her. Even as a child, this daughter of a goddess had a singular vocation. She danced before the statues of the gods, having inherited marvelous talents from her mother. She had seven daughters and three sons. Her sons became sacred musicians, her daughters dancers. Such is the origin of the present-day *devatas*."

As a matter of fact, if we begin with a minute observation of the costumes, we find not a difference but a mere modification. There are, in truth, women who dance and women who do not. The latter are the same as the former, except that they have draped their waistcloths so as to free their legs. Rolled up or not, the waistcloths are decorated with the same florets and borders. This is what permits us to say that the women are the same in both cases. And we find immediate confirmation in the *sampots* of modern actresses. It is the same piece of fabric that forms the *sarong* of the princess, or the sewn breeches of the prince.

Devata, Angkor Wat.

We can thus say that the women of Angkor are not either *apsaras* or *devatas*. No. They are all, depending on the ritual, celebrants dedicated to the temple for religious celebrations and the preservation of idols. Call them all *apsara*s, and we give them a celestial name that is perhaps not wholly appropriate. Calling them all *devata*, and we give them a more appropriate, terrestrial name.

Where indeed could the sculptors have found more charming models? What spectacle could have been more pleasing to the divinities? Ultimately, to give the stones the form of sacred celebrants was to make the stones themselves pray. Verily, all these women of the gods are exactly where they belong. At the doors they are vigilant guardians. Along a frieze they advance in an undulating procession. And close to the sanctuary, in magnificent stonework, they are crowned with the most beautiful tiaras and adorned with the rarest jewels.

Whether they dance or not, their hands are similar, always with an offering. Whether crowning them with seven points or decorating them simply with a flower in their chignons, the loving sculptors treated them with the same care. They have a strange smile, aloof, enigmatic, worthy of adoration. Their perfect breasts, which are those of Venus Anadyomene, have taken on a singular shine and the tone of flesh under the caresses of men and the kisses of barren women come to adore them. One is tempted to believe that they pulsate in the gallery shadows. They make a strange impression. Behind their harmonious orbs, hearts seem to continue to beat, full of tenderness, fervor, and love for the long-gone divinities....

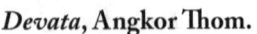

Devata, Angkor Thom.

Devata dancing. Copied and realized from a bas-relief of Angkor Wat.

Devata, Wat Nokor.

On a stele erected by the first of the Jayavarmans, it states that this prince made to the god of Samudrapura a gift of twelve civil servants and seventeen dancers whose names are mentioned. (Aymonier.)

On the great inscriptions of Bakou, Lolei, and Koh Ker (879, 893, 932 AD), Indravarman offers to Siva "forty-two of the dancers, singers, musicians, mentioned by name, who serve the priests; and seven of the second-order dancers, singers, and musicians who serve the public" (Aymonier).

On these inscriptions, the duties of the sacred personnel are indicated exactly in special terms borrowed from Sanskrit or in the common language. The *Rmman* (dancers) top the list.

An inscription (873 AD) found in Préah-Net-Préah announces a gift of four dancers, whose names are given, to the monastery erected to Siva (Aymonier). Finally, another mentions "beautiful, flawless women, skilful in song and dance" (Id.)

We can thus say that the women of Angkor were indeed celebrants, dancers, singers, and musicians; that they were offered to the divinities by fervent worshippers; and that the flawless were chosen from among the most beautiful.

We have seen that such is also the case with the women of the current Cambodian king. They are dancers, singers, and musicians, offered by his subjects, and the flawless were chosen from among the most beautiful.

They have not changed since the days when they haunted the temple of Angkor Wat. They have the same short-chinned face, the same broad little nose, the same full lips.

The type was admirably captured by the old sculptors. Its resemblance to today's type remains striking, despite the stylization of the sculptures. Only the stone eyes resist full examination. Perhaps the rains have slowly worn away the upper eyelids, which now seem closed, or perhaps the artists lacked the skill to render them precisely.

The present-day criteria of Cambodian beauty are a face round like the moon and three folds on the neck — the Greek folds! And what do we see on the women at Angkor? Faces round like the moon and necks marked with three perfect folds.

On the one hand, we have physical resemblances. On the other, the three grand gestures, illogical and haunting, that were essential to the religious celebrations performed by the ancient dancers, women who have remained young and beautiful despite the passing of centuries, despite profanations and death. Here is the foundation on which we can establish a direct lineage between dancers past and present.

The costumes, for example, have entirely changed. It is hard to explain how the authors could have found today's costumes similar to those at Angkor. How do they all finish their descriptions of the Angkor *devadasi*? "Such are the Cambodian dancers down to the present day."

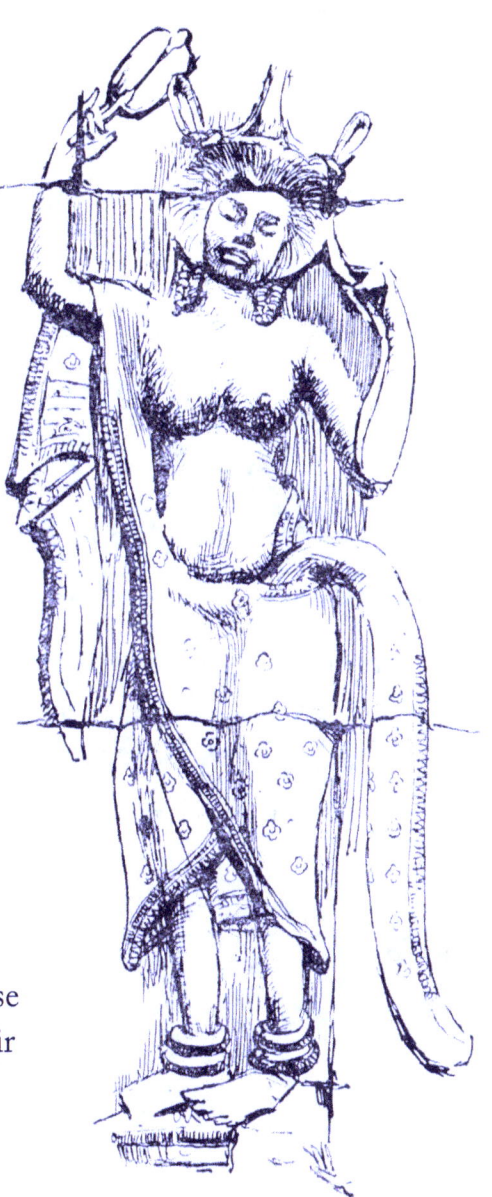

Devata **without belt, Angkor Wat.**

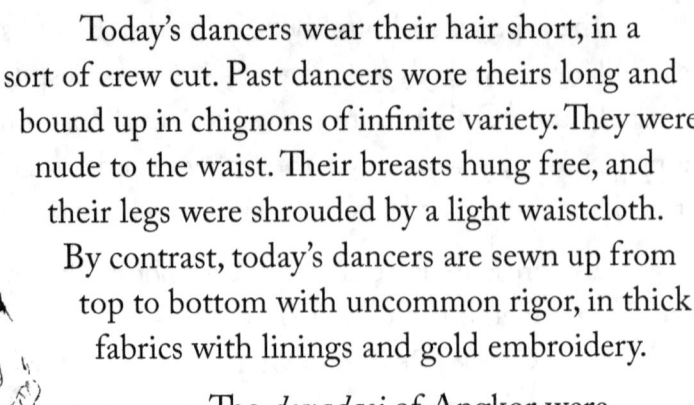

Devata, Wat Nokor.

Today's dancers wear their hair short, in a sort of crew cut. Past dancers wore theirs long and bound up in chignons of infinite variety. They were nude to the waist. Their breasts hung free, and their legs were shrouded by a light waistcloth. By contrast, today's dancers are sewn up from top to bottom with uncommon rigor, in thick fabrics with linings and gold embroidery.

The *devadasi* of Angkor were crowned with monumental tiaras, comprising rosettes and three, five, or seven points. Today's *lokhon* wear not special headdresses but those of the characters they portray.

The earrings were once enormous: lotus flowers either real or embossed life size. There is no trace of blooming-flower bracelets on sculptures made since then. Among ornaments, only the double *sautoir* has remained more or less the same since ancient times, and these are truly shaky grounds on which to claim complete similarity between old and new costumes.

Indeed, we shall soon see what the facts truly are, in detail. For now, let us restrict ourselves to the assertion that religious gestures have survived; that the type of Khmer woman sculpted at Angkor Wat is clearly determined; and, finally, that those women were indeed sacred dancers.

When the Hindu conquerors arrived in ancient Chinese Funan, which they would rename Kambuja, they brought along more than their gods, priests, legislators, and artists.

After the countless multitude of soldiers, elephants, and war chariots; after the Brahmins and their chignons, the gong orchestras, and the tom-toms; after the ark of the sacred fire; after the King, bearer of the divine sword, traveling under his parasols; after the ministers and the princes, there came, seated in ox carts or balanced in litters shaped like half-moons, the women, the dancers, and the courtesans.[22]

Princess in Palanquin, Angkor Wat.

A civilization took root in the wild, uncultivated Khmer soil. The priests, Brahmin Shivites, raised terrible gods before the aboriginal crowd, whose masters they had become. Imagine the native astonishment during the inaugural ceremony after the first temple was erected. Imagine the amazement of the first Khmer neophytes over what they saw near the priests and the conquering gods. There were women who had arrived with the priests, women covered with gold and precious stones, come to offer the white and pink flowers that grew in the local ponds. The people no doubt prostrated themselves, in the deepest admiration. And the first woman to dance on Cambodian soil became an object of adoration.

As they approached to burn ceremonial sticks of incense at the feet of the new gods, the Khmers would probably see divine dancers in great numbers, radiating their lunar beauty while adorning the altars, bathing the idols, preparing and maintaining the sacred implements, braiding garlands, stoking the divine flames, and taking their ritual ablutions in grand stone basins that reflected the towers.

22. Bas-relief of Angkor Wat: southern external gallery.

These were the *devadasi*. Offered to the temple while very young (DeBellouène), they were regarded as wives of the god. At puberty, their hymens would be broken on a marble phallus — the phallus of the god to whom they were devoted. After this painful ceremony, they would remain in the temple and maintain it (and still do to this day). They sang and danced to please the gods, calm their fits of rage, satisfy their desires, and transmit the adoration of the people and the crowds.

They would give themselves to the priests, who were the gods incarnate. The male children produced by these ritual fornications would be destined for priesthood; the female children, for the status of *devadasi*.

Were they truly sacred and inviolable? All the evidence suggests it. It is hard to believe that the people of the time would have allowed courtesans in their temples. Religious fervor was then at its height.

Sacrilegious thieves of donations to the temples risked the most terrible punishments. Acts of donation always ended with the warning. The old Hindu laws say:

> "Wherever women are honored, the Gods are satisfied;
> wherever they are not, pious acts are sterile."

What timid Khmer slave, what miserable clod of dust, already terrified by the unlimited and latent powers of the new gods, would have slipped into the bed of a *devadasi*?

In Angkor's heyday, dance was not only a religious practice but also a venerated art. The King would learn to dance. The stele of Vat Phou, near Bassac, tells us that Jayavarman was "the incomparable Master of all arts, starting with singing, music, and dance" (Aymonier). And Yasovarman, "Glory's favorite," who completed Angkor Thom, "would teach the princesses to dance while keeping time. The daughters of the greatest men in the land would dance in his presence" (Barth and Bergaigne). Moreover, was not Siva, the supreme god, known as the great dancer, and is he not often represented in an extraordinary choreographic pose?

Siva dancing.

But in what world did these princesses move, these daughters of the grandest families of the land, whom Yasovarman would teach to dance? Were they not offered to the King, and did they not comprise a harem that was completely separate from the sacred harem of the gods? Let us examine the documents.

For a long time previously, the poet Bharata had had poems performed. The Ramayana would be mimed, because during the Girivalgusamâgama festivals in Rajagrha the meeting of Giri, King of the Nagas, and his beloved would be celebrated.

According to Mr. L. Feer's translation of the Avadāna Çataka:

"The Perfect and Accomplished Buddha, named Krakucchanda, lived and dwelled in the town of Çobhâvati. King Çobha gave the dancers the following order:

'You must perform a Buddhist dance in my presence.'

And the dancers obeyed, performing a Buddhist dance so well that the King, though surrounded by his ministers, could not resist taking part.

The dance master appeared dressed as the Buddha and the dancers as Bhikkhus." [23]

So here is a true pantomime, with various characters and costumes.

23. Editor's Note: *Bauddham natakam* means drama or pantomime, rather than dance.

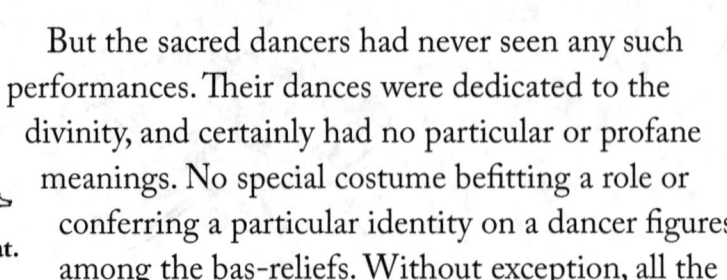

Costume. Angkor Wat.

But the sacred dancers had never seen any such performances. Their dances were dedicated to the divinity, and certainly had no particular or profane meanings. No special costume befitting a role or conferring a particular identity on a dancer figures among the bas-reliefs. Without exception, all the *devadasi* wear triple-point tiaras and skirts gathered like *sampots*, and they execute nothing but a single dance step.

It is inconceivable that the Khmer sculptors, with all their skill, and faced with the inevitable uniformity, the inevitable monotony, of their kind of decoration, would not have seized the opportunity to display all the characters, all the costumes, of the various plays performed by the celebrants whom they had chosen —if indeed such variety had existed.

There were thus two kinds of dancers: sacred dancers, living in the temples, and the others, profane, errant, or wives to the King or important personages.[24]

On this point too, legend will light the way.

"One night, Vishnu, incarnate in the body of a young, handsome man, found himself alone in a village, and sought to test the charity of men. Rudely turned away by every Brahmin on whose door he had knocked, he came at last to a poor, solitary hut, from which a charming voice emanated in song. He knocked, and a dancer opened the door. She welcomed him with good manners, offered him a meal, charmed him with her songs while he ate. Then, since the young man did not rise to leave, she offered him her bed for the night. The god loved her and promised his protection for her and all her descendants."

---

24. Down to the present day, there are in India both *devadasi* and *nautchny*, these last being the dancers of the rajahs.

Since all Hindu princes and kings are Sons of Vishnu, they must keep this paternal promise, and love and protect the descendants of the one who earned forgiveness for the rudeness of men.

The King of Cambodia, son of the Hindu Varmans, and thus grandson of Indra, according to tradition, continues to provide divine protection. This is the legendary reason for his troupe of dancers. We have seen that *lokhon* enjoy the same prerogatives as Hindu dancers: they approach the King, speak to him, serve him, charm him, and love him.[25]

We know that Hindu dancers are immodest in the extreme. There were — during the spring festivals, for example — orgiastic festivals, aphrodisiac customs, in which even *devadasi* took part. Did these customs spread beyond India? We find no trace of them in Cambodia. The Khmer people could not accept such debauchery. With the conquerors' departure, the unclothed dancers took to wearing closed costumes, as we shall see below. Nothing remains of the profane dancers. The Hindu *nautchny* returned to their country.

The Cambodian *nautchny*, wives and dancers of the King, have preserved only the pure and sacred traditions. Before they died, as their temples were sacked and their gods toppled, the ancient *devadasi* brought forth these traditions, so that the cult of their toppled divinities would continue to be celebrated, and the mysterious ritual that we have discovered would be preserved. The Cambodian *lokhon* needn't be ashamed of a past they did not accept, and from which they emerged as immaculate as they remain today.

---

25. The *nautchny*.

Dignitary (?) dancing, Angkor Wat.

I have stated that the Hindu *devadasi* and *nautchny* followed the conquerors into Cambodia. I now believe it necessary to provide some evidence. It is concrete evidence, though it flies in the face of historical probability.

The skirt worn by Manikka Vachaka Swami, apostle of the Siva cult, in a statue discovered in Pollonnaruwa, Ceylon, and preserved in the Colombo Museum is in every way similar to skirts worn by the dancers at Angkor. The same flare at the bottom, the same length, the same flowering of knots on the fabric belt over the waist and hips. And the peculiar way in which the hair of this statuette is parted and falls is found many times over on our own Khmer *devadasi*.

The ears of a Pollonnaruwa Vishnu of the same period (100 AD) are loaded with rings. We find the same jewelry on a dancer smiling to the east, on the terrace of the Bayon (Angkor Thom). The necklaces often depicted at Angkor Thom, each with several ranks of pearls and a circular pendant, are exactly the same as those of the Parvati brought back from Anuradhapura, in Colombo. This same goddess, moreover, has the very double *sautoir* crossed between the breasts that we know so well.

The same wonderful museum of Colombo also has in its collection a gold necklace imitating a garland of jasmine flowers.

Jasmine is the favorite flower in Cambodia, which has retained the foreign and secular custom of threading them into bracelets and pendants. We also find there a gold necklace with five rows of pepper-plant flowers, and another necklace of vine leaves.

In ancient India, then, it was customary to fashion flowers out of pure metal! And today we find the same custom alive and well in Cambodia, for the *lokhon*'s fifth bracelet is made in the exact image of a bracelet of triangular flowers arranged in series!

In the 5th century AD, Manikka Vachaka Swami was prime minister of the Pandiyan King of Madura until his calling to become a mendicant preacher and singer in the service of Siva, as he is represented in this 54.2 cm tall statue. Photo courtesy National Museum of Columbo. This photo does not appear in the 1913 edition.

Also of Hindu origin is the broad ornament worn by the princes of modern-day ballets. It consists of five or six metal bracelets joined together and opening with a common hinge. This method of mounting florets of precious stones on small helical springs, for perpetual quivering, is peculiarly Hindu. A hairpin at the Colombo Museum has seven such florets. Furthermore, the large pearls in filigree making up the Cambodian actress's third bracelet have thousands of counterparts among the treasures of Ceylon.

These uncommon jewels and costumes, which we have admitted are not originally Khmer, we now find present a few centuries earlier in the country from which history tells us the conquerors came. Is there any more room for doubt?

**A side of the skirt returning on the arm.
Angkor Wat.**

Two *Devata* heads at Angkor Thom.

The arrival in Cambodia of the dancers we are concerned with dates to the arrival of the first Varman, roughly in the fourth century AD. We have read their faint traces on the inscriptions, and have at last found depictions of them dating to the eighth century at Wat Nokor and Préah Khan and to the ninth century at Angkor Thom. On these principal edifices of the Khmer apogee, however, the characteristically Hindu type of the sculpted women — the high, narrow forehead, the thin nose, the fine lips — is clearly visible on the stone.[1] These are the exquisite faces of Ceylonese women.

Two *Devata* heads at Angkor Wat.

Little by little, the small number of civilizers was absorbed by the enormous mass of the people. New generations arose, raised with the new culture, the new religion, and the new art. There were pretty girls among the Khmers too. They gradually infiltrated the harems, as the foreign girls aged and died off. Ballet mistresses received new pupils. The same imported jewels kept sparkling, and new costumes were adopted, but the native race reclaimed its place.

Dance. Angkor Wat.

Devata, Angkor Thom.

Little by little, the last drops of blood — so rich, so fiery, and so vermilion in their foreign veins — were diluted in the vast stream of native blood. There came a day when Khmer artists could carve the temple walls in their turn, when indigenous *devadasi* offered the sacred flowers with the same grace and the rites that they had learned from their teachers. With the passing of three centuries, the types depicted changed. Not a single drop of pure Hindu blood remained, and upon the walls of newly erected temples (Angkor Wat) it was the Khmer woman, triumphant, with her convex forehead, broad nose, and full lips, who reclaimed her rightful place!

Thus did the Hindu *devadasi*, mothers of the Khmer *devadasi*, grandmothers of the Cambodian *lokhon*, arrive, live, and die.

Dancer dancing. Angkor Wat.

It is easy to imagine the envy that Khmer wealth must have provoked. The country was called Suvarna Bhumi, land of gold.[26] Buddhism was taking in neophytes in ever-greater numbers, and internecine wars were dividing the kingdom of Kambu. The Siamese, of the Thai race, originally from the north and untouched by the Hindu civilization, were the vassals and slaves of the Khmers, and shook off their yokes. Around 1351, it is believed, they rose up en masse and pounced upon their Masters, making them slaves in turn. Angkor the Great was taken. Its king fled to Laos, and three sons of the King of Siam occupied the throne.

Whether the Siamese invasion precipitated the introduction of Buddhism or not, one thing is certain. By the fourteenth century, Siva had been toppled, his images lacerated by chisel. On the walled doors of the sanctuaries, the smiling figure of Çakyamouni gleamed in the shadows. Before the Omniscient, the Brahmanic dancers had fled their deconsecrated temples. But when the triumphant warriors wandered into in the gynaeceum[27] and found the frightened women and dance troupes of the vanquished, they stopped the carnage. The women were too beautiful!

Moreover, had they not also respected the women carved on the temple walls? And so the royal Khmer dancers became the royal Siamese dancers.

26. G. Maspéro: *L'empire Khmèr: histoire et documents.* 1904.
27. From the Greek *gunaikeion*. In ancient times, a section of a large house reserved exclusively for women.

Warriors fighting. Angkor Wat and Angkor Thom.

After the destruction of Angkor, after the slaves had become the masters, after all power and pride had crumbled to dust, the Siamese victors acted as respectful and admiring guardians, preserving the fragile *lokhon*. Though the rituals and gestures, immortal as they are, remained the same, the costumes were subject to the influence of the new masters. Here is where we must seek an explanation for the great differences noted previously between the costumes of Angkor and the costumes of today. The former were Khmer. The latter are Siamese, as we shall soon see.

As soon as the masters died or fell from power, the half-naked dancers covered themselves. To understand the repugnance they must have had for appearing nude in public, it is necessary to grasp the sheer prudishness of Siamese and Cambodian women.[28]

---

28. **I shall cite only one example. On the occasion of a visit by Governor General Sarraut, the Superior Resident of Cambodia decided to organize a parade representing Cambodian history and heritage, and he entrusted me with bringing four Angkor dancers to life. In all of Phnom Penh, even among the women of low class, I could not find four actresses willing to appear naked to the waist, as the dancers are represented on the monuments. We had to cover them with shirts.**

The Khmer *mokot*, which decorates the foreheads of kings on the bas-reliefs, is thick and heavy. The Siamese sharpened it, lengthened it, and added stages in the image of their elegant *stupa* (towers).

The Khmer skirt from the sculptures of Bayon, tied in the front, was preserved, but the *sampot* made its appearance. Remember, the *sampot* is no more the costume of Cambodian women than the small white jacket seen today, which is also Siamese. The true Khmer garment is the *sarong*, the scarf (or *commin*). The long tunic they so often wear, meanwhile, is a Malayan import.

Finally, after 1600, when they were present even in Cambodia, the Portuguese introduced lace, velvet, fringes, and small metal disks to Siam, adding some Iberian pizzazz to the country's fabrics and ritual ornaments.

Warrior resting.

Clown dancers. Angkor Thom.

So many Cambodian dancers had left their unfortunate country that the last Khmer kings, up to Norodom, possessed almost entirely Siamese troupes. All the professors of Norodom's five hundred *lokhon* were Siamese. At his death, there were more than three hundred Thai actresses at the palace of Phnom Penh. Even today, all of the professors but two are Siamese! Ever since the minor Khmer kings achieved some measure of independence, hardly a century ago, the Siamese women, sole guardians of Khmer tradition, with their superior intelligence and refinement, have once again been teaching the Cambodians their lost dances and forgotten traditions, rebuilding the harems.

Some folk dancers remain deep in the countryside of the Mekong, but these have never learned the rituals. Their gestures are vulgar, raw, and joyous. Their spirit is the spirit of the people in celebration. Their joy is a joy of jubilation. These dancers cry out, perform conjuring tricks, laugh, grimace. They take us far away from harmony and rhythm. Curiously, however, despite all of the above, they still brandish the hand holding the sacred flower, in the same spirit of triumph.

But make no mistake. The dancers returning from Siam were indeed Khmer dancers. Have we not seen them make the gestures made at Angkor, when the Thais were only slaves? Have we not discovered that the original jewels and costumes were Hindu in origin? That they are the daughters of women from the country of all legends and all

138 *Cambodian Dancers*

Popular modern dancers.

poetry? The marvelous Ramayana scenes that they perform are not the work of the Thais! Their new masters could only substitute shiny stage rags for their noble fabrics, and the most beautiful and noble of these rags, the rich scarf, the beautiful floating scarf, is not their invention. Its origins date further back. It is the scarf worn by the Buddha when he preaches. It is the cascading gold fabric that the monks throw over their shoulder. It is a stylized version of the gracious *commin* that Khmer women wrap around themselves when they go to worship.

No. The Cambodian dancer is no foreigner, as we were momentarily tempted to believe. She is indeed the little Khmer idol, a jewel lost and found. She was the prodigal and abandoned child. She fell victim to the vicissitudes of her race. Though she can adorn herself with all the foreign pearls, with all the velvets of Portugal, she will dispel the illusion as soon as she raises her hand and flexes her legs. She detaches herself from the past, breaks with all contingencies, and recaptures all her nobility, all her grace, all the mysteries of which she is the sole expression.

Her destiny has been a play of shadow and light. She is the sole, fragile vestige of her country's glorious past. Of that not-so-distant past not a document or a jewel or a tool remains. Only she remains! She and, on the other side of the country, the immense ruins whence she came....

A few years ago, the *lokhon* went to dance in the noble central gallery of these ruins.[29] Oh, how the *devadasis* of stone must have shuddered! For among the new and foreign elements arrayed before them, which did not sanctify the centuries of their mystical past, the *devadasis* must have discerned something familiar. They must have sensed the presence of dancers who were still flesh of their flesh, and of the religious spirit that once had stirred them to dance!

---

29. Editor's Note - When Groslier wrote this in the early 20th century, modern *lokhon* had begun dancing at Angkor Wat more frequently due to the influence of French tourism and diplomatic activity.

The *mokot*,[30] headgear of royalty, is first mentioned in a contemporary Chinese account of the accession of Kiao-Tchin-Jou, in the fourth century:

"Covered with gold necklaces and cords, wielding a golden sword, the king would place on his head a high and pointed bonnet, decorated with golden flowers and precious stones" (Aymonier).

This is an accurate description of the royal headdress, a description that could apply even to the current headdress. It was depicted in the bas-reliefs of Angkor Thom, and then three centuries later on those of Angkor Wat. The cone is more or less elevated, but it is heavy and regular, rising over a headband. In sum, it is like to a modern *mokot* without the point. This point, as we have seen, was added by the Siamese. But the Khmers knew it quite well. Though they had not yet adopted it on the royal cone, it already served to decorate the diadems of the *devadasi*.

30. The *mokot* of H. M. Sisowath is made of gold, enamel, and precious stones. Its point is a spindly blossom of gold topped with a diamond. The chinstrap is enameled. The origin of this diadem, like that of the sacred sword, is lost to history.

On the marvelous statues of Angkor Wat — e.g., the exceedingly fine statue of a dancer to the right of the sanctuary's western door — the headdress's manner of construction is plain to see.

First, a broad diadem with a frontal headband encrusted with precious stones. This is more or less the same as the diadem in the modern *mokot* for women.

Then come five rosettes arranged in a crown, though not in a complete circle. These are probably held in place with a metal framework. The rosettes are encrusted with six large gems, which form the petals. Two new rosettes constitute a second rank above, and are placed between the first and second, and the second and the third of the lower row. Four points soar up from the first and fourth rosettes of the first rank, and from the two on the second rank. These points are formed by flowers that decrease in size as they rise. They are tiny gold flowers, whose every petal is again a precious stone. As is distinctly visible, each is mounted on a small stalk, exactly like those that quiver on springs on today's tiaras. From these ancient headdresses dangle pendants that mix or alternate with floral ornaments, pearls, and locks of hair, braided in long, multiple plaits.

Costume. Angkor Wat.

Although these past miters are completely different from today's, their components are closely related. I am convinced that the small stalks so clearly depicted in the stone-tipped flowerets are none other than delicate springs whose cousins we have already encountered in Colombo.

All the tiaras of Angkor are of three, five, or seven points, with one or two ranks of rosettes, but their variety is infinite. They follow the great law of Khmer aesthetics: "Uniformity in the whole, variety in the parts."

The points are fluted or not, equal or decreasing in size. The Siamese did nothing but alternate the levels with large connected sections, add nets and lace, and lengthen them a bit.

Costume. Angkor Wat.

Sometimes one of these points is simply stuck into a chignon. The tiaras of *devadasi* depicted in dance poses, meanwhile, are with few exceptions all similar. They have three rosettes and three points.

Bare-headed celebrants are depicted with a great variety of hairstyles. Their long hair is braided or divided into tufts, joined together into two or three chignons, gathered up and left to hang down in back, arranged in a halo around the forehead. They are often decorated with lotus or golden flowers, bunches of jasmine, pearls. We are far removed from modern *lokhon*'s little head of short hair. Here again we find the Siamese, this time cropping hair.

The tiaras of Angkor Thom, three centuries back, were more massive, higher. Many were decorated with triangular motifs; for example, broad sheets arranged in superimposed crowns, decreasing steadily in size to form a cone.

The *panntiereth*, the graceful crown of our time, also has its ancestor, frequently seen on the head of Siva or Vishnu. It is simpler, but its principle is the same: a headband closed in the back by a ribbon bow. It is clearly visible on a statue of a woman found in Ta Prohm of Tonle Bati. Mr. Aymonier mentions it, and Mr. Spooner made a sketch.

The finger rings are imperceptible. Let us not forget that the *devadasi* of Angkor have a maximum height of one meter, ten centimeters (3 feet, 6 inches), and are carved in sandstone. However skilful, the Khmer chisels could not have defined delicate rings on fingers. I have very rarely seen rings on a thumb. The other fingers show but a single ring.

Such is not the case with bracelets on wrists and upper arms. A large rosette in bloom and set with precious stones is carved on the outside. Another hides the clasp. Pendants in the shape of lozenges or triangles dangle from them. The bracelets seem articulated, made of interlocking metal parts, like scales.

Quite frequently the belts are made of successive plates, engraved and set. Dangling from each are pendants or strings of pearls.[31] Other, similar motifs dangle from the sautoir or the necklaces.

The artists had well understood the charm of dangling jewels that jingle, shine, and wiggle during a momentarily frozen gesture. They resemble tiny wings, flickering flames, for they reflect the light of the sanctuaries.[32] At present, these ornaments survive in the headdresses of young girls, in the *panntiereth*, and in the epaulieres of the bird-women.

A long pendant is depicted as being affixed to the belt and descending between the legs of all the *devadasi* figures dancing in the sky. The style is the same now, and is indeed used for the bird-woman.

The earrings were bulky and heavy enough to distend the ear lobe. They almost always took the form of a stylized lotus bud. They are quite beautiful and quite distinct on the great faces of Brahma at Angkor Thom.

Closely study the finesse and skill that went into carving these smaller-than-life-size stone jewels, the way in which the very prongs holding the gems are in some places discernable, and you cannot help but wonder what perfection the Khmer jewelers must have attained when working so pure and malleable a substance as gold!

---

31. Sanctuary, Angkor Wat.
32. The pendants are absent at Angkor Thom.

All precious stones were used. Not a single one from that time has reached us. They shine on only in a few inscriptions.

"… Dangling gold spangles threaded with brilliant aquamarines and pearls, ear pendants, necklaces … consisting of ranks of rubies " (Po-Nagar inscription, in Phanrang, Champa).

"… Gold belts, pearls, coral" (Glai-Lomov. 723 Saka).

On the list of ornaments and liturgical objects, drawn up by the order of the king in 890 Saka (967 AD), are:

"… Crowns, bracelets, rings, earrings, belts, ankle bracelets, all in precious metal enriched with gems."

The four Apsaras who left the town of Ramanaka invited Maitrakanyaka into their house for the night:

"Filled with all kinds of gemstones, lapis lazuli, conches, crystal, coral, gold and silver" (L. Feer).

The *devadasi* perfumed themselves with sandalwood like the modern *lokhon*. It was probably used in powder and dissolved in coconut oil:

> "The one … whose hidden chest exhales two perfumes, produced by an abundance of musk and fragrant sandalwood…" (stele of Glai-Lomov).

> "The dust raised by the army, clinging to the cheeks of the women, would take on the look of sandalwood powder" (Bhavavarman [550]).

Dancers from India, who have always danced without make-up, with their skin bare or lightly covered with saffron, found in Founan a white makeup that had certainly been imported by the Chinese, who still sell it today.

Though it appears nowhere on the list drawn up by the Chinese explorer of 1259, which nonetheless includes amber, sandal, and vermilion, we nevertheless learn that the make-up indisputably formed part of the sacred finery.

> "Glory to him … with a body of white immaculate, by effect of the ash that covers him…" (inscription of Loley [Bergaigne]).

> "Happy man … with the dazzling body, brilliant with an ash whiter than the swell of the Sea of Milk, whiter than the celestial river's foam, whiter than moonbeams" (inscription of Champa [Id.]).

Sadness. Angkor Wat.

The costumes of the *devadasi* were transparent. The sculptors rendered them with a simple contour, hewing to bodily forms and leaving the thighs and the triangle of the pubis perfectly visible. It is a simplistic but clear interpretation. Take the modesty of this people into account, and it is impossible not to equate the true significance of this manner of execution with its apparent significance. It would have been so simple, so much closer to their ideas, and so much easier for the sculptors to have treated the fabrics as opaque and heavy, had such fabrics been in use. Moreover, the sculptors clearly knew how to capture the differences. In Bayon, for example, they depicted the sarong wrapped around a peasant woman as consisting of a single piece, hiding every contour of the pelvis and hips.

Very often short pants are indicated, and on dancing *devadasi* the fabric that starts at the belt and passes between the legs is easy to follow. But it is impossible to specify what it does in the back, for not a single dancer in depicted from the back at Angkor.

Judging by my tests, the similarities found elsewhere (on the statuettes of the Colombo museum, for example), and the various practical combinations, I think that this long, light, and lined fabric was pulled up and attached at the belt, which it was wrapped around several times, to form two broad loops on each side. The ends were loose. This is the only secure way to obtain exactly the effect depicted on the bas-reliefs.

When at rest, the dancer would wear her *sarong* like a skirt, the two ends crossed in front. After passing under the belt, the two ends would emerge one on either side. These are the long pendants awkwardly depicted on the bas-reliefs. Indeed, what else could they be, since the embroidered edge on the bottom of the skirt continues along their entire length?

Four women depicted in the small southern chapel-like structure of the second level of Angkor Wat lack belts. The ends, supported by their arms, are clearly visible. Curiously, the Moï women of Darlac drape sarongs over themselves in the same way but let the fabric hang only from the left side.

The broad folds used by modern *lokhon*, and which create the pretty cascade that opens like a fan with the movement of their legs, did not exist at Angkor. They are of Malayan inspiration, and can be found held up by a belt on certain old statues of women. One such statue, located above Sambor, Mr. Aymonier believes he can date back to the sixth or seventh Saka century.

The *devadasi* of Angkor Thom almost always have a long, thin, and flexible accessory. They put it around the neck, hanging it on their shoulders. The celestial dancers shake it in the air. The sculptors carved it with lattice patterns, which are almost certainly supposed to be garlands of small flowers. As we know, Cambodian women love such natural ornaments. With skill and patience, they braid cylindrical flower bracelets of jasmine. Lengthened and thinned out, these would produce the motifs found at Angkor Thom, and absent at Angkor Wat.

All these flowers, as well as those decorating the alters and sanctuaries, were supplied by the gardens and parks that always surrounded temples and palaces. Moreover, the post of garland braider is mentioned in the Bakou inscription:

"Gardeners, braiders of garlands, florists…" (Aymonier).

Bird-woman. Angkor Wat.

The Khmer sculptors had the idea of carving into the stone a depiction of the legendary bird-woman. She is found under a figure of Siva, in the eastern external gallery of Angkor Wat. I could find her nowhere else.

Mr. Fournereau's work mentions a very beautiful Siamese statuette of Phra Pathom. This turns out to be the modern bird-woman exactly: same wings, same pendant, same feathers at the calves. The Siamese copy and modification are clearly visible. We see the first representation of the Ramayanic nymph by the Khmer, later interpreted by the Siamese and bequeathed, after the changes, to the current Cambodian ballet.

The Mythical *Kennari* Bird-woman. Edger Boulangier, *Un Hiver au Cambodge*, 1885. Note: This illustration does not appear in Groslier's original book.

There exists a Cambodian Satra, in epic verse, celebrating the construction of Angkor. It considers the temple as having been built in the image of Indra's heaven, as a dwelling for his son, Prince Préa Khet Méaléa. The following excerpt contains all the references to the *devadasi*:

> Numerous female statues…. Their figures are fine to see, their bodies white, supple, and rounded, endowed with every known perfection. Their heads are adorned or crowned with flowers. Some have their hair tied. Others have cut their hair at the follicle, shaved it in straight lines. Their waists are round and slender and graceful. Their firm and rounded breasts recall the flowers of the lotus.

Some, garlanded with fragrant flowers, have tied vines in their hair, lengthening it agreeably. Others have coiffed themselves with braided, threaded, rolled-up flowers. Still others comb their long, rich tresses. We see some who raise the edge of their skirt to knot it or who hold celestial flowers by their stems. Others gaze at each other and lean together, or seize each other by the shoulder in a quarrel over flowers. Others smile gaily, as if lost in the pleasantries of chat. For an attentive eye, the illusion is complete. You might even catch yourself thinking you've spied one making a soft, veiled confidence, then lowering her head, torn between love and decency.

Some carry parrots or fans as they walk. Others set their birds on the stems of flowers. Others carry lotuses or lilies by the stem. Their dresses are held up with belts. Covered with necklaces and ornaments of all kinds, they wear two circular bands on their ankles. Their many bracelets are engraved with flowers and vines. Covered with bands and rings, crowded together here, dashing about there, they appear to move, to stop. Supple, smiling, discoursing on love, they brim with feminine graces.... Some stretch their limbs, running through dance preliminaries. Always elegant, svelte, and well proportioned, they perform steps of every variety.

They are neither too big nor too small, well proportioned, in the flower of youth, admirable to behold. To contemplate them is to love them. Your eye never tires, your soul delights, your heart is never sated. Gaze upon them for a while, fill your spirit full with them, and you cannot resolve to leave them. No longer are they mere statues carved by the hand of man. They are living women, beautiful and pleasant. Doubt takes hold, and emotion works its paralysis....

I shall at last have said everything about the ancient dancers, their costumes, and their jewels once I have pointed out a great ring-shaped ornament, attached by a cord, and dangling between and under the breasts of certain *devadasi* at Angkor Wat.

What was it? I have been unable to find out precisely. Was it a small perfume or make-up box? Was it perhaps a hollow rattle that the celebrant would shake, making hard grains inside resound against its walls? Was it simply an amulet similar to the one that now hangs on the belly of our little Cambodians? This intriguing accessory can be seen only at Angkor Wat, and I have found no trace of it among the Ceylonese treasures.

Bending the arm on the bas-reliefs. Angkor Wat.

Whenever Khmer sculptors depicted a prince or princess indoors, they also depicted surrounding wives or attendants, all seated, and propped up on their arms. This is how maidservants position themselves in modern ballets when surrounding or listening to a prince or a Buddha.

But the similarity goes much further, for the characters frequently have an arm bent behind them. This hyperextension had thus already struck the ancient artists. They had no doubt regarded it as a sign of beauty and elegance.

We can trace the origin of the Cambodian *lokhon*'s arm-bending in the natural flexibility that I have already pointed out, and which did not escape the Khmer sculptors. As an exaggeration of natural flexibility, the hyperextension became the exaggeration of a form of beauty.

The modern grand salute was the same in ancient times.[33] These two sketches, of Bayon bas-reliefs (interior gallery, southern face, west wing), show characters in worship at the feet of Vishnu. The bodies are tilted slightly forward during the raising of the hands. In the second, the hands reach above the head. Elsewhere is an individual lying face down and flat. This was still the final phase of the Cambodian salute some time ago.

Ancient nymph flying.

Celestial dancers — and there are hundreds of them at Angkor — are all depicted in a single pose. The modern dancer suspended with wires and moved about in such a way as to simulate an aerial nymph holds exactly the same position. And she strikes the same pose in the dance when she portrays soaring into the air: knee to the ground, heel raised, body scarcely touching the earth.

Modern nymph flying.

The *devadasi* dancing at Angkor often have raised toes. We have not forgotten that this is one of the characteristics of the modern dance.

33. The *Apadāna Çataka* (trans. L. Feer) mentions a salute in which the hands are raised above the head several times. This salute bears the Sanskrit name *anjali*. The Cambodian salute now commonly used in stylized form in the dances is the same. Indeed, it even has the same name, *anhchuli*, a Khmer corruption of the Sanskrit name of the pious Hindu salute.

Today's terrifying warrior and giant poses resemble those of the characters set in the sandstone of Angkor. There is a direct line of descent, an absolute relationship between the parts and the whole. In fact, the line of descent is so direct that if *lokhon* in the modern aesthetic were suddenly to turn to stone, we could precisely superimpose their gestures on the gestures carved in the past.

The male and female dancers are depictions, like sculptures. They are animated sculptures. The art and spirit of the people determine both depictions in similar ways. The same divinities, beliefs, rites, and ideals govern the gestures of the individual-symbol, whether it is of flesh and blood or of stone.

The true Khmer orchestra, shown on the bas-reliefs of the monuments, can still be heard. The Siamese added xylophones and small pianos of wood, both formerly absent. Only the great harp, visible at Angkor, has not survived into modern times. What mystery lies behind its decline into oblivion? What snapped its strings? [34]

Nowhere could I find today's time beaters or their time-keeping sticks. However, some of the *devadasi* at Angkor are surrounded by characters, men and women, seated on the floor, often in a space delimited by a balustrade in the image of Naga — like the balustrades of bridges and temple terraces. Here and there, one of these characters will seem to follow the dance carefully, raising a finger. One such character, in an interior gallery at Bayon (eastern face, southern wing), has an open mouth. A narrator, perhaps?

It must also be noted that the congregation is always arrayed so as to face the orchestra, opposite the dancer. Thus are the choruses arranged today.[35]

---

34. The very detailed inscriptions of Bakou, Lolei, mention only string instruments and drums (Aymonier).
35. Bas-reliefs of Bayon, by Dufour and Carpeaux, plates 3. 11, 101, 120, 135.

Now the extraordinary ritual lies clearly before me!

The priests, dressed in immaculate vestments, their foreheads marked with three white stripes and the Saivite eye, have already eaten the grains of sacred rice. At the temple's summit, under a central tower looming like the bud of an immense lotus, in the dim sanctuary where the supreme divinity conceals his power, incense sticks by the thousands exude their slow, scented smoke. Gems flicker in the shadows like heavenly bodies, dance like flames, stare out like unfathomable eyes....

Bonze in prayer. Ancient statue. Angkor Wat.

On a golden bed supported by *garudas*,[36] the Varman, covered with precious stones, his hands resting nonchalantly on his divine sword,[37] attentively follows the ritual flow of events. He wears a sacred flower in his ear and has moistened his forehead, cheeks, and chin with lustrate water. The four pillars of the empire — the ministers, the superb princes, the great civil and military leaders — are capped with diadems glittering with gold sequins.[38] They proudly crowd behind the Varman, their sparkling mass spilling out into the courtyards.

---

36. Terrace of the Elephants, Angkor Thom. The current throne is also held up by *garuda*.
37. Bayon, interior gallery, northern face, western wing.
38. "This happy man … nevertheless has the colors of twilight on the gemstones of his toenails, for they act as mirrors for the innumerable and marvelous gold sequins of the *mukutas* and the *kiritas* of the troops of Suras…" (transl. Barth.).

All around, beyond the square windows with their stone bars and gold framework, gleams the sky of a setting sun. And down below lie a calm sea of trees and the dark waters of reservoirs sprinkled with lotus.[39]

The people stand innumerable, in silent veneration, scaling the twelve gigantic staircases, lining the foundations, filling the courtyards of the two lower levels, streaming through the galleries like a river. They wear modest clothing and carry *nandyavarta* flowers.[40] The warriors wear square breastplates, the peasants have wrapped coverings around their bodies,[41] the women are nude to the waist and carry their children on their backs,[42] people with offerings carry their vessels stacked in pyramids and platters loaded with fruit[43] — this entire mass of humanity, fanatical and unaware, stands in place, faces turned toward the proud sanctuary.

But suddenly a muffled murmur passes from mouth to mouth. The grand priest is seen, perched high atop a forty-step staircase guarded by lions, under a portico open to the crimson, twilit sky. Silhouetted there, he has made a sign.

Then, mysterious harmonies, dripping down the stones like the drops of some sonorous rain, fade before a procession that has suddenly appeared. Sixteen *devadasi* advance. The crowd is prostrate, like green rice bending in the wind.

Their gold pendants chime in the solemn silence. Magnificent breasts blossom like lotus flowers beneath their make-up, the sunset coloring them blood red. And three swans, passing in front of the sun, cast enormous moving shadows on the flagstones.

---

39. Third level of Angkor Wat.
40. Stele of Prah Bat (Bergaigne).
41. Bas-reliefs of Angkor Wat, western exterior gallery.
42. Bas-reliefs of Bayon, southern exterior gallery.
43. Bas-reliefs of Bayon, southern exterior gallery.

Two *Devata*. Copied and realized from a bas-relief at Angkor Wat.

Eyes fixed on their destination, the portico, the *devadasi* advance deliberately, in fear and bliss, on bent legs. They smell the fresh flower held between their hands as it lightens and blooms again. They start up the tall, carved steps. The people, closing in behind the dancers, to take in their perfumes of musk and sandalwood, to be caressed by the air that caresses them, watch the rise of the monumental, gleaming tiaras towards the divinity, the King, and the sun.

The harmonious troupe reaches the sacred threshold and collapse in salute. Prostrating themselves eight times, they make their offering to the guardian Spirits of the eight cardinal points. They proffer the divine flower, with rare foods and fruits, in delicate golden dishes. When they shift towards the west, they seem higher in the sky than the sun, that heavenly body still declining and floating on the horizon.

All their veneration, all their offerings, are expressed by the undulations and gestures of their bodies. The thoughts, imaginings, and fervor of the crowd, the priests, and the King are within them at this instant. The altar streams with lustral water. Something huge — something with wings, no doubt — seems to loom in the shadows above the idols. It seems to loom even in your dreams, at the threshold of that gaping hole of sleep, inaccessible in our waking hours. It is the unfathomable mystery through which the crowd, the priestesses, the priests, and the autocrat lived as they lived and did what they did.

What a spectacle! The huge, pale sky of Cambodia, the dying sun, the nine towers, the sacred academy, the King, the prostrate crowd. Beneath the great trees, the calm waters of the basins, with their trembling images of the structures above. Royal elephants, each enclosed in its golden carapace. Then, atop the sculpted mountain, before the shadow of the sanctuary where all powers dwell suspended, the sixteen symbolic *devadasi*, resplendent like stars in the night!

Yes, I see it quite well, the extraordinary ritual. As I contemplate it, my heart seems to acquire an uncommon serenity. An ecstasy not due entirely to my admiration penetrates me, and transforms me into something like one of those poor but blessed devotees. I needn't know more or understand.

Absolute Beauty stands complete before me. Nature destroying herself, beliefs and genius deceiving themselves— such things left me uneasy. I was vaguely afraid. It seemed necessary to seek forgiveness for venerating these monuments, the priests, the King. It seemed to me that they needed some justification, some right to be there, in such a show of pride and power.

Ah, but Grace appeared! I saw her fragile, mounting the steps. She whom no one can deny, topple, or curse, she who is near the gods — I saw her master the immense show of pride, ask forgiveness for it, and make an offering of it!

Of this absolute Beauty she is the sole pure expression, with no tyranny, war, or blood behind it. She was born of the virginal sea. She is all the poetry, charm, and enchantment of this people, their most distinctive work. Her rhythmic steps have left behind the most exquisite memories wherever their delicate traces can be found.

Alone, she returns from the past to offer us her flower, while all else about her crumbles....

Author's Note

This reconstruction was drawn from a scene in a religious dance that took place at the palace throne room in January 1911. Sixteen *lokhon*, through rhythmic gestures, offered fruits in bowls to the spirits of the eight cardinal points.

Attending this dance, performed at sunset three days in a row, I was able to determine that all of the *lokhon*'s gestures, unregulated by any words, were to a great extent the same, and were all, without exception, derived from the three great gestures of the past. Here, then, was peremptory verification of my hypotheses.

This ceremony was divided into three parts:

1st – The Grand salute, aimed successively at each cardinal point

2nd – The offering of fruit, at every cardinal point

3rd – A series of gestures, at every cardinal point, whose significance was again "offering" but this time without accessories

While this scene played out in the throne room — before the King, the supreme chief of the monks, the ministers, and Buddhist and Brahmanic priests — eight groups of four dancers performed the same dance to the same music in the courtyards, at the foot of eight altars, each group at one of the cardinal points.

A crowd of Cambodians, bearing offerings, was present.

Appendices

APPENDIX I - Biographical Materials

Le Khmérophile: The Art and Life of George Groslier
Charles Gravelle - Friend of Groslier and Patron of Cambodia
Timeline: Groslier Contemporaries in Khmer studies
Groslier Family Voyages
Works by George Groslier

APPENDIX II - Related Articles

1913 - Cambodian Dancers in France by George Bois
1914 - Review of *Danseuse Cambodgiennes* by Henri Parmentier
1929 - Theater and Dance in Cambodia by George Groslier
The Ouled Nail Dancers

APPENDIX III - The Future of Cambodian Dance

Dr. Paul Cravath Interviews H.R.H. Princess Buppha Devi

George Groslier
Photo in his museum office by Martin Hürlimann - 1926.

APPENDIX 1

Le Khmérophile:
The Art and Life of George Groslier
By Kent Davis

On February 4, 1887, the first French child was born in Cambodia. In a mystical way, the essence of the Khmer land infused itself deep within him. The child grew up to live, love and celebrate the art, culture, history and people of his birthplace. In the end, he gave his very life to Cambodia. His name was George Groslier.

Cambodia's Hidden Histories

On November 2, 2005 I entered Cambodia's 12th century temple of Angkor Wat for the first time. I had anticipated architectural grandeur at this Wonder of the World, but it was the temple's unexpected human side that overwhelmed me. As I immediately discovered Angkor Wat protects an artistic and cultural treasure unlike any other on our planet: nearly 2,000 images of ancient sacred women realistically portrayed in stone.

Who were they? What do they represent? Why did the Khmer empire honor the images of these women above all others in their fabulous monuments? Since that day, I've devoted my life to answering these questions. My goal is to understand the women, commonly called *devata* or *apsaras*, and to honor their Khmer culture in my work. It was on the path of this investigation that I encountered the now obscure genius of George Groslier.

My *devata* research soon led me to Cambodia's ancient, secretive and almost exclusively female tradition of sacred dance…dance literally performed for the gods to request their bounty here on Earth. This living tradition — passed from teacher to student for countless generations and practiced to this

Angkor Wat devata. Photo Kent Davis.

day — represents one of the purest connections between modern Cambodians and the ancient Khmer roots at the foundation of their culture. And within days of looking at this dance tradition I found yet another chunk of lost history, waiting to be revived.

From 1974 to 1985 a scholar named Paul Cravath researched and assembled the most comprehensive history of Cambodian dance ever written as his doctoral thesis. Once completed, however, his essential body of work was forgotten, ending up on microfilm only to be seen by a handful of researchers. In the course of my research I came across brief quotes of Paul's work that convinced me that it held some clues. Upon securing a printout of the entire paper I had another realization; just as the *devata's* unacknowledged importance was clear to me, it was also obvious that this precious body of historical work was important to share with the Cambodian people. I contacted Paul Cravath, now a tenured professor at the University of Hawaii. Our first conversation lasted for hours. By the time we hung up two commitments were written in stone: I would publish Paul's thesis and he would help me with the process.

By 2008, *Earth in Flower - The Divine Mystery of the Cambodian Dance Drama* was complete. The book garnered awards and much appreciation but my real reward was that Paul's meticulous research opened up so many new doors in my own studies. It was his work that introduced me to the first detailed study of Cambodian dance: *Danseuses Cambodgiennes, Anciennes et Modernes* published in Paris by George Groslier in 1913.

Passages Cravath quoted from the book inspired me to examine a rare copy of the original; a stunning collection of sketches, Groslier's first person accounts of Cambodian dance and dancers from nearly 100 years ago, and his vision of ceremonies that may have taken place at the origin of this sacred tradition. Later I learned that this ambitious project was Groslier's first book, published after two years of research in Phnom Penh in the company of other scholars, equally fascinated by this unusual art.

Groslier's study was appealing to read and visually brilliant but, to my dismay, only 30 copies of this historical record of Cambodian culture had ever been printed. Moreover, the book was never reprinted in French, nor was it ever translated into English or Khmer. As with *Earth in Flower*, I knew that this important history had been lost for too long — I was determined to reissue the book. By mid-2008, much of my new edition was complete but a critical item was missing; I simply wanted to include a photograph of George Groslier so that readers could see the man who produced this wonderful work. None were to be found.

I spent weeks contacting friends worldwide with no results. At that time, the Internet had a single small, grainy photo of Groslier with two children, but it was blurry and unusable. In September 2008, Isabelle Poujol at EFEO in Paris referred me to Brigitte Lequeux-Groslier, widow of George's youngest son, Bernard-Philippe. We spoke by phone and exchanged emails. She was kind but finally wrote to say that she had no photos of her father-in-law. But, perhaps I should speak directly with George Groslier's daughter Nicole? I literally jumped out of my chair when I read the next words "here is her phone number in Florida...."

Nicole Groslier - A Second Generation in Cambodia

There are "coincidences" in life…and then there are totally unlikely events that are so unbelievable that they would never be included in a "B" movie script. Mme. Groslier lives 25 km from my family home and both of us have been here for decades. Filled with emotion I gathered my courage and dialed her telephone number. A melodious voice greeted me, "Hallo?" To my relief, I immediately discovered that Mme. Groslier's English was perfect, having lived here for 28 years. And, yes, she would be happy to meet with me to discuss her father. On October 7, 2008, we met at her home for our first three-hour discussion.

It was a surprising development to go from seeking a mere photo of George Groslier to learning about him from his own daughter. Petite, elegant, articulate, energetic and quite charming, Nicole maintains a residence in Florida overlooking Sarasota Bay. Like her father and two brothers, Nicole Groslier was born in Phnom Penh. Her cabinets and walls are filled with Southeast Asian antiques, artwork and souvenirs from her father, her brother Bernard-Philippe and her own adventures. For the past two years it has been a privilege to frequently meet with her in this perfect setting to discuss her father.

Nicole spent the first 27 years of her life with George Groslier, nearly as much time as his wife Suzanne, who traveled back and forth between Cambodia and France. Due to World War II and his untimely death Suzanne never saw her husband after 1939 while Nicole shared George's final six years with him. Indeed, her love for her father and her Cambodian birthplace made this account come to life. Through her guidance, people would again know her father and, for the first time, they could see a personal side of the man who shaped the artistic foundation of modern Cambodia.

Transcripts of our conversations combined with her personal documents and photos became the framework of the following account. Especially helpful were her mother Suzanne's personal diaries and photo album notations that revealed details that occurred before Nicole was born or when she was still a child. In the end, Nicole herself was surprised by new revelations about her father's life that came from clues she provided.

The extended Groslier family embraced the research project as well, beginning with her daughter Margaret and son Patrick here in the US. In France, nephews Thierry, Sylvain, Antoine, Martin, Guillaume and Thomas (sons of her brother Gilbert Groslier) also contributed to this work by sharing a diverse assortment of documents and photos. All have my gratitude and respect.

Like many interesting projects, this one grew and grew. I went from knowing very little about George Groslier to having an abundance of archival information, much of which was unknown or unexamined for nearly a century. As his entire life took shape before my eyes my respect for him grew, as did my determination to share his story.

George Groslier spent his life documenting, preserving and reviving the art, architecture and culture of the great Khmer civilization. He shared his passion by training and inspiring new generations of Cambodian artists to take possession of their glorious heritage and change their nation. Yet despite the magnitude of his devotion and accomplishments few people today appreciate his contributions to Cambodia.

I submit this modest history as a small first step towards correcting this oversight. In the following pages you will come to know George Groslier — son, artist, author, husband, father, explorer, educator and true Khmerophile — who committed his life and work to Cambodia and her people.

Cambodia's Artistic Son (1885-1910)

The year Cambodia became a French Protectorate, Antoine-Georges Groslier and his wife, Angélina Sidonie Legrand, joined the colonial exodus from France to Indochina. Antoine began his work with the civil service on May 15, 1885.

At the time, Cambodia's very existence as an independent nation had long been threatened by Siam to the west and Vietnamese rivals to the east. King Norodom finally accepted French control in exchange for military protection. Though controversial, this map demonstrates that French intervention prevented Siamese expansion and, in 1904 and 1907, even reclaimed Preah Vihear, Battambang and Siem Reap; provinces that the Siamese had controlled since the 15th century. In 1887, French Indochina was formed with Cambodia and what is now Vietnam (at that time divided into Annam, Tonkin and Cochinchina). Laos was shortly added to the group.

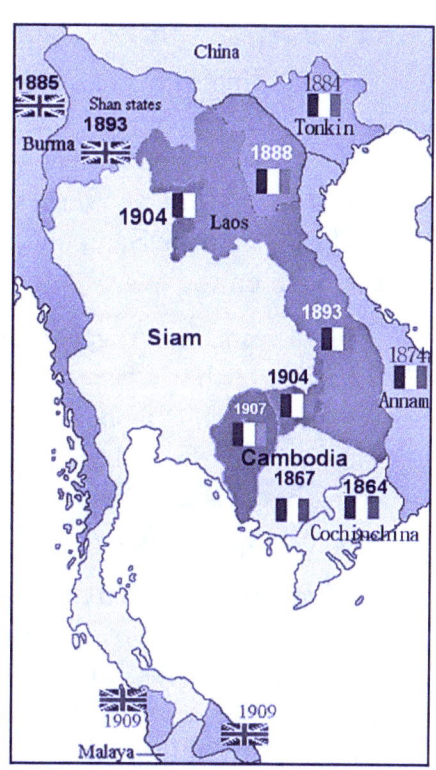

French Indochina - 1864-1907

George Groslier's baptism in Phnom Penh, 1887.

According to Suzanne Groslier's notes, the acting Resident Superior of Phnom Penh at the time was Mr. Huyn de Vernéville. When Angélina arrived there were few French women in town: the Resident Superior's wife Mme. de Vernéville, a nun of the Confrérie de Chartre named Sister Saint-Sylvère, and a woman (of questionable reputation) who ran the hotel on the quay.

Two years later Angélina became pregnant and on Friday, February 4, 1887 she gave birth to a boy. News of the event traveled quickly because this was the first French child born in Cambodia. According to Suzanne's notes, Sisowath himself, then Obarrach of King Norodom, visited the family to extend his best wishes. The child received his father's middle name (*sans* s) and was soon baptized as George Groslier.

Antoine was soon transferred to Kampong Chhnang, a post north of Phnom Penh were roads were almost non-existent and most travel was done by river. Angélina, an accomplished musician, requested (and received) one perquisite for this hardship: a baby grand piano, which was delivered by elephant. In 1900 the wife of Jean Commaille, the first curator of the

Angkor site in Siem Reap, made a similar demand from her husband. Given the sacrifices French spouses made in rural Cambodia at the time, asking for a piano may not have been unreasonable as it sounds.[1]

Angélina became pregnant with a second child but as the term progressed so did her worries due to the remote location and inhospitable climate. At the time, there was only one doctor in all of Cambodia, Dr. Gouzien, who later became a well known expert in colonial medicine. Towards the end of her pregnancy, Angélina traveled to Saigon to deliver her child. Sadly her daughter only lived for a few moments. At this loss she decided that jungle life was far too risky for her only son. With George scarcely two years old she hastily booked passage back to France, with no thought given to ever returning. She instilled this fear of the tropics in George during his childhood, and he himself took little interest in traveling to Indochina.

While nicer ships later plied the waters between Saigon and France the transport she found then was the hospital ship *Shamrock*. Suzanne later wrote down Angélina's account of one incident on the voyage:

> The steamer didn't have portholes that opened to the inside, as on today's ships, but shutters of a sort, which clapped onto the boat's exterior and were held in place by a chain on each side. One day my mother-in-law, who normally never left her son, had to step out for a few moments. When she got back to the cabin she couldn't see George anywhere. She ran about searching every place she could think of, even the closest gangways, and then raised the alarm.

> There was an extensive search of the ship but no results. Convinced that her son had drowned Angélina returned to her cabin to see the baby sitting quietly in the porthole, feet dangling outside the boat, hands grasping the chains. He was gazing out at the waves, perhaps looking at the flying fish or porpoises that frequented those waters. She didn't lose her cool or shout but crept up, grabbed him, pulled him inside...and gave him the spanking of his life.

After arriving in Marseille in 1889 details of George's early life are scarce. While George's Cambodian chapter had temporarily ended, his father continued working in Cambodia in a number of positions.

In 1893, Antoine was First Assistant to the Resident of Sambor province. In 1895 he was Chancellor of the Cambodian Girl's School in

---

1. Penny Edwards, *Cambodge: The Cultivation of a Nation, 1860-1945* (Honolulu: University of Hawaii Press, 2007). P. 138.

Exposition de Lyon poster, 1894

Phnom Penh. In 1897 he remained in Phnom Penh as Secrétariat de la Résident Supérieure as Chancelier de Résidence, a title similar to that of his co-worker Pierre Guesde, who would become the father of the Franco-Khmer writer Makhali-Phal the very next year. By 1906 he appears as a Government Commissioner in Luang Prabang, Laos with the pay rank of Civil Service Administrator 4th Class.[2]

Antoine probably traveled to France to visit his wife and son but there are no records of that. He is only seen in three photos in the family albums: at George's baptism in 1887; in an undated portrait; and with his new daughter-in-law Suzanne in Marseille, June 1916. Angélina certainly never returned to Asia but George was exposed to French Indochina from a very young age, attending his first colonial exposition with Cambodian exhibits in Lyon when he was only seven.

In 1904 George published his first book, an 80-page poetry collection entitled *La Chanson d'un Jeune*. From 1894 to 1905 there are no personal photos or other documents available. The biggest questions relate to the *Exposition coloniale* in Marseille in 1906 when Cambodia's King Sisowath and his dancers became a media sensation throughout France. The dancers performed near George's family home in Marseille and near his school and studio in Paris. Did George's father return to France for those events? Did the 18-year-old George see the exotic Asian dancers? Did their visit influence his future plans or the topic of his first book? No records have come to light that answer these questions.

---

2. *Annuaire du Cambodge* (Imprimerie du Protectorate, 1888-89, 1893-97, 1906-11)

Le Khmérophile 171

Angélina and George at the Exposition de Lyon, 1894.

Between May and November 1894 George and his mother traveled 300 km. from their home to the *Exposition universelle de Lyon*, which featured pavilions and exhibits devoted to Indochina, including George's birthplace of Cambodia.

Near the time of the Marseille Expo George began his studies in Paris under the guidance of Albert Maignan (1845–1908). Then in the last years of his life, Maignan had become a painter of great renown. A devotee of Oriental and Medieval art, Maignan amassed a large collection of antiquities, many of which came as rewards for funding archeological excavations. The artist's house on Rue de la Bruyère was a veritable museum with an immense studio decorated with showcases.

Maignan had a profound influence on George's artistic style and career. His student was so grateful that he dedicated his first book, *Danseuses Cambodgiennes,* to him. In fact, his teacher was directly involved in an event that changed George's life and the future of Cambodia; he supported George's application to compete in the annual Prix de Rome competition.

Initiated in 1663 during the reign of Louis XIV the Prix de Rome was an art contest of epic importance for hundreds of years. Organized by the *Académie de France,* its winners were awarded generous scholarships, working sabbaticals at the Villa Medici in Rome and prestige that all but guaranteed success as an artist.

Readers familiar with today's dramatic television talent competitions will be surprised to compare them to the ground rules of this rigorous contest. Entry to the Prix de Rome was limited to 100 students per year, all of whom had to be French, male, single, under 30, in good standing with their academic studies and endorsed by a well-known art teacher. The three trials to be endured at the Villa Medici were grueling to say the least.

The first test called for a painted sketch of an historical or mythological subject assigned by the supervising professor. The sketch had to be completed within a 12-hour time period, during which time students were actually locked into studios at the school. Canvases were signed on the back to maintain anonymity for judging.

At this point 80 students were eliminated, leaving 20 to advance to the second level five days later. Students were again locked in the same studios as before. This time, they were given four 7-hour painting sessions to portray a nude male figure, drawn from a live model, on an 81 x 65 cm canvas. Works were numbered, associated with each student's first painting, and again submitted for judging.

George painting in a garden - Circa 1905, Autreville-sur-Moselle.

George showed great promise as an artist but his parents saw no future in that line of work. Still, he persisted by attending the *Ecole nationale supérieure des Beaux-arts* in Paris, studying under the well-known artist Albert Maignan, and becoming a finalist in the Prix de Rome competition.

George (left) in the studio of his mentor, Albert Maignan, circa 1907.

For the final trial, half of the contestants were eliminated. The remaining ten students then worked on the most critical challenge for an incredible 72 days, during which time they received accommodation and private studios at the school. This assignment was to complete a large oil painting, 1.137 X 1.465 meters in size. Ten senior members of the Academy chose the subject in absolute secrecy and announced it to the assembled group.

In the first phase, contestants received a sheet of paper and were then locked in individual studios for 12 hours to produce a rough sketch of their final work. Next, they were given 72 days to work on their creation, only resting on Sundays and holidays. Their final canvas could not vary considerably in style or content from their original concept. The pressure of the situation actually drove some students to destroy their work out of frustration; a rash act that would cause them to be barred from the next year's competition!

As George's aspirations soared anticipating the Prix de Rome competition he rose to new heights in another unique way on April 9, 1908 (at right). In World War I, he came to experience a much more serious side of balloon technology.

George's fascination with Oriental art is clear in his studio at 50 Rue la Fountaine in Paris, circa 1908, as he attended the Ecole nationale supérieure des Beaux-arts. He appears to be wearing a man's *yukuta* (summer kimono) with *obi* (belt sash). *Japonisme* influenced the work of many popular European and American artists in that period including Monet, Toulouse-Lautrec, Gauguin, Degas, Renoir and others.

Finally, all the completed paintings were displayed under glass with the original sketches for viewing by the jury, journalists and the public. Unveiling the winner became a major annual event in France. After 106 days, the judges announced the winner of the Premier Grand Prix de Rome along with two runners up and one honorable mention.[3]

George Groslier reached the final level of the Prix de Rome competition. Realizing his dreams of becoming a professional artist, proving himself to his mentor, and showing his parents that art was a worthy vocation were so close. But in the end, he did not take the Premier prize and, like many others before him, he experienced this as a crushing defeat.

A formal portrait taken shortly before George's return to Cambodia in 1910.

George was in good company in his "failure": the artists Delacroix, Moreau, Manet and Degas competed without even an honorable mention. Jacques Louis David lost three competitions before finally taking the prize. Disappointed, George was now open to his parents' suggestion that perhaps a job in the colonial service held more opportunity than art. No doubt Antoine worked his internal connections and soon young George had an assignment: he would be returning to Cambodia.

---

3. *École nationale supérieure des beaux-arts* - **www.ensba.fr**.

Henri Marchal, a Cambodian assistant and George Groslier at Ta Prohm, 1910.

The Sacred Dance: Reunion with *Cambodge* (1910-1912)

In 1910, the Ministry of Public Education commissioned George for an educational assignment in Cambodia. He received an extremely small subsidy that he had to split with a traveling companion, the explorer and physician Dr Aimé-François Legendre (1867–1951) who was making his second trip to China. According to Suzanne's notes, George's stipend hardly amounted to more than his boat fare.

Their month-long passage was spent aboard the 142 meter long steamer *Ernest Simons*. When George returned to Cambodia his father Antoine was

Chief of the Province stationed at Ban me Thuot, in the Central Highlands of what is now Vietnam. While it seems likely that Antoine would meet his son there is no record of that in the family archives. All we find is Suzanne's note of his encounter with Sister Saint-Sylvère, the nun that brought him into the world, who greeted him saying "My dear child, how you have grown!"

George soon met Charles Gravelle, Jean Commaille, Henri Marchal, Roland Meyer and others through an association called the Angkor Society for Conservation of the Ancient Monuments of Indochina.[4] Group members frequently traveled to the Khmer ruins together, and two of his new friends — Gravelle and Meyer — were also avid admirers of Cambodian dance.

Whether George arrived in Cambodia with the intent of studying the dancers — based on their 1906 visit to France — or whether he was inspired by his new friends is unknown. The evidence shows that Gravelle, 23 years older than George, took an active and ongoing role in guiding and facilitating his dance study. He wrote the foreword to his book and helped with logistical arrangements for some of George's artwork. In fact, the dancer Ratt Poss, featured on the cover of this edition, became Charles' wife in 1923.[5]

Meyer, on the other hand, was a peer just two years younger than George. The details of their relationship are less obvious but, given their shared passions, may have been important. Meyer was becoming an adept Khmer linguist (he later published the first Khmer-French language primer) and seems to have been romantically involved with a royal dancer himself. During his first ten years in Cambodia Meyer wrote copiously, but kept his work to himself. In 1919, he finally published his epic novel in Saigon, *Saramani Danseuse Khmèr*.

While George's account of dance is vivid, it remains tactful. Meyer's tale, however, focuses on one particular royal dancer, revealing intimate details of her Cambodian life, including a detailed family history and secrets behind the palace walls where the sequestered dancers lived. His book also gives an in-depth account of the dancer's voyage to France with King Sisowath and his family in 1906. How much of Meyer's book is fiction and how much is fact is unknown but his graphic account certainly would have upset some people. Soon after the book's release Meyer left Cambodia for Laos. He continued to rise in the ranks of colonial service so whatever lines he may have crossed didn't have a permanent affect on his career.

So here we have three intellectual French men, all writers, all living in the same small town, belonging to the same club, traveling together, and

---
4. *La Société d'Angkor pour la conservation des monuments anciens d'Indochine.*
5. See Charles Gravelle's biographical profile in Appendix I.

George at the Bayon, Angkor Thom, 1912.

sharing a special devotion for Cambodia's sacred dance — and especially for the dancers. That said, exact details of their creative collaborations in this field, if they existed, remain unclear.

George completed his official duties and his personal study of the royal dance in 1912. While he made many friends during his first return visit to his birthplace, Suzanne comments that the Ecole Française d'Extrême-Orient (EFEO) "took a dim view of his mission, assigned as it was to an amateur outside their institution. They made a lot of trouble for George." Suzanne's notes refer to the next incident as "the Cœdès affair," implying that George Cœdès, an EFEO worker one year older than George, was directly involved:

> While in Cambodia, George collected some Khmer pottery, mostly in fragments, and held a public exhibition in Phnom Penh before his departure. As he was preparing his return to France, the EFEO arranged to have an embargo put on the crate containing the aforementioned pottery on the very day of his departure. This embargo, instigated by a dispatch (see the complete records in the trunk), accused George of exporting the pottery for himself, though the addressee on the crates was clearly the "Ministry of Public Education."
>
> George had time to rush over to, I think, Mr Tricon's house.[6] Tricon, an auctioneer in Saigon and a friend of his father's, took a bailiff to see the crates and have them officially sealed, so that no one could seize them. On George's arrival in Paris, Minister Albert Sarraut made the necessary arrangements and the crates were then sent to France...at the EFEO's expense.

Leaving the pottery behind was a small issue. When George boarded the *Amazone* for his month-long trip back to France he carried a more valuable treasure; his personal research including hundreds of original sketches, numerous paintings and the manuscript that would soon become his first book, and the first study of Cambodian dance.

Once back in France, George returned to Paris and established a relationship with a publishing house founded by historian Augustin Challamel (1819-1894). Challamel produced many books and catalogs on French colonial topics, including works by Khmer history scholars Auguste Pavie, Charles Carpeaux and S. E. Thiounn. In 1913, Challamel created 30 copies of George's first book, *Danseuses Cambodgiennes - Anciennes et Modernes*, funded by a subscription from the Minister of Colonies and the "High Patronage of His Majesty Sisowath, King of Cambodia."

Back to the Jungle (1913-1914)

---

6. In 1921, Albert Tricon and Charles Bellan would publish *Chansons cambodgiennes*, a Cambodian songbook. In 1913, George included one of their songs and a sample of their translated lyrics in *Danseuses Cambodgiennes*.

George's studio in Paris, 1913.

Cambodian scenes now dominate George's growing collection of canvases, with Angkor Wat featured in four paintings.

George's studio in Paris, 1913.

To the left of the *mokots* (crowns) and books we have George's painting, *Les danseuses*, featured on the rear cover. Below is his sketch, *Malika-The Legendary Little Princess*, a favorite of his daughter Nicole that hangs in her entry foyer today.

George's desk in his Paris studio, 1913.

After his first visit back to his birthplace Cambodian culture dominated George's life. His art objects blend his European youth and his growing future in Asia.

Items of interest from left to right (defined with a high resolution scan):

1. Two Cambodian dance *mokots* (crowns).
2. Two bird bodies and a carved stone bird. Significance unknown.
3. A *repoussé* container - This metal container with hammered design appears to be Cambodian. George later revitalized this local art in his school.
4. Bookshelf - Titles include the *Catalogue Officiel Salon de 1910* and *1912*, published by Baschet for the *Societe Nationale des Beaux-Arts*; an essential art research tool. To their right is Jean Commaille's 1912 book, *Guide aux ruines d'Angkor* published by Hachette.
5. Certificate (above) - With the images of a head, two angels and text this may be recognition for his Prix de Rome participation.
6. A woven Asian basket hangs below the certificate.
7. Two Chinese or Annamese marionettes - Possibly gifts from his father.
8. Photo of a balding man leaning against a balustrade, possibly his father.
9. Triple framed paintings (top) - These three architectural studies seen on his studio wall in 1908 are now matted and framed. The number 442 in the lower left hand corner implies that they were part of a competition.
10. Painting of unknown subjects. A seated women and standing man.
11. (below, behind oil lamp) The photo of George with his teacher, Albert Maignan, that appears earlier in this article.
12. Desktop - In addition to personal papers we see a typewriter, a brass oil lamp, a small cast metal pot on a tripod, ink bottles and a knife. At the back is a metal human figure carrying something on a rod across the shoulders, but the style is unrecognizable. Another framed certificate is behind. At the center of the desk are three photos of a young girl, but her identity is unknown.
13. (above) Three photos behind a clock and next to two crucifixes - George's mother (center) and father (right). The woman at lower left may be an early photo of his mother.
14. Painting of a statue of a horse and rider.
15. Art from the chapter *Leur Histoire* in *Danseuses Cambodgiennes*.
16. A primitive stone figure, an oil painting of a dining room scene, and an indigenous basket with a *khaen* resting inside. The *khaen* is a musical wind instrument made from bamboo tubes now in popular use in Northeastern Thailand.

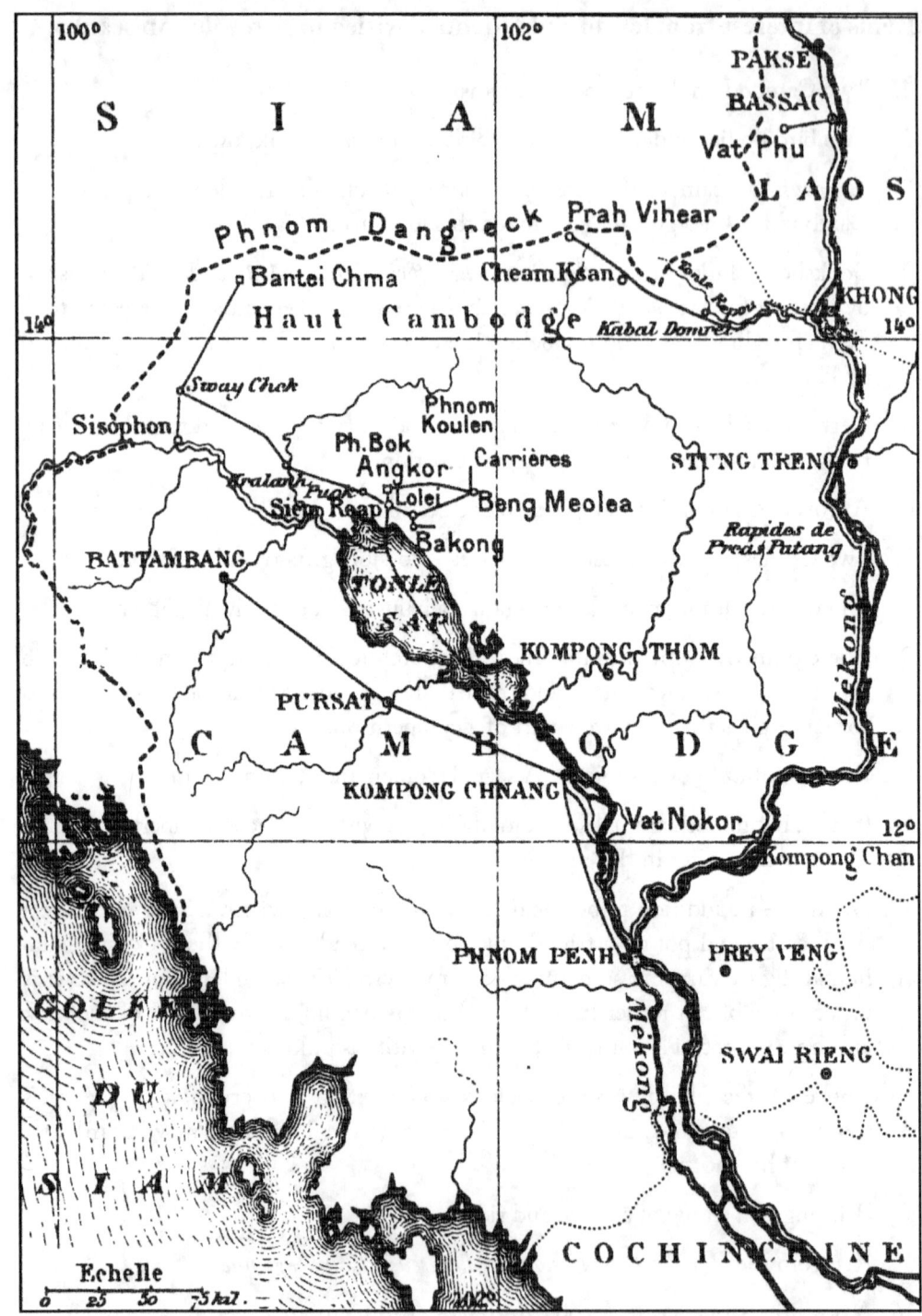

George Groslier's missions, April 1913-January 1914.

Albert Sarraut, the Minister of Public Education (and soon to be Governor General of Indochina) was so satisfied with Groslier's previous work that he issued a new title to George: Project Manager in Cambodia for the Minister of Public Education and Fine Arts.[7] On April 1, 1913 George boarded the steamship *Paul Lecat* again bound for Cambodia with new assignments.

Over the remainder of the year, he traveled the length and breadth of the country documenting Khmer monuments and recording his impressions and adventures. He traveled on his own, isolated in remote jungles, rivers and mountains in primitive and demanding conditions assisted only by native helpers. Many of these experiences would later appear in his 1916 book *In the Shadow of Angkor: Notes and Impressions on the Unknown Temples of Ancient Cambodia*.[8]

In early June 1913, George set out for the Khmer temple of Wat Phu, now in Laos, via the Mekong River. By the end of July he found himself hiking 50 km to the foot of Preah Vihear, a majestic Khmer temple perched at the top of the Dangrek Mountain range overlooking Cambodia and Thailand. As it turned out, his notes of this mission held great benefits for Cambodia half a century later. At the time, George was filled with other concerns as he wrote in his diary entry of July 25:

> After tomorrow, I will arrive at Preah Vihear. I feel the darkest premonitions. For more than three years I have dreamt of studying this temple. From Angkor, when the weather was fine, I would often look to the north, barely making out the Dangrek chain. I knew the temple was perched atop like an eagle's next, and I would feel both an irresistible desire to go there and a sort of irrational fright.
>
> Every time I thought of this temple, two ideas — like quarreling sisters: one superb, one tragic — would rise up in my mind. I knew how hard it would be to reach the spot, high on a peak, at the edge of an abyss. I would imagine its desolation, and the bitter, lashing wind that had already passed over all of Cambodia and Siam. I knew, too, that the trails leading up to it were the trails of wild elephants, that they served as gathering places for Siamese rebels, that the tiger was king of that land. Divided as I was between desire and fear, the first word written on my mission's itinerary was *Preah Vihear*.[9]

This mountaintop temple was particularly significant because

---

7. *Chargé de Mission au Cambodge par le Ministère de l'Instruction publique et des Beaux-arts.*
8. Groslier, George. 1916. *A l'Ombre d'Angkor: Notes et Impressions sur les Temples Inconnus de l'Ancien Cambodge.* **Paris: Challamel.**
9. Ibid., p. 39.

the French negotiated for the Siamese to repatriate it to Cambodia following their 1907 treaty. George arrived on July 26, 1913 and spent 11 days working at the site. He submitted his report to the Archeological Commission of Indochina that November. In 1916, he included parts of his experience in *A l'Ombre d'Angkor* with a detailed account in his 1922 book, *Art et archéologie khmers*.

Decades later Cambodia gained its independence from France in 1952. French troops left the country and within two years the Thai government took advantage of the situation by occupying the sacred site. Cambodia's recovery of the temple, however, was already ensured by previous actions of King Norodom Sihanouk. Upon assuming leadership he quickly charged Cambodia's only internationally qualified Geographical Engineer, Nginn Karet, with establishing the Khmer Geographic Service (*Service Géographique Khmer*) under the auspices of the Khmer National Armed Forces (*Force Armée Nationale Khmère*).

Thai soldiers remained on the temple site so Cambodia was forced to submit a formal protest to the International Court of Justice in 1959. Arguing on behalf of Cambodia was American attorney Dean Acheson accompanied by experts, including Karet, whose work was recognized by the international authorities. The procedure examined documents going back to the original grant of land in 1907 so George's careful study became a key piece of evidence. The court established that Thailand had unfairly encroached on Cambodian soil and ruled in their favor on June 15, 1962.[10]

George at Preah Vihear, August 1913.

From Preah Vihear George returned to Angkor by early September resuming the

---

10. International Court of Justice, Case Concerning the Temple of Preah Vihear (Cambodia vs. Thailand). Vol. II, pp. 468, 478, 509-510.

studies he had begun on his first mission. With the greatest challenges of his extended trek behind him the 26-year-old artist now roamed the jungle-shrouded temples of Angkor Wat, Angkor Thom, Ta Phrom, Takeo, Phnom Bakeng and Preah Khan, penning lively accounts that blended his subjective impressions with objective details.

> [The Khmer people]... resemble this forest. Like her, they are full of mystery. In their gestures, in their types, in their habits, in their implements, you sometimes discover a vestige of ancient times surviving to this day, mixed in with modern custom. You stumble upon it suddenly, as if in the depths of a forest. It might be a jewel, a humble bit of pottery, the shape of a statue's lip, a corrupted word of Sanskrit. The whole country holds vigil over its own sleeping past, deriving no profit from it, but unwilling to let it go.[11]

As Maxime Prodromidès observes, what set George Groslier apart from other authors was his close contact with the Khmer people with his passion split between the art and life of the country. Echoing Henri Parmentier's 1914 review of *Danseuses Cambodgiennes*[12] Prodromidès asks:

> Is this a travel diary, a breviary of subjective archeology, an ethnological meditation? Mixed works do not lend themselves to classification. Too much science, cry the pure writers. Too much poetry, cry the scientists. Groslier fortunately indulged in both, never minding the contradiction.[13]

George's gift to Cambodia was his duality. He was an artist and a scientist, painting his subjects with oils and words, presenting practical descriptions with emotional experiences. George investigated ancient heritage while making it relevant to Cambodia's present and future, always with respectful consideration for the Khmer people who he knew were the true heirs to the legacy.

In December he traveled 40 km east of the Angkor group. After fifteen hours in an ox-cart he reached Beng Mealea, the "lotus pond" temple entirely collapsed upon itself in deep jungle. Only accompanied by "troops of monkeys," George spent two weeks there alone, exploring the mysteries of this complex temple:

> If you search carefully, and dig them out from under the crushing heaps, you could exhume a great many masterpieces. Not only would they be intact, but they'd be in much better condition than the works

---

11. Groslier, *A l'Ombre d'Angkor*, p. 86.
12. See Appendix II.
13. Prodromidès, Maxime. 1997. *Angkor: chronique d'une renaissance*. Civilisations & sociétés. Paris: Kailash.

we can now observe at our leisure. Since destruction followed so closely on the heels of construction, the collapsed blocks in effect protect one another. If you slip through a hole in the rubble where its possible to do so (and this is the case at the sanctuary of Beng Mealea), you find a smiling *devata* and a polygonal post, ringed with lotus flowers. Protected from centuries of rain, as they have been, by the colossal superstructure, the sculptures have kept their shine, their polish, and the vigor of their execution. Out in the open, meanwhile, tilting lintels have exposed their graceful surfaces – the gestures of a god, a lotus blossom – to the rains and to falling branches. Everything has been erased.[14]

George's words leapt from the page when I first read them: I believe I met this particular *devata* at Beng Mealea in March 2006. As Groslier noted 93 years before, most of this temple's lintels and *devata* are badly weathered. But in the ruins of a northwest corner tower I discovered a hole formed by collapsed stones and covered by foliage. At the bottom of a well-hidden and well-protected opening I saw her:

Her exquisite features expressed her Khmer heritage so perfectly she was chosen to become immortal. No one had spoken her name for nearly 900 years but certainly thousands had admired her beauty; her almond eyes, the gentle cleft in her chin, her benevolent gaze, her full lips and deep smile conveyed warmth that set her apart from other women. Once adorned with a golden crown, jewelry and accoutrements this flower of the Khmers became divine. She answered her king's highest calling in the temple of Beng Melea.[15]

There in the sweltering jungle, surrounded by the shrill sound of cicadas, she was timeless, having survived the collapse of her civilization, countless wars and centuries of weather. Through all of that, she still offered me peace and her benediction. Sadly, her story does not end well.

In his solitary time at the temple George only noted rain and falling branches as enemies of the stones, but later in his career he would become well aware of the danger of human predators. One year later I returned to the site to introduce this miraculous hidden survivor to my wife Sophaphan. As she climbed the rubble she shouted to me that there was nothing to see. Where an ancient beauty once stood, we now found a

---

14. Groslier, *A l'Ombre d'Angkor*, p. 115.
15. See the complete article and photos at www.devata.org: "Death of an Angel: How antiquities theft destroys Cambodia's past…and future."

The hidden angel of Beng Mealea in March 2006. One year later she was destroyed by a looter. Photos Kent Davis.

faceless section of bare stone left by looters — the angel of Beng Mealea was now gone forever, leaving only a reminder that heritage is irreplaceable.[16]

George then traveled another twelve hours south by ox-cart arriving at the brick temples of Loley and Bakong in the former Khmer capital Rolous. He noted the fertile plains that dominated the area near the Tonle Sap lake. A few more days of study and his itinerary directed him to his final destination, a vast temple that would fascinate him for decades to come: Banteay Chhmar.

George traveled for weeks across the flat plains of Cambodia, celebrating a solitary Christmas day in the middle of a harvested rice field. Upon reaching Banteay Chhmar he spent ten days drawing site plans of the huge temple, one of the largest the Khmers would ever build. In 1924, George would be the first to travel there by automobile but as this mission ended he was limited to one-ox-power transport.[17]

Before returning to Phnom Penh to organize his notes George ends

---

16. For information on promoting positive tourism practices and preserving cultural heritage please visit www.HeritageWatchInternational.org.
17. See Darryl Collins' article, "The First Automobiles to Reach Banteay Chhmar, 1924" in Udaya, Journal of Khmer Studies, No. 9, 2008.

his meditation at Angkor Wat on January 22nd 1914:

> The shadow of Angkor, beautiful and sweet, vibrant with memories. Heroic, supremely long, the shadow of Angkor favors all artists. They should go there. If not, they should think of it and concern themselves often with new flights of imagination and with getting to know other examples of human genius.[18]

Back at the capital in February, George received another honor from the Résident Supérieur de Cambodge (RSC): a contract to augment the work of painter François de Marliave in the Throne Hall of the Royal Palace with additional scenes of his own design. George's contribution was to be three paintings depicting Brahmanism, Buddhism and the relationship between the two in Cambodia. The outbreak of World War I that summer changed plans all over the world, including these. The proposed paintings were never finished. François was mobilized by the War and in June George was also headed back to France on the steamship *Magellan* to enlist.[19]

---

18. Groslier, *A l'Ombre d'Angkor*, p. 185.
19. Muan, Ingrid. 2001. *Citing Angkor: The "Cambodian Arts" in the Age of Restoration.* Doctoral Thesis, Columbia University, New York. Pp. 64-67.

George's Buddhism panel concept for the Throne Hall, 1914.

Suzanne Poujade skating.

A World at War, Suzanne Poujade and a Wedding (1914-1917)

For new perspectives we now shift our attention to George's future wife in France, with the benefit of direct quotes from her personal journals.

Suzanne Poujade's father Jules was born in Paris in 1870, the youngest of the six children of Jean-Pierre Poujade and Anne Fertand. Her great-grandfather had been the Emperor Napoleon's calligrapher and her grandfather, Jean-Pierre (1818-1869), later assumed the same respected position. Following this family tradition her father Jules, her Uncle Edmond, Uncle Arthur and Aunt Pauline all became recognized as gifted calligraphers and artists. As it turned out, when Suzanne was born on June 8, 1893 she became the "only Poujade child" as Jules was the only Poujade of that generation to have a successor.

Her early family life was pleasant but she recalled that her father never liked the idea of leaving Paris…until he "invented the weekend." The family purchased a lakeside home in Enghien-les-Bains, a popular resort area just north of the city where Suzanne was baptized.

As a girl, Suzanne "had a solid frame but was alarmingly thin" so the family doctor recommended sports as the cure. As a result Suzanne pursued both tennis and ice-skating, going on to win French national championships in both categories as she relates:

> We really loved it, and it ended up costing our families a fortune. There was no training back then, and we pretty much made it up on our own. Except for some tennis lessons from Brodequis, the elder in Dieppe, that is. Ice skating you'd learn from your friends as best you could. With Pigueron, my couples partner, I won five gold medals at the French championships and several medals at the Paris city championships. In tennis, just before 1914, I got into the top league after winning the qualifying rounds and then played in the world championships of 1914 winning three gold medals. [20]

The start of World War I quickly changed Suzanne's life, as it did for George as well in distant Cambodia. Suzanne's personal diary records her experiences at the beginning of the War:

> In 1915, the first German planes[21] appeared over Paris. Their arrival affected Maman in particular, greatly upsetting her stomach, and we embarked on our first exile. We headed for Lavaur [in the *département* of Tarn in southwestern France], where Papa still had a great aunt and some cousins. We were lucky enough to have to change trains a single time at [Aubrais], so the trip took only twenty-four hours! Of course, the trains were so crowded that there were people riding on the outside stairs and the roofs.
>
> At Lavaur we separated, Maman going to that great aunt's house, and I to the Bonhommes' because they had a daughter my age, Gabrielle. The great aunt, who was blind, had me kneel in front of her and ran her fingers all over my face, so that she could recognize me. As soon as we were settled, Papa naturally set out for Paris again, not wanting to abandon the Institute and its

German aerial attack on Paris in 1915.

---

20. Suzanne donated her medals, news articles and documents to the archives of the Musée National du Sports.
21. Suzanne used the word "taube," German for "dove," the common name used for all German aircraft at that time.

Suzanne Poujade (center), George's future wife - At the beginning of the War, Suzanne worked as a nurse in Lavaur, 44 km east of Toulouse in southwestern France. The French army suffered terribly with more than 6.1 million men killed, wounded or missing — more than 70% of their entire fighting force.

staff, since things were in full swing there. I immediately sought out Doctor Iversinc to volunteer for an infirmary he was organizing in an old seminary. The wounded had begun to arrive, especially from the Fifteenth Infantry Regiment.[22]

So I was really taken aback a few days later when I ran into two friends from Paris there, on the streets of that little sub-prefecture. It was the two youngest Francès sisters, Marguerite and Germaine. ...A few months later, they were back in Lavaur and bored, looking for something to do besides knit for soldiers. Me, since I was no longer a minor, I'd now begun working at the makeshift hospital at the Collège Chaptal, thanks to Dr. Theirry de Martel.

Someone — I don't know who — pointed out to the sisters that while many soldiers found packages of woolen articles and food very useful, some soldiers just wanted pen pals to help them pass the time in the trenches or the back lines. Asking around, we found out where to go to get letters from soldiers seeking a to start a correspondence with a *marraine de guerre*[23]. The sisters, however,

---

22. *15e régiment d'infanterie de ligne.*
23. For more acts of female contribution and heroism in this conflict see Margaret Darrow's book *French Women and the First World War* (ISBN 9781859733660).

"A few words from you give me great joy." Beginning in the spring of 1915, the French media promoted becoming a "War Godmother" as an act of patriotism. Women were encouraged to correspond with soldiers to boost morale and many weddings resulted.

were far too timid to go there alone. As the acknowledged leader of the bunch, I went with them and they selected their letters without any interference from me.

Guite [Marguerite] began a correspondence, but it stopped because the soldier wasn't very interesting. Germaine continued hers with Théo Briant, the future Breton poet.[24] We went back to get a new pen pal for Guite, who couldn't decide between two or three letters. She would give me one, take it back, give it to me again, and so on. When I'd had enough of this, I just put one letter away in my muff and refused to take my hands back out, citing the cold.

Since aviation was all the rage back then, Guite had selected nothing but aviators. One soldier said that he'd travelled a great deal, and that's the one I inherited. And that's the story! The letter was signed 'George Groslier, Fifth squadron'....

---

24. A photo in Suzanne's album shows that correspondence also ended with marriage in August 1916, just two months after Suzanne and George were wed.

Viewed in high resolution, the photo of George seated on an observation balloon basket revealed a silk shoulder patch confirming his service in the dangerous new art of balloon warfare. With the help of World War I balloon expert and author Richard DesChenes, the following details emerged.[25]

The French were expert balloonists, who quickly saw the advantages balloons provided as observation platforms to report enemy positions and direct artillery fire. At first they used spherical balloons to observe battlefields, but these were hard to control: spinning and bouncing with the wind when tethered on a cable. They were raised and lowered by a group of soldiers and, because they couldn't go up very high, they were excellent targets. Commands and observations were shouted through a megaphone, as they had no other communications; radio communications had yet to be invented.

This instability led to the development of sausage shaped balloons. These used drogues trailing from back to stabilize them in the wind — like the tail on a kite — allowing them to rise out of the range of ground based gunfire. "Kite balloon" became the accepted term for that style. A German design with a large tail-rudder replaced the drogues. Finally, a French army engineer named Major Albert Caquot invented the three-lobed fin design that became the standard for all the armies during the first war.

His addition of the lobes — inflated by air passing through a scoop on the leading edge — oriented the balloon to point into the wind, creating a more stable tethered platform in winds up to 60 MPH, at altitudes up to 5000 feet. The French also developed the motorized winch truck that could spool cable in or out at 30 ft per second. Soon, the 3/8" woven steel cable had a telephone line embedded in its core.

Caquot balloons could only lift about 500 pounds depending upon the quality of gas and air temperature. The balloon basket carried up to

---

25. The patch and French basket team photo are also from the archives of Richard DesChennes — www.Camp-John-Wise-Aerostation.com.

Balloonist George Groslier at Versailles Aerostation in 1915. He is equipped with a Lebel 8mm rifle, the first small bore rifle adopted by any nation and introduced in 1886. His holstered pistol was probably a Model 1892 8mm Revolver. WWI expert Richard DesChennes notes "it was very unreliable, as was the ammunition. They generally had it attached to a lanyard, which would allow it to be swung as a club when it wouldn't fire."

Balloon observation revolutionized battle tactics.

two crew members (often small in stature) equipped with parachutes. Upon an enemy air attack on the flammable balloon, the crew would attempt to parachute to safety. Easily spotted as key observation platforms, balloons became important targets of enemy aircraft.

The balloons themselves were at first defenseless, only protected by antiaircraft guns and friendly aircraft. Later, the French added mounts for a moveable machine gun but, according to DesChennes "they were not really practical, as you could only carry a few hundred rounds of ammunition. As the gun was fired, the balloon would rise as the shells were expended due to lost ballast. Hydrogen then had to be vented to compensate."

When America officially entered the War on April 6, 1917, it assigned many men to French balloon companies to learn how to operate and run the airships, forming the foundation of the US Army's Balloon Corps. Blimps and balloons enhanced superiority in air-to-air, air-to-ground and ground-to-ground combat situations by improving reconnaissance. Ultimately balloon technology contributed to the stalemate of World War I's extended trench warfare.

Letters between Suzanne and her aviator soon blossomed into a serious relationship. In an unusual twist of fate, the young woman who initiated this long-distance relationship entirely by chance also shared one of George's connections to Southeast Asia.

A rare 1915 photo showing a French balloon with machine gun and mounts.
Photo Richard DesChennes.

Suzanne's father, Jules Poujade, had many friends in high circles including Georges Clémenceau — a prior Prime Minister of France who would regain that office the very next year — and Albert Sarraut, who directed George's first two expeditions to Cambodia. Sarraut would lead George to even greater things in his post as Governor General of Indochina after the War. Sarraut was certainly familiar with George's professional work and perhaps this romance further enhanced his personal awareness and esteem for the young man.

Suzanne's notes don't document the details of their first face-to-face meetings but they obviously went well: a wedding was arranged for May 27, 1916 in Paris. George's father Antoine was by then retired from his posts in Indochina so the Poujade and Groslier families met there, with the newlyweds returning to the Groslier home in Marseille afterwards. George arranged time off for the event and, somehow, also arranged the publication of his delayed second book: *A l'Ombre d'Angkor: Notes et Impressions sur les Temples Inconnus de l'Ancien Cambodge*.

George and Suzanne Groslier on their wedding day in Paris - May 27, 1916.

The wedding gave a brief but welcome break from George's wartime responsibilities. Soon afterwards he returned to his aviation unit, the Fifth Squadron, stationed in Bar-le-Duc about 60 km south of Verdun. The town was the railhead and key supply point for the Battle of Verdun, a horrific conflict that left 250,000 dead and 500,000 wounded between February and December 1916. Despite the danger Suzanne was determined to be near her new husband.

> I was able to join him there using identity papers in my maiden name, to avoid detection under my married name. It turned out to be a good idea, because the police detained me for an entire day on my arrival, demanding to know what I was doing so close to the front. George found some local letters for me with the name Dardart as an excuse but it was this strange name that they didn't like. By the end of the day I was allowed to go into town, but that proved difficult under the heavy bombardment. It was particularly bad on Pentecost Sunday (June 11) at the end of the mass. More than a hundred people died in the square in front of the cathedral.

Romania entered the War in late August. A little more than a month later, George suddenly received transfer orders to that front on an Air Force assignment. His mission leader was none other than Albert Sarraut, who was serving in France for the War. They were scheduled to sail the next day and Suzanne scrambled to follow her husband. She learned that a support team of nurses, secretaries, and others were also being transferred, but they wouldn't accept her in the group. Several months later she learned that most of them died of typhus.

Suzanne was, however, able to accompany George as far as the port of Brest where George embarked on the *Catherine II* on October 10, 1916. Several days later the Swiss press reported that the ship had been sunk. Two agonizing weeks passed with no additional news:

> I was, of course, devastated. Then on Tuesday, October 24th I awoke knowing that George was safe and sound. I proclaimed it far and wide, but nobody believed a word. Everyone felt sorry for me. But it was that very morning, that very hour, that the *Catherine II* entered the port of Arkangelsk (1,000 km north of Moscow). Days later I received a letter from George confirming it.

In her previously panicked state, Suzanne also reached out to her father for help. Through his influence "a Mr. de Panafieu at the Ministry of Foreign Affairs sent, under George Clemenceau's signature, a telegram asking for news of George Groslier, soldier Second Class." Meanwhile, George's circuitous route took him from Russia's northern port 2,400 km south to Romania where "the telegraph caused a great hullabaloo in Bucharest and George was suddenly named corporal!"

As 1917 began, George was stranded on the dreaded "Russian Front" — a bleak theater of winter warfare — and making every possible effort to return to France. The Russian economy was nearing collapse and the February Revolution that forced Tzar Nicholas II to abdicate was about to begin. George learned that Alexander Fydorovich Kerensky[26] was due to travel to France and volunteered to accompany him, but the plan failed. George's commander then assigned him as a diplomatic courier but train travel was impossible as all waited for provisional rails to be laid on the ice.

Suzanne eventually received a letter from Petrograd (now St. Petersburg) explaining this but by now the Revolution had started and she was ill at ease. As required for diplomatic couriers, George was dressed

---

26. A Russian politician and prominent leader in the Revolution.

As a courier during the Russian Revolution in 1917, Suzanne commented that George bore an uncomfortable resemblance to Joseph Stalin.

as a civilian and carried nothing to show that he was French. Adding to Suzanne's worries: "George bore some resemblance to Stalin!"

Finally, he was able to travel north to the ice-free port of Romanov (now Murmansk). There he boarded a small ship for an exhausting voyage that, to avoid enemy ships, sailed north of the l'île de l'Ours[27] then on to Oslo before arriving in Liverpool, England.

From there George telegraphed his wife with news that he would soon arrive in Paris by train.

> "At Saint-Lazare station, I didn't even recognize him when he passed in front of me, he had lost so much weight. He was in civilian clothes, too, and I'd never seen him dressed like that before!"

In April 1917, George's icy duties in Russia were about to rewarded with a more appealing assignment. Albert Sarraut was charged with assembling a French Air Force team in the Far East. Knowing George was an aviator familiar with Cambodia who even spoke the language, Sarraut had him reassigned to the mission. Suzanne was, however, once again banned from going along but this time it didn't stop her.

Today, jets take us around the planet within a day, but in George's era travelers spent weeks on the ocean enroute between France and Indochina, giving him time for undistracted reading and writing.[28] While the ships weren't opulent they were generally comfortable and safe, albeit less so during the War. On April 29, 1917 George and Suzanne departed from Marseille headed to Cambodia aboard the *Porthos,* the fairly new sister ship of the *Athos* on the Marseilles-Saigon-Haiphong line. With the War still raging Suzanne relates a harrowing voyage:

> Bright moonlight forced the commander to zigzag through the Mediterranean, which was chockablock with German submarines that would torpedo anything they could. A supply ship close to us was sunk. According to dispatches from the neutral newspapers, it was the Porthos that had been hit. Our families thought us lost and learned the truth only a long time afterwards.
>
> Moreover, the Porthos was ill ballasted and listed badly to port. In entering the Suez Canal we had to squeak through a graveyard of ships of all kinds. Only the masts protruded from the water, with crosses on them.

---

27. Bear Island is in the Barents Sea north of Norway.
28. See Appendix I for Groslier family ship itineraries showing passages ranging from 23 to 39 days between Marseille and Saigon.

George Groslier during World War I, 1916.

Inevitably Indochina's most well-known people traveled this route and on her first voyage with George, Suzanne made note of two fellow travelers. Dr. Aimé-François Legendre, who shared George's first return to Cambodia in 1910, was again headed for China. She also became friends with Felix Challaye (1875-1967), an Orientalist and professor of philosophy who had just published *Le Japon Illustré*, a lavishly illustrated book about Japan where he was headed again.

By their first year anniversary on May 27, 1917, George and Suzanne Groslier arrived in Cambodia to begin their new life.

Life must be lived forward,

but can only be understood backwards.

Søren Kierkegaard - 1813-1855

Reflections on George Groslier at Mid-Life

Researching George Groslier's vision of Cambodian dance and recreating his book in the English language was in itself a fulfilling project. But the privilege of learning about the author from his daughter, family and personal photos has been a rare and emotional experience. The process revealed many surprises that were unseen before this reexamination. One milestone, for example, was on Wednesday, April 12, 1916 — a bit more than a month before George and Suzanne married — a profound day that all of us experience without ever realizing. It was then, at 29 years of age, that George reached the exact midpoint of his life. Today, reflecting on the entirety of his time on Earth, a certain logic and balance begins to take shape.

Through a coincidence of birth, George became the first French child born in Cambodia, an interesting historical footnote but meaningless on its own. We are all born somewhere and, in fact, George's mother quickly removed him far from Asia. In France he grew up essentially fatherless in his early years, pursuing his education. George's mother doted on him and he returned her love with gifts of art and poetry, always keeping her photo on his desk. Over time, the family homes became a gallery of George's works with his mother as the proud curator. Still, her protective instincts encouraged her to prejudice George against the unhealthy tropical Asian climes that stole his only sister at birth and, for many years, separated her from her husband.

But the die was cast. The soul of the Khmer land had infused itself into this child and by the age of 23 he was drawn back to his birthplace. As Charles Gravelle so eloquently wrote to George in his Foreword to *Danseuses Cambodgiennes*, "you returned here as if marked by destiny...a Buddhist, or rather Brahmanic, providence." Equally curious were the natural artistic abilities that took shape in George. The Poujade family produced generations of fine artists and calligraphers but George was the first among the Grosliers (although perhaps his mother's musical talents gave her the sensitivity to nurture his artistic side).

By his 29th year George had proven himself as a son, student, artist, author, civil servant and soldier. His education and career had taken him around the world, absorbing a diversity of cultures and ideas. He worked among France's artistic elite in Paris, studying under a true master and successfully participating in his country's most respected artistic competition. On the other side of the world he sought to understand the gentle beauty of an ancient people, documenting their female tradition of sacred dance and later spending months in isolation, trekking the jungles of Cambodia conducting archaeological and geographical surveys while recording his personal impressions. Finally, he served his country at the bloody Western and Russian Fronts of World War I, never speaking of the war or his duties with his daughter Nicole. Always an active participant, George experienced the best and worst things that nature and humankind represent.

Close to midlife, as the ship carried him from West to East, his life also began to transform. The son had now become a husband and, in the coming year, he would be a father. The soldier would become a scholar, the student would become a teacher, and the loyal follower would be given the power to lead, allowing him to become an idealistic proponent of the Cambodian arts. It was all to unfold, as if by design, but of course George never saw his future as he lived it. None of us do.

George Groslier in the salon of his official residence, adjacent to the National Museum and School of Cambodian Arts. All three Groslier children grew up in this home where George spent the rest of his life.

Albert Sarraut (1872-1962), Governor General of Indochina (1912-1919). Official portrait by M. Mascré-Souville.

A New Commitment to Cambodia (1917-1919)

When George arrived in Phnom Penh in May 1917 Albert Sarraut quickly ended his military mission. In his book, Prodromidès defines what was perhaps George's *true* mission all along, stating that

> his task, then, was to spark a renaissance, in the very midst of the French colonists and their latent hostility. Henri Marchal had already had a world of trouble convincing the officers and administrators of his own country of the value of Cambodian decorative arts. They had laughed in his face. George Groslier went over their heads and made a convert of the governor general, Albert Sarraut.[29]

---

29. Prodromidès, *Angkor*, pp. 120-121.

In fact, George, Sarraut and Marchal were like-minded — it's hard to say who converted who! In his first term as Governor General of Indochina (GGI) Sarraut had proven his commitment to indigenous cultures in many ways; in 1912 he secured considerable funding for public works and renovation of the royal palace.[30] Albert Sarraut believed that the future of colonial rule lay, not in assimilating cultures, but in "understanding [them] so that they may evolve, under our tutelage, in the framework of their civilization."[31]

George, of course, had a long history with Sarraut, first working for two years in Cambodia as his employee for the Ministry of Public Education, then as a soldier under his final command and now through his marriage. As Suzanne wrote in her diary,

> Sarraut had long wanted to create a school of Cambodian art. On their arrival, he decommissioned George from the military and entrusted him with the task, to which he added the founding of a museum (the Albert Sarraut Museum in Phnom Penh).

So it seems that the man wielding the political power had finally found the perfect artist-administrator to fulfill their mutual goals.

George was, at last, *officially* empowered, but he and his associates had shared their distinctly "un-Colonialist" passions for respecting the local culture and maintaining the purity of Cambodian art for many years. Members of his original group of friends — Marchal, Gravelle, Meyer and Commaille (now deceased) — expressed similar views in their writing. Now, the current *Résident-supérieur* of Cambodia (RSC) François-Marius Baudoin was also ready to implement these sorts of policies as Penny Edwards confirms:

> From 1917 to 1942, Groslier had shaped his career as a rescue mission and established institutions, principally an art school and museum, which he described as a life raft to save Cambodia's national arts from vanishing.
>
> ...on Groslier's return from war service, GGI Sarraut entrusted him with the portfolio of art education in Cambodge, seeing in Groslier a potential solution to the "crisis" in native arts. Published the previous year, Groslier's book *A l'ombre d'Angkor: Notes et impressions sur les temples inconnus d'ancien Cambodge* had stressed the tenacity of Cambodian artistic tradition. Now, perhaps propelled by a heightened sense of mortality after experiencing

---

30. Edwards, *Cambodge*, p. 45.
31. Edwards, *Cambodge*, p. 149, quoting from Sarraut's book, *La mise en valeur des colonies françaises*.

the vast carnage of World War I, Groslier rose vigorously to his new responsibilities. Those arts he had only years ago described as "immortal" now seemed to Groslier to be on the verge of vanishing. He would devote the rest of his life to the conservation and containment of Cambodge's artistic tradition."[32]

On analysis, George's strategy of characterizing the state of Cambodian arts as in "crisis" was nothing less than brilliant. His technique, misunderstood by some modern scholars, was incredibly effective at attracting — and receiving — positive media attention, public sympathy and support and, ultimately, considerable arts funding from the ethnocentric French Colonial administration. As Edwards points out, George framed his new tasks within the context of a "rescue mission". First, he established clear needs — boldly proving fault and obligation on France's part — then he rallied popular support and got the funding required for his institutions. Perhaps Sarraut himself mentored George on effectively navigating and manipulating the previously indifferent bureaucracy.

As the first stone of Cambodia's national museum was placed on August 15, 1917, George (center, with back to camera) had already initiated the national survey of the arts that would justify the costs to France. Seated to George's left are Francois Marius Baudoin RSC and Albert Sarraut GGI. His Majesty King Sisowath is directly in front of George, but not visible. To George's right holding the cane is Cambodian administrator Thiounn Sambath. Suzanne is seated next, possibly with Gene Stoeckel far right.

---

32. Edwards, *Cambodge*, pp. 145, 148, quoting Groslier in *Arts et Archéologies Khmèrs*.

Muan presents his position in the following paragraph, quoting some of the astounding rhetoric George used to confront the very colonial powers that employed him:

> In the Cambodian context in particular, the "spirit" of "the native" (which after all "contained the spirit of his forefathers") had to be treated with an "attitude of respect" since remaining examples of Angkorian art showed that this spirit had created "a classical art", "of the same standing as ours", "as complete and as old as ours". By what "foolish national vanity" then, Groslier asked, could the French — those supposed "children and propagandists of all liberties" — "presume to introduce [their] aesthetic formulas" into an established civilization whose own art had been "tested and tried" "through centuries of independent practice?"[33]

George and his friends had frequently discussed these concerns years earlier, particularly in relation to commercialism and the influx of Western manufactured goods. In *Danseuses Cambodgiennes*, 1913, he emotionally described the disruptions he perceived on his very first visit to Cambodia as an adult:

> But everything here that has withstood time, wars, and religions has now succumbed to civilization...the people and the mandarins no longer understand their own theatre. The aged King, now nearly blind, is absorbed in all sorts of worries. He has new expenses and two cars in the garage. His successors, raised in France and dressed in European style, will fail to remember when they are crowned that they are the Sons of Indra...Our steamships and automobiles generate a smoke in which champa flowers wither....[34]

To him, the West clearly threatened Cambodia's cultural integrity and the ability of traditional crafts to survive. Muan's quote from "*La tradition cambodgienne*" shows that George's convictions remained the same in 1918:

> The native who, since the time of Angkor, had need of nothing and received nothing from the West, living by his own resources and through his own means, suddenly discovered that he had all kinds of needs: a pair of shoes, a watch, a sparkplug, a yard of English crepe, a bicycle, a hat. By 1915, one could not find a dignitary who did not possess or at least consult the catalogue of the Manufacture d'Armes de Saint-Ecienne.[35]

---

33. Muan, *Citing Angkor*, p. 36.
34. Groslier, George. 2010. *Cambodian Dancers: Ancient and Modern*. Holmes Beach: DatAsia. Pp. 106-107.
35. Muan, *Citing Angkor*, p. 25.

With the local clientele shunning indigenous crafts for mass-produced European items, George sounded the alarm over a crisis that could permanently end the country's ancient artistic traditions and crafts. As always, his focal point was the Khmer civilization, and he clearly used the term "Khmer" to differentiate between what he perceived as the native culture of Cambodia, as opposed to Chinese or Annamite influences from the outside.

Even in his position of authority George didn't hesitate to place blame squarely on the shoulders of the colonizers:

> Our appearance on these shores provoked such a disturbance, that the past can no longer guarantee the future....[The] turmoil [of] Western civilization installing itself [had] completely upset Khmer society.[36]

Within the rational structure of French bureaucracy, his first priority was to establish proof of the need. In the summer of 1917, George and RSC initiated a national survey to quantify the present state of traditional arts. Not surprisingly, their analysis came back painting a very grim picture of diminished artistic ability throughout the land...but it was a grim picture that George promised to correct if France supported his efforts.

Institutions for Cambodia's Past and Future (1920-1922)

George would attempt to restore cultural integrity with two solutions: a museum to define and preserve Khmer arts and an art school with production facilities to perpetuate them. According to Muan, George believed that Cambodian art

> is "transmitted from generation to generation" over centuries. Such transmission was "not just obedience to an established formula" nor was it "the desire to imitate". Rather, for Groslier, it spoke to "something stronger, more imperious — a latent aesthetic" which revealed a "Cambodian temperament", an "ancient soul".[37]

The style of his new institutions was based on his concept of art as a legacy inherited from the Khmer forefathers of the land as, perhaps, George felt that he had absorbed his destiny from the land:

> The passing down of artistic knowledge from generation to generation required only the "simple contact" of a master and an apprentice in order for "an alphabet and formulas" to be learned: "the atavism, the milieu, the omnipresence of the art, did the rest". Exchange between master

---

36. Ibid., p. 22.
37. Ibid., p. 29.

and apprentice consisted of commands which were "not personal", but which showed that "they were thousand times older than the master", stemming from "a distant origin, sacred and mysterious". Thus "the master obeyed the teaching just like the student".

"Art was in the air" and "all breathed it" with a "strange universality".[38]

Passionate? Idealistic? Even spiritual?

Yes. George Groslier's vision of Khmer art and culture was all of these things, as he had already made quite clear by expressing his profound personal feelings in his first books, *Danseuses Cambodgiennes* and *À l'ombre d'Angkor*. What is remarkable is that his passion for Khmer heritage and his effort to cultivate artistic distinction for Cambodia never diminished — and now he charged ahead, finally empowered to create the reality he saw. With much fanfare, the museum opened its doors to the public on April 13, 1920.

George's vision (shared and supported by his mentor and peers) was for the museum to build traditional collections from the full range of Cambodia's ancient works of art: sculptures, bronzes, inscriptions, ceramics, jewelry, fragments of monuments, wooden objects, paintings and manuscripts. His administration helped end the era when colonials looted antique treasures as they pleased. He enlisted Cambodians in preserving their own heritage by providing an organization to catalog the nation's historical resources:

> The Khmer land is so laden with history and art that [the Cambodians] in their everyday labors, simply by digging wells, foraging for tubers in the forest, or founding villages, stumble upon pottery, bronze utensils, or carved stones. We have taken steps to ensure that such finds are declared to the government and gathered in Phnom-Penh.[39]

With this directive, George took part in establishing laws to control Cambodian artifacts, and to keep them on Cambodian soil. Now recorded under the auspices of the museum, Prodromidès notes that this "was a way to give all Khmers a stake in that past."

His museum preserved Cambodia's past while the School of Cambodian Arts, next to the museum, served the future by training new generations of artists. Within the school, George established a series of workshops or guilds based on the "six great arts of Cambodia" including jewelry, painting and temple planning, metal work and casting, sculpture of all kinds, furniture making and carpentry and weaving.[40]

---

38. Ibid., p. 31.
39. Prodromidès quoting Groslier, *Angkor*, p. 121.
40. Muan, *Citing Angkor*, p. 126.

Albert Sarraut Museum on grand opening day, Tuesday, April 13, 1920.

George (far left) and Suzanne at the Museum Inauguration.

His goal was to revive the craft industry that, according to his survey, was withering in the face of a flood of Western imports. The workshops created more than art objects: under George's plan the workshops created retail products in Cambodian style for purchase by tourists and residents of Cambodia alike. The idea was not new; in 1906, four years before George returned to Cambodia, his friend Jean Commaille wrote a paper about organizing a vocational arts school. [41] Twelve years later George turned Commaille's idea into a reality, but his vision for the organization of the school and workshops was controversial, to say the least. In George's plan, *Cambodian* teachers and managers would fill the key positions!

Since the turn of the century, colonial powers had systematically excluded Cambodian master artists (at least by name) from participating in large public projects. In 1906, two Frenchmen designed the iconic "Palais du Cambodge" at the Marseille Exposition, although a contingent of anonymous native artists did much of the decorative work. In 1908, a competition was held in Phnom Penh to create a monument recognizing King Sisowath's reign and the recovery of extensive territories from Siam the previous year. Visiting French sculptor Théodore Rivière received the award, completing his entire project in France before shipping it back to Cambodia where it was installed at the foot of Wat Phnom.[42] Years later, George himself was commissioned in the redecoration of the Throne Hall, but the events of WW I interrupted and the work was never completed.[43] In fact, most buildings and prominent paintings at the Royal Palace, even those on the ceiling of the Royal Dance Hall, were the work of French hands as Muan's surprising archival research proves.[44] As George later noted in his two part essay *"La Fin d'un Art"*:

> Not a single sculptor, not a single carpenter, in short not a single Cambodian artisan [was involved in the construction of the Palace as] all had been confided to European architects and entrepreneurs.

Naturally, Cambodian hands labored extensively throughout every French project, but they were unaccredited and forgotten while the French were recognized — such was the nature of the colonial beast. Equally, it is no surprise that in 1920 George and other French men were appointed to the managerial roles at the museum and school.

---

41. Ibid., p. 37.
42. Ibid., p. 51, p. 53-54.
43. See page 193.
44. Muan, *Citing Angkor*, p. 62.

George implemented radical new policies appointing a majority of Cambodian staff and teachers to the School of Cambodian Arts. They remained in place ten years later when this photo was taken in October 1930. Photo National Museum of Cambodia Collection.

What is surprising is that George accepted this for the sake of appearance while setting up his own agenda, as seen in his words and actions. In 1917, George installed the former royal architect Tep Nimit Mak as an administrator, and later assembled Cambodian master artists to teach. The institution grew and George maintained his hands-off approach, as Muan describes:

> Despite his own training as a painter, Groslier would never teach at the school "I am not Khmer", he declared, and the "fundamental principle" of the School was "only to make Cambodian art and only to have it be made by Cambodians".

> The one restriction placed upon these "masters" was that they "purge all Western influence" from their teaching.... "We don't expand on the pedagogical methods of the [Cambodian] master", Groslier declared: "No change is to be brought to their habits, their working methods, or the materials they use"

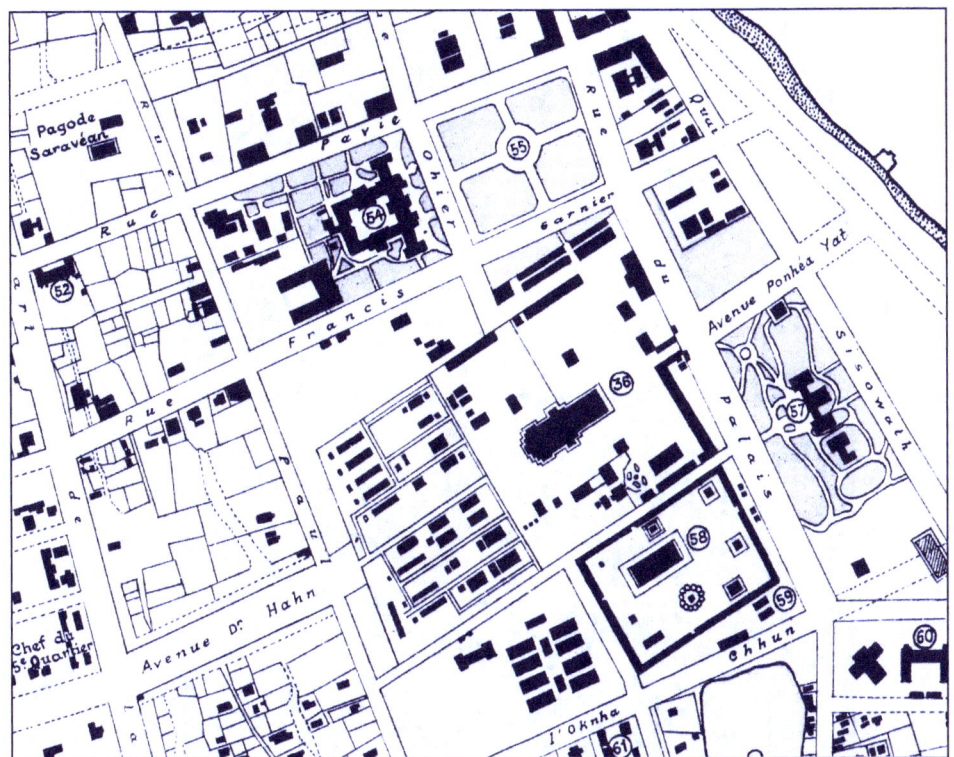

The Sarraut Museum (54) lies west of the festival grounds (55), directly north of the Royal Palace (36). The School of Cambodian Arts and workshops are just behind, with the Groslier home at the corner of Rue Pavie and Rue Paul Doumer. Circa 1925 map by A. Portail - US Library of Congress. See page 277 for photos of the home today.

> The doctrine of the "impenetrable sphere" of pure "Cambodian art" is shown clearly by the absence of French personnel in official photos taken of the School and its students shortly after it was put under Groslier and his French colleagues"[45]

So, within a single city block, Cambodia now had a national museum, an art school, workshops producing merchandise in Cambodian style, and one other important feature: George's residence. His workplace and home were inseparable for the rest of his life. It was here that he and Suzanne raised their family, beginning with the birth of Nicole Groslier on Saturday, June 15, 1918.

The little girl grew up surrounded with local customs, spending much time with her nannies who taught her to speak Khmer and enjoy

---

45. Ibid., pp. 77-78.

"Petite Nicole... in a Cambodian fruit bowl — old style — on a Cambodian table — new style — of the School of Cambodian Arts...Voila...isn't that an original photo? She's beginning to say "ba ba ba" to anyone who'll listen and promises to be as much of a chatterbox as her mom!" Suzanne's note on the back to her parents in France, Dec 4, 1918.

In 1922, Grosliers arriving at the Sarraut Museum to welcome WW I hero Marshal Joseph Joffre on his tour of Indochina. Nicole's entrance certainly gave the guest of honor some competition! From left we see Auguste André Silice, future director of the School of Cambodian Arts; Jean Stoeckel, a museum associate interested in Cambodian textiles; M. Debé; and RSC Baudoin.

Cambodian food, much like her parents. Obviously delighting in his new paternal role, George included Nicole in many grand events, but that was only fitting: her godfather was none other than Albert Sarraut.

Over the next four years George continued developing his museum, school...and his family. On September 8, 1922 he and Suzanne had their first son, Gilbert. The next month, on October 31st, Cambodia welcomed another child who later changed the country's history — Norodom Sihanouk.

I had this group photo on the staircase to the top of Angkor Wat for a year before discovering its secrets in Suzanne's notes. Taken in January 1918, we see (from left) RSC François-Marius Baudoin and his daughter; Suzanne Groslier (three months pregnant here, so Nicole is on her first visit to Angkor Wat!) and George in pith helmet. At the top, looking a bit impatient with the photographer, is Albert Sarraut. Next we have the stylish, but unknown "Mlle Vibert" and at the lower right a rare photo of Roland Meyer, who would publish his epic novel *Saramani* the next year.

Nicole, barely two months old, with her proud father on her first official pilgrimage to Angkor Wat, seen here among the *devata* of the Cruciform Gallery.

Helen Churchill Candee's *Angkor the Magnificent* and other books feature images from this circa 1922 photo shoot. In this rare version, however, Nicole Groslier takes center stage, holding hands with two of the king's prima ballerinas.

François de Tessan Interviews George Groslier (1923)

François de Tessan was a well known journalist who established his reputation as a correspondent reporting on American issues for the French press. In 1923 he traveled to Indochina to gather material for his book, *Dans l'Asie qui s'éveille; essais indochinois*. Mr. de Tessan's contemporary account is especially significant because he gives us a French perspective of cultural efforts in Cambodia, a first-person look at the newly established museum and school, and an interview with George Groslier himself describing his views and work. I include it here unabridged and translated to English for the first time. Mr. de Tessan's text appears in italics with George's comments in quotations.[46]

The Museum and School of Cambodian Arts

It has been three years since the inauguration of the Musée Albert Sarraut *(Albert Sarraut Museum) and the* Ecole des Arts Cambodgiens *(School of Cambodian Arts), both created in the name of a clearly stated ambition: to bring about a renaissance of Cambodian aesthetics in every form.*

Suppose that 16th century France had been three-quarters abandoned, crushed, buried under ruins. Suppose now that four hundred years later — after a long slumber during which all had been forgotten — a small group of foreign scholars, architects, historians, and administrators got it into their heads to resuscitate our chief national monuments, to revive our styles, to reeducate a population detached from its past, by rediscovering the traditional aspirations and leading the people back to their flamboyant cathedrals. Yes, imagine all of the above, and you will understand the design of Cambodia's present-day leaders.

Since the thirteenth-century, the Khmer civilization had been relegated to oblivion. Its temples and palaces vanished beneath the jungle or crumbled. Its customs were lost. Its artisans no longer knew the secrets of the ancient crafts. And suddenly, some audacious Frenchmen fired up by the discovery of Angkor decided that it was not impossible to reconnect the strands of time. They read the texts, deciphered the inscriptions, penetrated the archeology, studied every manifestation of Khmer thought, and concluded that it could shine once more.

So they began a campaign among present-day Cambodians, revealing their own souls to them and inviting them to return to the very source of their ancestral genius. They took Cambodians by the hand and explained the marvels of their own country

---

46. This extract appeared as Chapter XXV, *"Le Musée et L'école Des Arts Cambodgiens"* (pages 318-328) in François de Tessan's book, *Dans l'Asie qui s'éveille; essais indochinois* published by La Renaissance du livre, Paris, 1924. Translation by Pedro Rodríguez.

that they hardly even suspected. So all this came about during the reigns of Norodom and Sisowath. It must rank among the brashest and most seemingly paradoxical undertakings ever essayed by reconstructors bitten with the bug of historical verity. And it is succeeding, as the museum and art school of Phnom Penh attest.

At the Albert Sarraut Museum are all the vestiges of Khmer art; all the patterns of local industries and all the rare pieces that may serve as models. Notably, all the relics of the great flourishing period of the Varmans *— the kings of Cambodia — have been assembled. Much remains to be done if the collections are to be enriched with all that remains scattered throughout the Cambodian provinces and all that awaits discovery buried in the ground! Work has just begun.*

In his Voyage au Cambodge, *Delaporte characterized Khmer art as:*

> "Born of a mixture of India and China, spare, ennobled by artists whom we might call the Athenians of the Far East, this art has remained the purest expression of human genius in that vast swath of Asia stretching from the Indus to the Pacific. True, it departs from the great, classical works of the Mediterranean basin that for so long have commanded our admiration. We do not find any majestic colonnades, or the great, calm surfaces of Greece or Egypt. Instead, we have laborious, complex, tormented forms: superimpositions, multiple levels, labyrinths, low, open galleries, lacy towers, stepped pyramids with countless spires; an extreme profusion of ornaments and sculptures, a constant play of light and shade that enriches the whole without affecting its majesty and that enters into a marvelous harmony with the intense light of the luxuriant vegetation of the tropics. It is, in a word, another form of beauty."

Cambodian architects, sculptors and decorators can come to the museum of Phnom Penh for useful lessons. There, ceramists, founders, embroiderers, goldsmiths, chiselers and all other artisans can find samples of the masterpieces bequeathed by their ancestors. This direct instruction is equally effective for the personnel hired to guard Cambodia's archeological treasures. It is a remarkable effort to popularize all aspects of Khmer art.

The true epicenter of this artistic revival, however, is the school. Directed by Mr. George Groslier, it was inaugurated by His Majesty Sisowath and, in the name of the French government, by Resident Superior Baudoin. It is an impressive complex. The lovely main building is 66 m long and 54 m deep, with a sculptured foundation two and a half meters tall. The rules of Cambodian architecture for interlocking roofs, superposed pediments, bands of undulating panels, mullioned doors, and sculpted door and window frames have all been carefully observed, from roof to gutter. The spire for the central part of the school is 38 m high. Galleries surround the buildings. The main pediment comprises four hundred thirty-eight pieces, sculpted separately and then assembled. The middle door, 5 m 10 cm tall, is marvelously sculpted.

Mr. George Groslier drafted the general plan and decoration. In addition to the museum, whose interest we have already mentioned, the complex contains various workshops, a library, a remarkable collection of photographs, a sales office, and buildings to house grant recipients. All open onto an inner courtyard that has been transformed with gardens and a lawn.

It is in this setting that those who strive for a Cambodian renaissance work. To attend classes at the school, they must be fifteen years old and literate in the Cambodian and, if possible, French languages (French remains optional). After a three-month apprenticeship devoted entirely to drawing, they are divided up among the various classes and workshops where they learn jewelry making, sculpture, artistic metal casting, modeling and weaving. Every six months they take examinations, and after two years the worthy receive a diploma in fine arts.

Mr. Groslier, who graciously welcomed me to the school, provided a thousand details on the students' lives and qualities. This director is not only an artist himself, he is an apostle and a pleasure to listen to.

"As you can see," *he told me,* "we have settled in and are well equipped. But for two years, at its very beginnings, the School of Arts was functioning in a dark, nondescript warehouse a third the size of what was needed. There we worked without complaint and with whatever means fortune bestowed on us. We did our bronze founding in mud ovens. Every night during the rainy season we had to remove every piece of silk from the looms, because of leaks in our worm-eaten roof. It was a tedious task for masters and students alike. We had recruited a handful of professors and artisans to get the classes going. Not one failed to show up. Not one quit their job. Not a one. In fact, these educators were so enthusiastic that they refused their vacations. Outside its walls, all of them promoted the school, recruited students and sought ancient and rare objects."

How did you assemble that first nucleus of instructors?

"It certainly wasn't easy, but here's how I did it. Cambodian art — like every other Asian art — evolves neither in principle nor in essence. Collective thought will not abide individual interpretations of a given form. It is no longer necessary to show that these arts do not copy nature in accordance with our 'verisimilitude,' our science, or our methods of observation. Usage, the most remote traditions, and especially rites have meticulously fixed the meaning of all human work, so that it always remains a symbol. These forces have set the forms, sizes, and proportions once and for all. If, by chance, the Cambodian artist begins with nature, he transforms it radically. He will stylize it in accordance not with its context, its logic, or the laws of its organization, in our manner, but with a set, independent program transmitted from generation to generation. The problem for me, then, was to seek out old artisans and isolated artists, in the backwoods of this country, who still commanded a part or even a crumb of the aesthetic traditions.

"Though disturbed by five hundred years of struggle, desolation, and servitude, these traditions had more or less survived into our time. But one of the greatest blows struck against them has come from the Cambodian aristocracy, who for the past half-century have been turning away from their artists. No more private troupes of actors and actresses. No more gold smithies or sculptors in mandarin households. In the monasteries, very rare are the bonzes or sculptors who, as in times past, execute their own Buddhist pulpits or pediments. In short, with no more outlets there were no more producers.

"To organize the Service of Arts, we had to seek out artisans who in some cases had set down their tools and returned to the rice paddies. And the traditions, if still living in memory, were now relegated to the fragile minds of the old, who had become the final repositories. When these men, so neglected by their compatriots, felt our understanding, our encouragement, our love, they made great efforts to help, and little by little the resurrection came about!"

And the students?

"Oh! The School of Arts has never lacked for students. We have always surpassed our official quotas, even as we've raised them! Note well that the school has never sought out students, never made the least official call for them — except, of course, for the twenty-five pensioners from the provinces. There have never been notices nor circulars. Still, in 1918 we planned for eighty students and, three weeks after the school opened its doors, there were one hundred seven.

"Despite the selection and entrance examinations, we have never managed to reduce the figure. Our coffers and some dismissals allowed us to spread them out. In 1919, the official quota of eighty was raised to one hundred. Well, since then the school has never had fewer than one hundred forty students. We had those extra thirty all year long. Not wishing to leave the premises, they stayed on as aspirants inside the school walls, working, awaiting the opening of slots that never opened! I take responsibility for my own management irregularity regarding these excessive admissions. But how do you close the door on a strapping eighteen-year-old lad who says to you: 'I cost the school nothing. I only ask for a little square meter of space and a little piece of paper'?

"Like the masters, students refuse the official vacations to which they have a right. Consult the school's personnel registers, and you will see an average of 1% unauthorized absentees per month, and 7% authorized absences, instead of 10% regular absences [in other schools]. You will also see that expulsions for indiscipline or lack of skill have declined steadily since 1918.

"With students so filled with zeal and self-esteem, and so skilled with their hands, how can we complain? When the time came to sculpt the central gate of our new school, all we had to do was say to them: 'We are going to copy a door from Angkor. Your job is to prove whose sons you are and that you are worthy of your fathers.' And the team of sculptors hopped right to it, like men possessed."

Mr. Groslier also provided a number of other useful facts about the school's overall program and national goals. The School of Arts instructs artists and promotes Cambodian works but does not sell them itself. If the school kept the profits of the renaissance it is bringing about, it would ruin the last remaining private workshops or become the competitor of its students. Its policy has the opposite aim. It accepts commissions only to transmit them to independent workshops whose development and flourishing it favors. It also commissions works itself.

"Independent artisans," *he continued,* "have been grouped into six corporations, corresponding to the six great industries of Cambodian art. Each has a unanimously elected chief, responsible for dividing up and delivering the work. The corporations have been brought together in general or partial assemblies. Rates have been set. The first meeting, advertised on flyers, attracted forty-five individuals. There are more than two hundred who have found work thanks almost entirely to the Direction of Arts.

"Of course, for our efforts to come to full fruition, it is important that the independent workshops employ all the youths that we will have trained. We have no pretensions to perfection, but orders are picking up and we have reason to be proud! We have sent parcels to all the countries of the [French]

Union, to Siam, China, and even to Korea, and not a single one has been sent back. There's the proof that foreigners appreciate Cambodian art.

"Not a single piaster leaves the country through the reawakening of these industries: the wood is in the forest, silver bars serve as money. The sole value of the merchandise is to be found in the hands and heads of the artisans. What we have, then, is money coming in for the benefit of Cambodia alone. In exchange, we provide only what is necessary to assert the country's renown. What we sell, only we can sell. Rice, cotton, and rubber can be got elsewhere. But sculpted furniture and boxes in the Khmer style, these are made only on the banks of the Mekong. Their originality, which increasingly refined work will only make plainer, will become an even greater source of wealth. Thus the School of Arts combines an elevated ideal with realistic objectives for the prosperity of Cambodia."

One can only approve of the double principle, especially after touring the workshops, busy as beehives, where, under the guidance of Mr. George Groslier and his collaborators, neophytes devote themselves heart and soul to again making the honey of the ancient Khmer civilization.[47]

Milestones East and West (1923-1929)

With museum, school and family well-established in Cambodia, George devoted his attention to other areas. Over the next six years he spent a little more than 19 months outside of Cambodia, publishing several more books, addressing personal and career obligations, and experiencing the mortality of a number of people who influenced his life.

Still, 1923 began with an auspicious and joyful event. On January 24, his longtime friend Charles Gravelle wed former royal dancer Ratt Poss, apparently after admiring her for more than a decade. Today George's 1912 portrait of her graces the cover of this book. The couple had a happy, albeit short, life together, as detailed in Gravelle's biographical sketch following this article.

---

47. This concludes the unabridged extract from François de Tessan's 1923 book, *Dans l'Asie qui s'éveille; essais indochinois*.

Pierre Loti enjoying a smoke from a Turkish nargile one year before his long-awaited first visit to Angkor. Photo Wikipedia.

Shortly after George's interview with François de Tessan, a French naval officer named Louis Marie Julien Viaud died on June 10, 1923 — a man far better known by his penname Pierre Loti. Hailed by contemporary critic Edmund Gosse as "unquestionably the finest descriptive writer of the day", Loti wrote more than forty books during his career. In 1891, the *Académie française* — the prestigious 40-member body presiding over the French language and its literary works — elected Loti as their youngest member to fill Seat 13 for the remainder of his life.[48]

Loti's vivid descriptions of travel, romance and adventure in the exotic Near and Far East captured imaginations around the world, spurring many others on to Asian adventure. As Loti revealed, his own youthful dreams were inspired by an etching he saw in papers that belonged to his older brother, who served in Indochina — one image cast its spell on him along with the words "In the depths of the forests of Siam, I saw the evening star rise upon the grand ruins of mysterious Angkor".

At the age of seventeen Loti enrolled in the naval academy at Brest and pursued a career as a naval officer, but decades of adventure preceded the fulfillment of his boyhood dream. Finally, his ship was stationed in Indochinese waters in 1901 and he seized the opportunity to visit the jungle temple of Angkor in person. In 1910, Loti retired from a lifetime of service

---

48. On his death, Loti's seat was taken by Paul Claudel, whom George Groslier hosted for his tour of Angkor in February 1925.

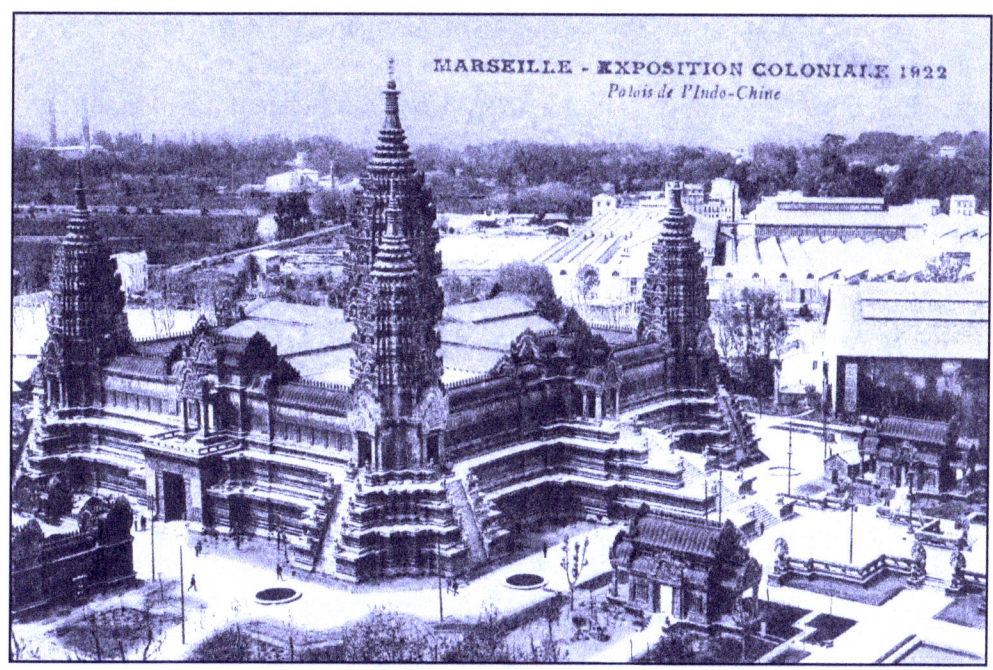

Angkor Wat replica at the 1922 Colonial Exhibition in Marseille. This event was the first major European marketplace for artisans from the School of Cambodian Arts.

in the French navy and, as George was completing his study of Cambodian dance in Phnom Penh, Loti released his book, *Un pèlerin d'Angkor* in 1912.[49]

Author Roland Meyer cited Loti's books as an inspiration in his own life. So did Marguerite Duras, the French writer born in Cochinchina in 1914 who lived to see her semi-autobiographical novel, *l'Amant* (*The Lover*) transformed into an award-winning feature film in 1992. While George made no mention of Loti that I have found, it is almost certain that this man's style and passion made an impression on the young scholar.

In addition to books about Asian adventure, much interest in Indochina stemmed from the colonial expositions, such as those held in Marseille in 1906 and 1916. World War I interrupted travel but a third Marseille exposition in 1922, this time with a replica of Angkor Wat, rekindled tourism as well as international interest in Cambodian art. Inevitably, this attracted avarice along with admiration.

---

49. In 1913, Loti's book was published in English under the inappropriate title *Siam*, rather than his original title, *A Pilgrim of Angkor*. In 2003, Silkworm Books issued a beautiful new edition of the work as *A Pilgrimage to Angkor*, edited and revised by Michael Smithies.

Some disrespectful tourists defaced monuments by leaving their mark as graffiti, others took home small pieces of the history they saw. These problems continue today, with groups like Heritage Watch International still seeking practical solutions including educational programs for natives and tourists alike. One of George's strategies to combat these problems involved organizing workshops at the School of Cambodian Arts. There, indigenous artists created accurate Khmer art reproductions for resale. Through a network of shops, these high-quality art objects gave tourists an authentic alternative to stealing the country's irreplaceable heritage while generating income for Cambodian artists.

> The system of the Corporations initiated by Groslier in 1918 was eventually, by almost all accounts, extremely successful. In their first year already, the foundry, weaving, and jewelry Corporations were deluged with a "veritable rain of commissions" and it became clear that there was a market for "native" objects presented to foreigners in accessible environments.[50]

Satisfying tourist demand, however, only addressed part of the problem. As more museums and private collectors sought Khmer masterpieces some were attracted to the vocation of antiquities trafficking, regardless of local heritage destroyed by their acts. The most infamous tale of that era involves a talented 23-year-old Parisian writer who traveled to Asia to seek adventure and fortune by plundering Angkor. As Maxime Prodromidès writes in his detailed account, this incident

> singled out George Groslier to play a decisive role in an affair that would shake literary and colonial France, the École Française d'Extrême-Orient, the Conservation d'Angkor, the Musée Albert Sarraut, and, later, Indo-China itself.[51]

The young perpetrator, André Malraux, went on to become a prominent French writer and statesman who was ultimately buried with honors at the Panthéon. In fact, his painful experience with the corrupt colonial court system is what inspired him to become involved in politics, and within two years of his arrest he had become a major force in promoting civil rights and independence for Indochinese citizens. But in Cambodia, his attempted cultural theft was of such magnitude that it permanently scarred his reputation. Upon hearing Malraux's name, Nicole Groslier instantly remembered hearing of her father's encounter with "*le petit voleur*" (the little thief). The Franco-Khmer writer Makhali-Phal called him by the same name in her papers and, when

---

50. Muan, *Citing Angkor*, p. 169.
51. Prodromidès, *Angkor*, p. 123-124.

A teacher and three students from the NKFC Conservatoire, a local school preserving Cambodia's sacred dance tradition, respect their Khmer gods and ancestors at Banteay Srei. Photo Kent Davis.

introduced to him in Paris in the 1930s, refused to shake his hand.

The incident revolves around the remote, 10th century temple of Banteay Srei where Malraux cut out two pairs of the finest stone *devata* (sacred female images) in Cambodia. Today, Banteay Srei preserves some of the most exquisite and well-preserved examples of Khmer stone carving to survive until modern times, but at that time it was in a state of total disrepair.

In 1923, George Groslier finalized the arrest of André Malraux for his theft of four devata cut from the temple of Banteay Srei. Photo Kent Davis.

Surprisingly, the story began in Paris when the eighteen-year-old Malraux read an article in the official publication of the Ecole Française d'Extrême-Orient (EFEO). World War I had slowed reporting on archeological activities so postwar issues of the *Bulletin* grew in size to present previously unpublished studies. It was the massive 1919 issue (613 pages) that engaged the teenager, who already had a personal fascination with Oriental art. To him, one article stood out; a lengthy piece written in 1916 by Henri Parmentier entitled "The Art of Indravarman". Under the subheading "Isolated Monuments" Parmentier examined a dozen temples including the well-known sites of Prasat Kravan and Pre Rup. The twelfth site in the series was one that locals called Banteay Srei — the Temple of Women — only discovered accidentally in 1914 by the Colonial Geological Service. Parmentier described its particularly fine carvings on three sanctuaries and libraries within a walled enclosure. As the text and photos showed, the site was neglected and overgrown with much of the structure collapsed. The article revealed no further EFEO plans for the site.[52]

In addition to Prodromidès, American professor Walter Langlois also provides clarification on the events that followed.[53] According to his research, the article prompted Malraux to begin a careful analysis of the

---

52. EFEO *Bulletin,* Tome XIX. 1919. Hanoi: Imprimerie d'Extrême-Orient
53. In 1969, Langlois founded the *Revue André Malraux* journal to study his life and literary works. See www.revueandremalraux.com

laws governing archeological sites in Indochina, using the *Bulletin* itself and official publications as his primary references. Through this inquiry, "he became convinced that this temple was — legally speaking — abandoned property."[54] By the summer of 1923 he had organized an expedition to Cambodia with his wife Clara and an associate, Louis Chevasson. He had even secured the blessing of the Colonial Office, which issued him a "certificate of requisition" that would supposedly ensure the cooperation of the Colonial Administration in Indochina, with the main stipulation being that he covered all the expenses of his journey.[55]

While this sounds quite legitimate, Malraux was actually structuring the justification for his trip around legal loopholes that he perceived. While one motivation may have been an interest in Oriental art, it seems that the most important factors were a youthful craving for exotic adventure and, above all, the desire for financial gain. Clearly, the temple of Banteay Srei was his hidden objective through each manipulative encounter he had with colonial administrators as well as with top Cambodian art scholars.

Malraux traveled to Saigon and then on to Hanoi to register with the proper authorities, following protocol. Along the way, George and other officials became aware of Malraux's hidden goal in time to prevent him from succeeding. According to Suzanne's notes, George became involved when Henri Parmentier himself escorted two self-proclaimed "tourists" to meet him at the museum. They impressed her husband as "intelligent visitors" but

> George added a small caveat, and I swear on the head of my children that he said this before we had any other information. He noted that this gentleman often remarked on the "commercial value" of the statues and other pieces in the Museum.
>
> That very evening, there was a dinner at the Resident Superior's house, where the "tourist" air that Malraux had affected earlier seemed greatly at odds with his presence as a guest.
>
> The occasion for this dinner was the visit of Mr. Finot, director of the *École Française d'Extrême Orient*, on his way back from Siam to Tonkin, where the EFEO was headquartered. After dinner, I was surprised to see the Resident Superior take Finot's arm, then my husband's, and lead them aside for a conspiratorial chat in one of the verandas. Afterwards, quite naturally, I approached George and asked

---

54. Langlois, Walter G. 1966. *André Malraux: The Indochina Adventure*. London: Pall Mall Press. P. 6.
55. Ibid., p. 11.

with a laugh what all the secrecy was about. He just gave me an evasive answer and clammed up.

The story, filled with deception, intrigue and drama, reached its denouement on Sunday December 23. After looting a ton of stone carvings from the temple, Malraux was headed to Phnom Penh by boat with his loot onboard — four priceless *devata* carefully divided into pieces and crated — planning to embark to Thailand via Kep. As the boat cruised south, George received a tip and raced to Kampong Chnang by car, arriving at 12:45 PM to intercept the *Hainan* moments after its arrival.

Onboard, he found the crated *devata* falsely labeled with the name of a chemical company in Saigon. Without revealing himself, he ordered the captain not to unload anything until the boat reached Phnom Penh, then departed to arrange the details of their arrest. At 10 PM, the police took the group into custody upon arrival and

> ...as Bernard-Philippe Groslier wrote in his diary in 1957, shortly before his appointment as curator of Angkor: "Who remembers today that my father had Malraux arrested?"[56]

The perpetrators soon met George under circumstances quite different from their last encounter.

> The next day, 24 December, by order of Judge Jodin, the cargo was taken to the Musée Albert Sarraut (truly omnipresent) for appraisal by its director, George Groslier.

> On that Christmas Eve, then, the Resident-Superior and Phnom Penh museum took back from that infamous duo, the young Malraux couple, the little sculptures with which, fancying themselves Santa Claus, they had hoped to stuff the stockings of Western antique dealers.[57]

The ensuing courtroom drama rocked the colonial world at both ends. On Monday, July 21 the judge handed down his sentences: "for Malraux, three years in prison and a five-year prohibition of residence in Indochina; for Chevasson, eighteen months in prison. Both young men were ruled ineligible for a suspended sentence, and they had to relinquish all claims on the sculpture in favor of the government."[58]

The tactics of the colonial administration and prosecutors, however,

---
56. Prodromidès, *Angkor*, p. 124.
57. Ibid., p. 160. The original metaphor had "Father Noël" stuffing gifts in shoes (*souliers*) rather than stockings, as is customary in France.
58. Langlois, *André Malraux: The Indochina Adventure*, p. 36.

had blatantly ignored the principles of justice as they were administered in France. A secret investigation into Malraux's "bohemian" lifestyle, his associations with "Bolsheviks", and even the fact that his new wife Clara was a Jew of German origin all became part of a secret dossier, unseen by the defense. The prosecution used this to demonize the defendant as an enemy of the French state, making Malraux a scapegoat while avoiding points of law that could question the entire legitimacy of French control in Cambodia.

Both defendants immediately requested that their case be heard by the Court of Appeals in Saigon. As word of the verdict spread to Paris more than fifty prominent literary figures signed a petition for their release. At the Saigon trial Malraux's sentence was reduced to a year and Chevasson's to eight months with the right to appeal for a suspended sentence. The sculpture was ceded to the state.

The pair returned to France, appealing to the highest court in the land, but the outcome is unknown and the entire event eventually faded from view. Neither man served time in prison for their deeds but the trials did raise difficult questions about the rights French "protectors" had to antiquities found in their colonies. As Langlois asks, "...if these two young men were to be imprisoned for taking the sculpture from Banteay Srei, should not the same penalty be exacted from the various Governors, High Commissioners, and administrators of Indochina who had done the very same thing to similar monuments?"[59]

That question was left unanswered but it was obviously becoming harder to remove historic heritage from Cambodia. Another positive outcome was that Parmentier, as head of the EFEO's Archeological Service, wasted no time in initiating the restoration of Banteay Srei temple in 1925 while expressing his regret that the task hadn't been done sooner.

In 1930, Malraux incorporated parts of the incident into *La Voie royale*, a novel about two looters trekking the Cambodian jungle in search of treasure. In 1935, the book appeared in English as *The Royal Way*, with Time Magazine reviewing the tale in which the protagonists "eventually discover a temple with valuable bas-reliefs, which they hack off and load on their bullock-carts". But by this time, Malraux's youthful sin was forgotten; the reviewer mistakenly thought that the author "could supply at least the scenery for *The Royal Way* from his archeological explorations in Cambodia and Siam."[60]

I could not find George himself commenting on the affair. While he was always pro-active in preventing historical objects from being removed from

---

59. Ibid., p. 50.
60. Time Magazine, "*Books: To Death*", Feb 18, 1935.

George and Nicole at their home by the museum in 1923, the year he helped arrest André Malraux for looting Banteay Srei.

George arriving at Banteay Chhmar on Sunday, March 9, 1924, as reported by Darryl Collins in his 2008 Udaya journal article, "The First Automobiles to reach Banteay Chhmar". Photo: National Museum of Cambodia Collection.

Cambodia it seems unlikely that he would have approved the unjust tactics the colonial government used to pursue their case. On July 26, five days after the initial sentencing George and his family sailed for France from Saigon.

George now entered an especially prolific period, publishing *Angkor* in the *Les Villes d'Art célèbres* series in the second half of 1924. 1925 saw him issue two major books; *La Sculpture khmère ancienne* and the massive two-part work of *Arts et Archéologie Khmers*. He also released his first novel, *La Route du plus fort* (*The Road of the Strongest*), a story that asks questions about the act of colonization that he could not explore in his academic works. These were the last of George's books that his proud mother would see; Angélina passed away at the age of 60 that year.

In May 1925, another death may have resonated within George, especially in the wake of the Malraux trials: the explorer Louis Delaporte died at the age of 83. Also skilled as an artist and musician, Delaporte was actually on one of the earliest missions to Angkor with Captain Doudart de Lagrée in June 1865. His vision, however, was the

George with Gilbert and Nicole at their home's garden pond in 1925. In the background, a replica of a 10th century statue of Shiva and Uma from Banteay Srei made by the School of Cambodian Arts stone workshop (the original is in the National Museum of Cambodia).

Suzanne with Nicole, Gilbert and the family's newest addition, Bernard-Philippe.

antithesis of goals George would pursue throughout his own life. In a letter to the Ministry of Education seeking funding for a return trip Delaporte offered to acquire for the Louvre

> a collection of statues, bas-reliefs, real and fantastic animals, pillars, ornamental sculptures, all entirely new [to Europe], and of the greatest artistic and archeological value…. Where England failed, France can succeed with ease and at little cost…. Our protégé and friend the king of Cambodge will undoubtedly put the statues we covet… at our disposal, and will even help us transport them through the forest.[61]

As Edwards documents in *Cambodge*, Delaporte was quite an efficient colonial looter, as were many of the early French visitors. For decades he and others chose the best of Cambodia's treasures and transported them to France where a number of new museums were established, including the Musée Guimet which still holds the world's finest examples of sacred Khmer art. George did not mention Delaporte's demise, but continued his efforts to put Khmer art and history in Cambodian hands, and to change colonial attitudes that had begun a lifetime before.

In 1926, George and Suzanne had their third and final child on May 10, 1926: Bernard-Philippe Groslier. All three children — like George himself — came into the world from conception to birth entirely in Cambodia. Like his father, Bernard was educated in France but he, too, was destined to return to Cambodia to devote his life to understanding and preserving the history of his birthplace. At the end of the year, the Grosliers took their first family trip with the new addition, relaxing on a seaside holiday in Kep with friends including Jean and Jacqueline Stoeckel.

Crisis and Catharsis in Cambodian Dance (1927-1928)

In 1927, George once again became involved in Cambodian dance under extraordinary circumstances — indeed a situation evolved that would have been unimaginable to the young man when he was researching *Danseuses Cambodgiennes* just fifteen years earlier. To put these events in context we will briefly change our focus to Cambodian dance history with the guidance of Dr. Paul Cravath and his work, *Earth in Flower*.[62]

---

61. Edwards, *Cambodge*, p. 30.
62. Special thanks to Dr. Cravath for his personal guidance refining the observations that appear in this section.

As Cravath points out in his Foreword to this new edition, George's 1913 book about Cambodian dance was "the first commentary in any language — Asian or European — on one of the world's most refined performing arts whose roots stretch to antiquity." George approached his study with youthful innocence, energy and tenacity, mixing objective observation with emotional subjectivity.[63] What is unquestionable is the respect and awe George held for this ancient art, which he conveys throughout his text. In his heart and mind he saw each dancer transformed,

> ...no longer a woman but a divine statuette, gradually animated by Art, beliefs, the past of a people who admire and venerate in her their most beautiful imaginings and the most perfect expression of their religion and life.[64]

George saw the sacred qualities inherent in the dance, but when he attempted to articulate them his words became vague and even metaphysical. At the end of his book he envisions the power ancient dance may have held:

> ...It seems to loom even in your dreams, at the threshold of that gaping hole of sleep, inaccessible in our waking hours. It is the unfathomable mystery through which the crowd, the priestesses, the priests, and the autocrat lived as they lived and did what they did.
>
> ...Yes, I see it quite well, the extraordinary ritual. As I contemplate it, my heart seems to acquire an uncommon serenity. An ecstasy not due entirely to my admiration penetrates me, and transforms me into something like one of those poor but blessed devotees. I needn't know more or understand.
>
> Absolute Beauty stands complete before me.[65]

George caught a fleeting glimpse of something that few people in his time or since have realized: Cambodian dance in its purest state is a sacred tradition. Paradoxically, the dance has retained precise movements and gestures over the centuries but lost its meaning. What shocked George was seeing the sacred nature of these dance rites vanishing as secular realities replaced them.

> What will artists and poets do tomorrow in this chosen land? They will be told that, only yesterday, there still remained one hundred twenty Vestals in whom the entire past and all its rituals were preserved; that these Vestals could sometimes be seen emerging from their mystery

---

63. Henri Parmentier even criticized George's personal passion for the subject in his 1914 review, which appears in Appendix II.
64. Groslier, *Cambodian Dancers*, p. 51.
65. Ibid., p. 157.

and dancing slowly in splendid costumes with graceful harmony, under streaming lights; that in a few corners of the earth colors, eurhythmics, enchantments, and dreams persisted... but that now it is gone![66]

Some scholars have criticized George's dramatic comments about the "demise" of Cambodian dance, with debate focusing on the accuracy of the number of dancers he reports.[67] The fact that construction of the huge Chhanchaya dance pavilion at the front of the Royal Palace complex began in 1913 indicates that there were clearly enough dancers to justify the expense. George was certainly aware of that project in his research.

My interpretation is that George was expressing his concern not over the *quantity* of dancers, but over the *quality* of the dance itself. His warnings attempted to raise an alarm that the *sacred traditions* of the dance ritual were deteriorating. George observed among the Cambodian people that they "no longer understand their own theatre" and "are gradually detaching themselves from their monks and their gods. Their concerns are now with the material."[68] His words ring painfully true today. Ultimately, however, he doesn't fault Cambodians for this loss, instead placing the blame for this social upheaval upon Western influence.

To spiritually aware Cambodians, and clearly to George himself at that time, the dance represents a sacred tradition, albeit one with most of its true meanings lost somewhere in a distant past. Cambodian dance never entirely stopped fulfilling its ritual duties but for most people of the past century its significance has become more closely linked to four more tangible functions: pleasure, performance, profit and politics.

First, in regard to pleasure, the palace-sequestered dancers were members of a harem whose duties included providing comfort, pampering, amusement and companionship to the king. According to Cravath,

> rarely were there less than a hundred dancers resident in the court during the reign of Sisowath. Their position was one of high prestige as an indispensable part of his entourage, and he surrounded himself with dancers every minute of the day. Twenty of the most beautiful — together with a few musicians — attended Sisowath in shifts....[69]

---

66. Ibid., p. 107.
67. In a similar way, others criticize Groslier's expressed concerns over the demise of traditional Cambodian art, again seeking to disprove him by questioning the statistical accuracy of his reports without considering their context within the goals of his mission to revive and empower native arts and traditions.
68. Groslier, *Cambodian Dancers*, p. 106.
69. Cravath, *Earth in Flower*, p. 131.

This tradition of monarchs surrounding themselves with women goes back to the kings of Angkor and beyond. The prominent placement of female images in the largest temples of the Khmer civilization strongly suggests that women were closely connected to powerful forces and ideas in ancient times. The modern troupe therefore served as a potent symbol of royal power to subjects and neighboring nations alike. As Cravath observed, the intimate relationship between the king and the dancers — some of whom were his wives or would bear his children — made this "the one realm into which the French could not easily penetrate."[70]

While the king's dominion over these women was absolute in the 19th century this began to change as Western influence increased. In 1906, the newly crowned King Sisowath accompanied his royal dance troupe to France exhibiting them for public performances (to foreign audiences no less), marking a huge change in their sanctity and visibility. After their return from France, however, "he made little effort to either increase the performance quality of the palace troupe or to make them more visible to the general public." By 1911, Sisowath allowed dancers to leave the company at will for the first time, even encouraging younger ones to attend school.[71] Roland Meyer describes such events in his novel, *Saramani*, but Charles Gravelle's marriage to a royal dancer is an even better indication of the new conventions.[72]

The second interpretation of Cambodian dance is the most obvious, especially to Western minds: understanding it from a superficial level as a performance art. Indeed, all dance studies must dwell on this area because there is so much to understand including choreography, costumes, characters, plots, casting, jewelry, staging, music and venues. For the French, especially those far removed from Cambodia, it never occurred to them to look any deeper than these elements. The "*ballet royale*" was nothing more than an exotic entertainment developed by a foreign culture with the added bonus of mystical dancing girls to add romance, fantasy and intrigue to the mix. The sacred female images at Angkor Wat and other temples were also viewed by scholars entrenched in inaccurate Western perspectives: like the dancers it is assumed that the stone images of those sacred women were simply put there to amuse and entertain viewers with their beauty. But as

---

70. Ibid., p. 134.
71. Ibid., p. 128.
72. See Gravelle's biographical sketch in Appendix I.

Dancers at the 1922 Colonial Exposition in Marseille.

George wrote, more profound meanings are there for those willing to observe, think and understand.

Earlier, when the dance was the private domain of the king, he used it to affirm his power, only sharing his dancers' divine skills with the public on special occasions. With the advent of tourism inspired by colonial exhibitions in France, more and more people came to Cambodia expecting to see dancers. Like any theatrical production, the supply was adjusted to meet these demands and the demands of entertainment producers everywhere...profit.

Monarchies and democratic governments alike revolve around money. Religious orders, too, for that matter. But now, what was once a spiritual and cultural practice in an Eastern society had become a high-profile asset that was increasingly driven by Western interests. Over the past century, a number of observers reported varying troupe membership figures, accounting for dancers, students, musicians, costumers and others in the entourage. Their numbers are somewhat inconsequential; what really came to matter was "the bottom line".

Cravath estimates that Sisowath spent 7-8% of his annual budget supporting the troupe early in his reign. Throughout his time on the throne the king "appears to have supported his dancers — as well as French financial restraint allowed — to fulfill ritual functions, indulge his own pleasure, and guarantee transmission of the art". [73] By 1922, Sisowath was too feeble to accompany his troupe to the Colonial Exposition in Marseille. Cravath notes that it was a "pallid affair compared to that of 1906" with only a small troupe. With the French controlling his purse strings, Sisowath found it increasingly difficult to support his dancers. Actually, the colonists were setting the stage for a new act in this drama.

The primary reason for dance was no longer about sacred rites to please gods or to honor kings. Nor was it about pampering the king himself, or entertaining the masses with captivating but costly theatrical performances. The French realized that the dancers were indeed symbols of power. So the story of the royal dancers evolved into one that was politically motivated. And in that game the French administrators held all the advantages.

Having their fate intertwined with Earthly governments was not new to sacred dancers in Khmer history. When the Siamese vassals overran Angkor in the final battles of the 15th century the dancers were abducted and transported to Ayutthaya. Those who lived became Thai subjects in the service of foreign kings, and the Khmer dance tradition was changed to meet the tastes of the new masters. Throughout the region's history, as the fortunes of Cambodia, Thailand and Laos rose and fell, the control of royal dancers, and even the right to maintain troupes, was invariably decided by politics and power.

As King Sisowath weakened with age and his reign drew to a close the French encroached more and more on his ceremonial powers and dignity. Tensions increased between the two factions. Through fiscal control the French insisted that the Resident-Superior was frequently seen at the king's side as an equal. Soon, he even shared the royal box with the king at performances of the Royal Ballet, which had become as essential to the pomp of the French state as to the Cambodian.[74]

Towards the end of Sisowath's reign George documented seventy-five royal dancers.[75] These women surrounding the king remained the last symbol of sacred Cambodian power untouched by the French. Indeed, during

---

73. Cravath, *Earth in Flower*, p. 131.
74. Ibid., p. 134.
75. See "Theater and Dance in Cambodia" in Appendix II.

Le Khmérophile 247

This November 1927 photo shows the royal troupe, now under French control for the first time, gathered for a dress rehearsal at the Royal Palace.

Sisowath's reign many Siamese influences were finally eliminated from the dance and there was a "translation of a significant portion of the performance repertoire from Thai into Khmer — in some instances a return to its original language." But even as Thai influence was removed the French were preparing to stake their own claims.[76]

On August 9, 1927 King Sisowath died with his fifty-two-year-old son Monivong next in line for the throne. With his formal coronation not scheduled until July 20, 1928, the French used the regnal transition to execute an amazing coup by gaining complete — if short-lived — control of the royal dance troupe. This level of French interference with the royal dancers was unprecedented. Their first step was to appoint a French director to re-establish disciplined rehearsals and to restore the troupe to its former level of excellence: quite logically they chose George Groslier.[77]

Edwards and Muan make no mention of the incident and even Cravath's sources are limited. Suzanne Groslier didn't write about George's brief responsibility for the dance troupe in her notebooks and other documentation is not available at this time. While we don't have records of

---

76. Cravath, *Earth in Flower*, p. 134, p. 136.
77. Ibid., p. 137.

George's personal feelings about this appointment we do have a clear picture of George's commitment to Cambodian customs through his prior actions and statements.

When he became director of the museum and art school, for example, he quickly appointed Cambodians to key positions, summarized by his statement that "I am not Khmer" as the explanation of why he himself never taught there. In two major articles he wrote about Cambodian dance in that period he maintained the reverent attitude used in his first work in 1913. His first article was published in the French newspaper *Mercure de France*, appearing just before the coronation. The second was a formal presentation about Cambodian theater at the Sorbonne.[78] All these factors make it unlikely that he ever coveted a position managing the dancers — it seems more believable that he would have seen the French takeover as disrespectful and even sacrilegious.

The French government, on the other hand, clearly sought total control — as Cravath points out they could have simply increased the king's allowance if they wanted to improve the troupe and its appearance.[79] Despite the fact that almost none of the dancers could speak French to any extent, they went ahead with their plan.

Among the seventy-five dancers of Sisowath's troupe even Khmer literacy was almost non-existent. Groslier noted that only four could read and of these only two could write. Of the eleven dance instructresses, only one could read and write.[80] This was not unusual for a tradition based on oral transmission and direct teacher-to-student instruction but it certainly put the continuity of the art in a precarious situation, especially if it was usurped by foreigners. By the time Monivong was crowned only two of the previous reign's premiere dancers, "supreme in grace and technical knowledge" remained. Cravath presumes that "the other dancers took advantage of the time-honored option of departing the palace following a monarch's death".[81] Despite changes in personnel it appears that the number of dancers was quickly restored as seen in two photos from George's family albums. The relationship between the dancers and the king was, however, broken.

---

78. See "Theater and Dance in Cambodia" in Appendix II.
79. Cravath, *Earth in Flower*, p. 137.
80. See "Theater and Dance in Cambodia" in Appendix II.
81. Cravath, *Earth in Flower*, pp. 139-140.

A French photographer and an official from the École des Beaux-Arts (perhaps André Silice) review the new troupe in November 1927, already in rehearsals for King Monivong's coronation the following July.

By the July 1928 coronation ceremonies the extent that the French had degraded King Monivong's sacred power became painfully clear.[82] Now the French government openly challenged the king with the official account stating that "today the religious dignitaries of Cambodia are no longer the only consecratory of royalty; the Governor-General of Indo-China and the Resident-Superior assume almost the role of chief priests during the five-day ritual of investiture."[83] While the dancers had effectively been under French control for nearly a year, Monivong endorsed the official documents transferring control of the dancers from the Royal Palace administration to *l'École des Beaux-Arts* during his coronation, accepting the terms "because it seemed a possible way of saving the ballet."[84]

On the evening of July 23, the fourth day of rituals, the new *corps de ballet* with fresh costumes offered their first performance to an international audience of European and Asian guests. In a strange twist, however, these forty royal dancers were acting in an entirely new role — they were now French civil servants.

---

82. Monivong's coronation ran from Friday July 20 until Wednesday July 25, 1928.
83. Cravath, *Earth in Flower*, p. 139, quoting Alfred Meynard's 1929 translation of the official coronation publication.
84. Ibid., p. 139.

The official photo from the French coronation publication showing Resident-Superior Aristide Eugène Le Fol with King Monivong at the Royal Throne Hall.

Earlier that day, George also did something quite odd: he boarded the ship *Angers* in Saigon en route to Marseille. So not only does he seem to have deliberately avoided the coronation (which was scheduled months in advance), he also arranged to be conspicuously absent from the premier performance of the dance troupe that the French now controlled.

Was George expressing his disapproval for French interference in the sacred customs of Cambodia? Did he literally distance himself from these events to make a statement? There were certainly many good reasons why George would have been unhappy with the French takeover of the Royal Ballet. And as Cravath documents, many changes were taking place that were clearly at odds with George's vision of this ancient art.

Under French control, rehearsal schedules became unusually strict, first to prepare for the coronation and then for appearances at an important international exhibition in Saigon in 1928. A surprising account published the next year in the United States reported that the former court dancers

> recently... became sufficiently modern to protest about their working conditions. They went on a strike and appealed to the French resident for a readjustment of their status. As a result they are no longer the dancers of the palace but a sort of state troupe whose performances are under the direction of the protectorate. [85]

Cravath quickly defines the real problem, which may have eluded French administrative minds:

> ...the traditional *raison d'être* of the dancers had been eliminated. Their overall function as attendants of the king and performers of ritual dances over which he presided had been replaced by a social role allowing them a personal freedom for which they were ill-prepared.
>
> Eschewing the protectiveness of the palace, however, thirty of the forty dancers under the French administration chose to marry. The Khmer dance tradition on a more fundamental level than mere performance was rapidly deteriorating [86]

The end of French control of the troupe was triggered by a scandalous event during the Saigon Exhibition. The jewel-keeper — now managed by the French — fled to Thailand...taking more than twenty-five kilograms of gold and silver ornaments with him! The colonial powers quickly returned control of the troupe to the royal palace administration

---

85. Robert Casey. *The Four Faces of Siva*. Indianapolis, Bobbs-Merrill, 1929. P. 156.
86. Cravath, *Earth in Flower*, p. 140.

where only Cambodians could begin the long process of restoring its dignity and strength.

George, meanwhile, did not return to Cambodia for nine months following his unusual departure during King Monivong's coronation. His year ended in France on a sad note with the loss of his father Antoine, who died on December 14, 1928 at age 72. Two months later George presented his Valentine's Day paper on Cambodian theater at the Sorbonne, finally returning to Cambodia in early April. That presentation seems to have been George's last direct connection to Cambodian dance.

He and the family arrived back in Cambodia in early April 1929. Two weeks later, his Paris publisher Emile Paul released George's second novel, *Le Retour à l'argile* (*The Return to Clay*), lauded by Milton Osborne for realistically capturing colonial drama in an urban setting, which was uncharacteristic of his previous works.

> It traces the slow absorption of Claude Rollin, an engineer sent to Cambodia to build a bridge, into the country's indigenous society as he responds with growing warmth to its ambience, and finally to a Cambodian woman who becomes his mistress. This is the "return to the clay", an abandonment of the falsities and vanities of the western world, as Claude comes to see them. The Phnom Penh in which this story takes place is largely the city of the Cambodians, of bamboo huts and boats on the Tonle Sap, rather than that of colonial society. It is portrayed with sympathy by Groslier in contrast to what he had written fourteen years earlier, in his first non-fiction book about Cambodia. Then, in *A l'Ombre d'Angkor*, he had stated that he had no wish to write about Phnom Penh, which "offered so little of interest" by comparison with the country's ancient temples.[87]

It's not surprising that George's thoughts were more focused on city lifestyles at that time. His primary goal was increasingly to promote the products of the art school guilds with an eye towards the upcoming colonial exposition, which offered the possibility of opening world markets to Cambodian art. By 1929, more and more tourists were increasing the demand for his school's products. The original retail locations in Phnom Penh were now supplemented by sales offices in Angkor and even Saigon.

Despite this success he seems to have seen Cambodia's growth in a mixed light, penning an article reflecting on how much the sleepy country of

---

87. Milton Osborne. *Phnom Penh, A Cultural History*. Oxford University Press, New York, 2008. P. 100.

The Groslier children dressed up for a costume party in February 1928, seen on the porch of their home: Nicole, Jean (a family friend), Gilbert and Bernard-Philippe.

"I know why you built a snowman in Meaux in 1929, Madame!" Nicole was quite surprised by my explanation when I realized that these two photos coincided with her father's Sorbonne presentation on Cambodian theater on February 14, 1929.

"The big boy who took a voyage in the tiny boat." February 1930.

his youth had changed. In a 1929 article he observed that in 1900 there were just fifty kilometers of roads in Cambodia and no cars. By the end of his first visit in 1914 there were six hundred kilometers of roads and 30 cars. As the decade drew to a close he noted "2400 kilometers of roads with 1840 tourist cars, 820 buses and 270 transportation trucks"[88] In the face of this modernization he maintained his vision to preserve and market traditional Cambodian arts and crafts.

In addition to losing his parents, the decade held one more personal loss for George that he would face alone. On September 17, 1929 his wife and children, accompanied by their cook and nanny Ba, returned for France. This time they would stay there for nearly three years, living in a family home in Château-du-Loire, about 200 kilometers southwest of Paris. A few days later George began a new voyage of his own.

This journey was one of solitary observation and meditation on the mighty Mekong River that had flowed from the Himalayas to nourish Cambodia since the beginning of time. Again, George sees a poetic side in the capital city as he begins on the morning of Saturday, September 21.

> Phnom Penh, stretching out in the rising sun, appeared to me nearly submerged, like a narrow scarf gently wavering at my departure, the roofs of the Royal Palace and the spire of the Silver Pagoda, with their yellow and green tiles, glistening like sequins. And then, from hour to hour, the weather changed and each bend of the river was overcast by a different sky.[89]

His official function was to inspect pagodas along the route, but Cambodia's natural beauty and pace of life captivated him as it had twenty years earlier; he found peace communing with the land that gave him life. He planned his trip to experience the river at the height of its waters after the rainy season, then returning in the spring for a second adventure when water levels had fallen. Taking notes along the way, he drank in the Mekong's natural beauty while interacting with the diverse people, fish and animals that made the river their home. In 1931 he published his experiences as *Waters and Lights: Journal of a Voyage on the Cambodian Mekong*. Reminiscent of his earlier work, *In the Shade of*

---

88. Muan, *Citing Angkor*, p. 23.
89. *Eaux et lumières: journal de route sur le Mékong Cambodgien*. Société d'éditions géographiques, maritimes et coloniales, Paris, 1931. P. 1.

Angkor, he once again shared his most personal thoughts and impressions with readers.

His notes end the first leg of his trip on October 20. By sad coincidence that was also the day that George's longtime friend, Charles Gravelle, who assisted George with his first book, passed away shortly after his sixty-fifth birthday. He spent the Christmas holidays far from his family and entered the new decade alone in an increasingly westernized Cambodia.

The Apogee of the *"Mission Civilisatrice"* (1930-1938)

As the "Roaring Twenties" passed into history Cambodia had become far less insular. World transportation, communication and politics had greater influence over the local culture, economy and government. Europe's financial boom after World War I led some leaders towards megalomania, overconfidence and greed. France continued making huge investments in its colonies despite an increasing number of people who perceived their *mission civilisatrice* (civilisatory mission) less as altruism and more as a quest for power and profit — symptoms of which were seen at King Monivong's coronation.

Britain's colonial empire was already weakening; Egypt gained its independence in 1922. That same year in India — the crown jewel of Britain's colonies that fueled the French desire to dominate Indochina — a man named Mohandas Gandhi was arrested for peaceful protests against foreign rule. Italy accepted the dictatorship of Benito Mussolini in 1925 as the erstwhile French art-thief André Malraux began his work furthering the cause of Indochinese independence. Meanwhile, in Germany an obscure orator two years younger than George was successfully organizing citizens dissatisfied with hardships and humiliation suffered after World War I. His name was Adolf Hitler. Nationalists led by Chiang Kai-shek ruled China by 1928. In Russia, Joseph Stalin's control was almost absolute. The decade of prosperity was punctuated by the October crash of the United States stock market in 1929, an economic crisis that soon spread. Soon, the decade of global change even affected the tiny tropical paradise that just seventy years earlier was practically unknown to the West. It seemed that much of the

The breathtaking replica of the top level of Angkor Wat featured at the Colonial Exposition in Vincennes from May–November 1931.

world's growth and optimism were an illusion, yet momentum continued in France where a major international exhibition was on the horizon.

But first, George had a commitment to the Mekong. From February 15 to March 15, 1930 he again took to the river in his small boat to complete his expedition. Then he returned to begin preparing for his demanding responsibilities in planning Cambodia's participation in the upcoming Colonial Exhibition, scheduled to open just outside of Paris in Vincennes on May 6, 1931. The event was to be the most spectacular colonial show in history and George wanted Cambodian art to steal the show. Another ally on the exhibition organizing committee was Pierre Guesde, a former administrator in Cambodia and the father of the Franco-Khmer author and poet Makhali-Phal.[90] The expo's highlight was a full-sized reproduction of the top level of Angkor Wat and a Cambodian pavilion that was

> planned by Groslier in collaboration with the architect of the Exposition and members of the Department of Public Works (whom Groslier claimed did nothing). Decorative details and the sculpted wood entrance of the building were completed by ateliers at the School of Cambodian Arts. A meter-high "traditional painting of the principal episodes of the life of the Buddha" was completed by the atelier of *dessin*, rolled and shipped to be included in the displays. The entire middle gallery of the exhibition space was reserved for "*Arts cambodgiens*".[91]

The official architects, Gabriel Blanche and his father Charles, had designed the Indochina pavilion for the 1922 Marseille exposition as well. As postcard credits show, Blanche's firm is prominently associated with the Angkor Wat model while George is only connected to the Cambodian pavilion itself. Suzanne's personal notes confirm that

> Preparations for the Cambodia pavilion as well as the sculpted parts of the replica of Angkor Wat were made a year in advance. The entire team of craftsmen, Cambodian and French, arrived in time for us to be ready ahead of everyone else.

George's tireless work in Cambodia, however, didn't guarantee the family any benefits in preparing for his arrival in January 1931. Suzanne wrote that

> Despite our friends' best efforts, however, it had been impossible for us to find an apartment. In the meantime, I lived in a furnished room on Rue Emile Desvaux. Bernard and our nanny, Ba, lived in a their own small house, and Gilbert stayed with his godfather, Leon Cirou. Since there was no room for Nicole, she was unable to join us and stayed behind at her high school, Victor Duruy, where she was a boarder.

> One night, [a neighbor] woke me to say that the tenants of the villa next door seemed to be slipping out in the dead of night. At

---

90. For information about her work please visit www.makhali-phal.org.
91. Muan, *Citing Angkor*, p. 176.

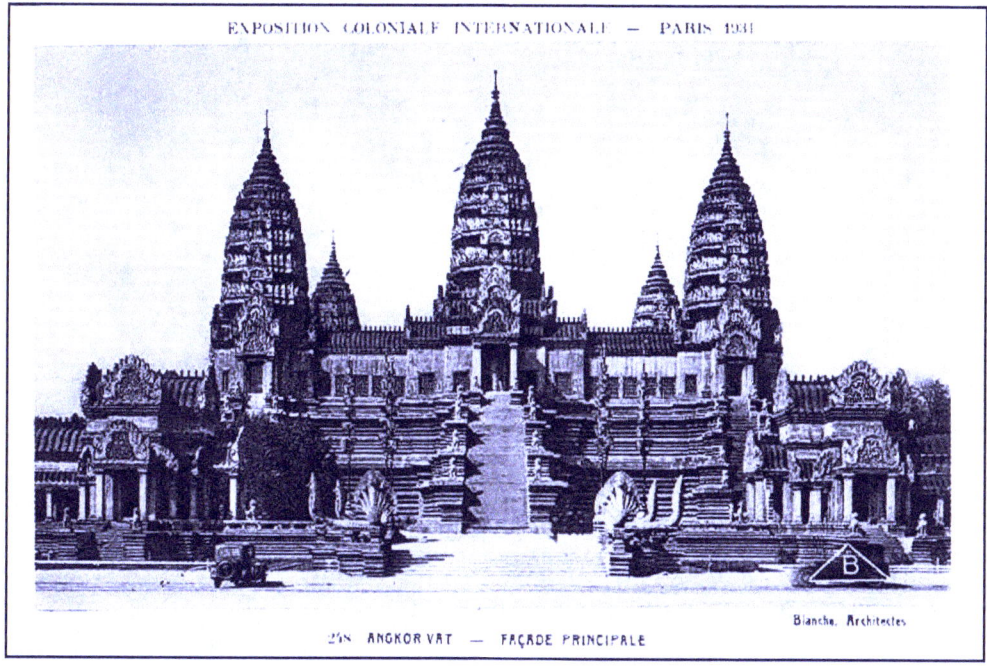

For the 1931 French Colonial Exposition George Groslier designed the distinctive *Pavillon du Cambodge* in a style reminiscent of the Albert Sarraut Museum in Phnom Penh (now the National Museum of Cambodia).

Commemorative coins struck for the 1931 Colonial Exposition featuring the ever-present Cambodian dancer as the symbol of the nation's heritage.

dawn, we were already at the office of the agent administering affairs for Rue Desvaux, a private street, and rented the place for ourselves. I was finally able to write to George that we had a roof over our heads.

In considering the historic context of this exposition the modern term "irrational exuberance" comes to mind. As France mounted this magnificent celebration of their colonies and wealth, neighboring countries were entering devastating economic depressions that would set the stage for the next world war. Britain, Germany, the Netherlands, Russia and the United States all faced staggering unemployment, poverty and even starvation. Beginning the very next year as many as ten million Ukrainians would die under Stalin's rule during the Holodomor,[92] an event that many scholars believe was intentional genocide by famine. The exposition also gave a platform to the growing number of people who saw colonialism as an archaic and brutal practice of strong nations oppressing weaker ones.

Such was the tumultuous world George lived in, but his politics remained quite simple; he followed his life mission to preserve Cambodian art and culture and to create vocations for the artists who joined him in that process. Despite the gloomy economic situation the exposition attracted 33 million visitors from around the world and it was a major success for Cambodian arts. More indigenous crafts were sold there than in the best prior year for all the shops in Phnom Penh. Based on this demand a

---

92. From the Ukrainian words *holod*, 'hunger', and *mor*, 'plague.

167 TEMPLE D'ANGKOR-VAT ET PAVILLON DU CAMBODGE

permanent sales office was opened in Paris catering to a "metropolitan public [who] have thus shown themselves to be very favorably inclined with regards to Cambodian art".[93]

Other Cambodian artists needed for a successful colonial exposition were, of course, the royal dancers who played a major role in captivating French imaginations since their first continental appearances in 1906. Exposition planners knew they were essential for the 1931 expo, however there was a problem. Since the debacle of the French takeover of the royal troupe in 1927 — and subsequent return of its control to the palace in 1928 — the dancers had become nearly unavailable for French needs. When invited to participate in the exposition King Monivong declined, claiming that his troupe was still depleted.

Fortuitously for the French, a dispute in the royal court developed over succession to the Khmer throne. One contender was King Sisowath's youngest son, Prince Yong Kath, who had married a former royal dancer named Princess Say Sangvann. The princess, who maintained her own amateur troupe, decided to escape the drama by withdrawing from the court. Next, she made her troupe's services available to the exposition

---

93. Muan, *Citing Angkor*, p. 176.

planners who quickly accepted her offer.

At the exposition in France, however, her dancers were "officially presented as the genuine Royal Ballet. By admitting that they engaged independent artists, the French authorities should have recognized their failure in one of the missions claimed by colonization: to protect the splendid Indochinese heritage from the wrongdoings of time and indigenous barbarism."[94] The public were none the wiser. Upon their return to Cambodia

> "the troupe was granted a subsidy by the French government and declared to be the official 'one and only true' Khmer dancers with exclusive rights of performance for distinguished guests both in the salon of the Resident-Superior and at Angkor Wat. Definitely a coup. The greatly overshadowed palace troupe retained the prestigious title of 'Corps de Ballet Royal' and continued to perform ritual ceremonies, but clearly to French authorities they were extraneous."[95]

This move clearly separated the commercialized Cambodian dancers performing to entertain tourists from those in the palace, who were relearning the true purpose of their art to perform sacred rituals in support of the king and the country. For the rest of his life, George doesn't seem to have had any involvement with the dance. The only exception was that the artisans in his school continued producing the masks needed for the performances.

In the literary field, George acquired three personal honors in 1931. He was awarded membership in the *Société des gens de lettres* (Society of Men of Letters), a private association founded in 1838 by Honoré de Balzac, Victor Hugo and Alexandre Dumas to protect the rights of writers and their works. Next, his 1928 book *Le Retour à l'argile* (Return to Clay) received the Grand Prize of Colonial Literature and finally the *Académie française* recognized his book *Angkor*, published by Laurens in 1924.[96]

As the Exposition was winding down in late October, George headed back to Cambodia but once again his family remained in France. Suzanne had become active founding a charitable organization called the *Entraide Féminine de la France d'Outre-mer*.[97] The group established offices in Marseille

---

94. Anne Decoret-Ahiha. "*L'exotique, l'ethnique et l'authentique: Regards et discours sur les danses d'ailleurs*". Civilisations, Num. 53. 2004. p. 160.
95. Cravath, *Earth in Flower*, p. 142.
96. Suzanne Groslier's personal notebooks.
97. Woman's Aid of Overseas France.

and Bordeaux to assist women returning to France from colonial duties under adverse conditions; some were ill, others were abandoned by their husbands or suffered difficulties due to family emergencies. The group provided a "safety net" for the women, giving them help in desperate situations and offering a form of social security. The group became a successful public service organization and Suzanne worked with them until 1975.

Meanwhile, the exposition's benefit of increased demand for Cambodian products created new problems. George "the artist" was immersed in the responsibilities of George "the production manager". From the minute he stepped off the boat on November 17, 1931 his life increasingly revolved around administration as he balanced quantity and quality to provide a steady stream of artistic goods from his school's workshops.

After studying this man's artistic works for years I began to wonder how happy George was with the expanding business obligations he had created for himself. Perhaps he sometimes felt as if he'd painted himself into a corner. But his isolation ended a year later in September 1932 when Suzanne, Nicole, Gilbert and Bernard returned to Cambodia, with mother and daughter involved in an interesting mission of their own.

Before their departure, Suzanne's social connections from charitable work in Paris led to an unusual request from a certain Countess Jean de Pange: could Suzanne chaperone Mariette Hao, daughter of a wealthy Cochinchinese family, on her journey from the Convent des Oiseaux at Notre Dame to Saigon?

Suzanne, her three children and Mariette boarded the *André Lebon* in Marseille on Friday, August 26, 1932 and set sail for Saigon. Mariette was just four years Nicole's senior, and the two girls became fast friends on the 25-day boat trip and stayed

Mariette sent this personal photo to Nicole after her wedding on March 20, 1934.

in touch over the years. As Suzanne wrote "No one could then have foreseen that the Emperor of Annam, Bao Daï, would fall in love with Mariette and marry her, despite religion, caste, and everything else that separated them." And so it was that the French-educated Vietnamese Catholic girl, Jeanne Marie-Thérèse (Mariette) Nguyen Huu-Hao Thi Lan, was destined to become Hoang Hau Nam Phuong, the "Southern Perfume Empress" and the last empress of Annam.

For the next three happy years the family photo albums again showed outings, celebrations and events in and around Phnom Penh. In 1934, George's creative side manifested with the publication of a short fictional story entitled *Monsieur de la Garde, roi*, which was "inspired by the royal chronicles of Cambodia". *L'Illustration* magazine published the work in two installments in Paris.

In early 1935, the Grosliers traveled to a temple George first visited twenty-one years earlier: Banteay Chhmar, a shrine that held a special place in his heart. Located in northwestern Cambodia bordered by the Dangrek mountain chain the location is particularly remote. Although his trip in January 1912 was by ox-cart George later took the first automobiles to the site in 1924. Now he was able to take his entire family to see the historical mystery that he later wrote about in *L'Illustration* magazine:

> We come across fewer and fewer villages, and finally none at all. In summer, torrid heat and no game. In winter, violent storms reverberating in the mountains. These are the most desolate places in Cambodia. Yet here lie the ruins of an imposing group of monuments from the ancient empire, and one of them not only is the largest known in Cambodia (larger even than the Angkor group) but ranks among the largest in the world. This temple is currently known as Banteay Chhmar.
>
> By what series of events did the builders settle eight centuries ago, at the height of Angkor's power, in so desolate an area, only to abandon it later and bequeath it to us much as they found it? This is one of the most intriguing puzzles in Cambodian history.[98]

This was the last Cambodian adventure they shared as a family. On June 9, 1935 they all headed back to France and Gilbert would never set foot in Cambodia again. A year later, George returned to Cambodia alone. It wasn't until Christmas 1937 that Suzanne returned, this time with only Nicole and Bernard as Gilbert remained in France to pursue his studies.

---

98. *L'Illustration*, April 3, 1937.

American artist Lucille Douglass later sent George one of her Angkor Wat engravings as thanks for his hospitality in 1927.

Suzanne records an unusual event worth sharing here, but the precise date is not known. It involves an adventurous American artist named Lucille Douglass who first met George in 1926 on her way to Angkor. Douglass, forty-eight years old at the time, was enchanted by the vestiges of the Khmer civilization. She was traveling with Helen Churchill Candee, the American author who had released her acclaimed book on Cambodia, *Angkor the Magnificent,* the previous year. Candee was now back in Cambodia working on her next book, *New Journeys in Old Asia*, which Douglass would illustrate. Both women visited George at his museum and apparently a bond of friendship formed between the two artists.

On her return to the US, Douglass's etchings of Angkor were exhibited in Washington D.C. under the auspices of the French ambassador. In 1931, they were even featured at the Colonial Exhibition in Paris. Following an illness of several months, Douglass passed away at the home of a friend on September 26, 1935, but her friendship with George wasn't over yet.[99] As Suzanne relates

> In the living room there's an engraving of Angkor Vat, which Miss Douglass dedicated to George and I. She was a painter and George had helped expedite her travels, providing her with introductions to various people, etc. Accustomed as we were to receiving not the least thanks, or even a postcard, we were astonished to receive that engraving.
>
> We were even more astonished a few years later, when the American Consul at Saigon came to Phnom Penh and asked to see George. Miss Douglass,

---

99. Goldfarb, Stephen. *"From Tuskegee to Angkor: The Odyssey of Lucille Douglass"*. *Alabama Heritage*, Issue 81, Summer 2006.

it turned out, had died and had arranged to have herself cremated. The Consul brought with him a small urn containing her ashes and asked whether it would be possible to grant her dying wish: to have her ashes scattered from a plane as it flew over Angkor. And that's what was done.

Suzanne's dramatic note, however, contradicts another account of the artist's final resting place, which instead involves none other than George's friend Henri Marchal. According to a document in the Birmingham Public Library

> Anne Morgan arranged for Lady Marston to take the ashes to Angkor Wat. In Feb. 1936 Lady Marston spoke with M. Marchal, the conservator at Angkor, and his assistant, M. Lagisquet, and they selected a mango tree on the grounds, Lady Marston sprinkled the ashes in a circle, and said a few words, and marked the location on a map to share with Lucille's friends at home. But having her ashes scattered from a plane sounds like Lucille — she loved flying.[100]

It seems unlikely that Suzanne could have come up with such an unlikely story involving an airplane over Angkor. I also note that George was in France from July 1935 until September 1936 and Suzanne herself didn't return until Christmas 1937. Are the dates wrong in the account above? Were white lies told about the mango tree while Ms. Douglass sat on a shelf at the American Consul's office in Saigon awaiting a more dramatic fulfillment of her last wish? We may never know but by both accounts she is now resting at Angkor in peace.

In 1938 Suzanne added an amusing note about George and Jean Giraudoux, a multi-talented literary figure who is regarded as one of the most important French dramatists between the two wars. Apart from his writing, Giraudoux worked with the Ministry of Foreign Affairs. While on a tour of embassies in the Far East he took a break from his mission to visit Indochina:

> As a simple tourist, then, he went from Hanoi directly to Angkor and from there to Phnom Penh, where the Resident Superior invited him for lunch. But Jean was running ahead of schedule and the Resident's private secretary (a solid Auvergne name that I cannot recall) waited for him at the city gates in vain, finally starting to panic and setting out on a search.

> Meanwhile, Jean had gone straight to the museum to find George, whom he knew already, and stayed there for a long visit. Not minding the time, he came to our house for rest and refreshment. Towards one-thirty or two it occurred to the police chief and the Colonel to check and see if Giraudoux had taken refuge at our house, since his horror of official formalities was well known.

---

100. Personal communication with Vicki Ingham, a researcher preparing a full-length biography of Lucille Douglass.

![Banteay Chhmar elephant trip photo]

Banteay Chhmar elephant trip, 1935. Berets, not pith helmets, were *de rigueur* on this outing! At the top are George and Nicole following Bernard and Gilbert.

The End of Art and Dreams (1939-1945)

As 1939 began, Cambodia was a tranquil oasis compared to the rest of the world, and it would remain so for six more years. Europe, however, descended into madness and violence. At the end of January Adolf Hitler raved in a Reichstag speech that war would soon lead to "the annihilation of the Jewish race in Europe". In March the Nazis took Czechoslovakia, but it was their invasion of Poland that dragged all of Europe into the conflict. On September 3, Britain and France officially declared war on Germany and World War II began. Closer to Cambodia the Japanese continued escalating their ten-year campaign against China and occupied Hainan Island in February.

George and Bernard-Philippe in their final photo together at the museum, 1939.

Nicole got this sporty car for her 21st birthday and began exploring Cambodia on her own.

Gilbert, now 17 years old, had been in France attending high school for four years. In June, Suzanne and Bernard-Philippe, only 13, headed back to join him. George would never see his wife or two sons again. Nicole remained with her father in Cambodia. It's not clear if the family celebrated her twenty-first birthday together on June 15th but her gift was certainly an indication of the mood in Cambodia; she received a 1936 Peugeot 302 cabriolet and soon began exploring Cambodia on her own. Nicole's photos over the next few years show her and her distinctive car on a number of adventures from the beaches of Cambodia and Annam to the temples of Siem Reap.

Despite grim events in Europe, George continued promoting Cambodian art and apparently was quite successful.

> A network of foreign outlets also came to be established as a result of the interest shown on the part of merchants visiting the 1931 Exposition.... By 1940, outlets or representatives of the Corporations had been established in Port-Said (Egypt), San Francisco, Santa-Barbara, Los Angeles, Washington (USA), Algiers (Algeria), Papeete (Tahiti), Bangkok (Thailand), Batavia (Dutch Indies), Singapore, and Medan, among other places.[101]

---

101. Muan, *Citing Angkor*, p. 176.

Bernard-Philippe and Gilbert in Vouvray-sur-Loire with an uncle on March 24, 1940. Six weeks later, the Nazis would invade France.

But the network he had worked years to develop would soon vanish as the War reached global proportions. The fate of his family became a far graver worry for George on June 14, 1940 when Nazi troops entered Paris. The western allied forces had completely lost control over the European continent. Prime Minister Philippe Pétain quickly sued for peace and established an armistice with Hitler. The agreement surrendered two-thirds of France to the Nazis while Pétain was allowed to control an area in the southern part of the country.

During this time Suzanne and the boys escaped the violence by first traveling southwest of Paris and then moving into the southern region under the newly formed Vichy government, which continued to administrate the French colonies, including Indochina. Pétain's collaboration with the Nazis, however, prompted Britain's leader Winston Churchill to take aggressive action. That summer he ordered massive attacks on the French navy to prevent it from falling into Nazi hands. Many of the ships that had carried the Grosliers back and forth to Indochina in peacetime came to rest at the bottom of the Mediterranean Sea.

In 1940, the pro-Nazi Vichy regime—which actually insulated Cambodia from the effects of the war—appointed Jean Decoux as

Governor-General of French Indochina. By August the Japanese were demanding the right to move troops through Tonkin (now Vietnam) as part of their war against China. Decoux cabled Vichy for help but none was forthcoming — Germany was already pressuring the French to give full cooperation to the Japanese. On September 22, Decoux signed a treaty giving Japan free movement through the region's transport hubs. Initially, some Indochinese Colonial troops and Foreign Legionnaires fought against the Japanese but by September 27, 1940, the three Axis Powers — Germany, Italy and Japan — signed the Tripartite Pact pledging mutual cooperation and resistance ended.

King Sisowath Monivong, who held no political power, grieved for his nation and grew increasingly demoralized. He retired to Kampot and died on

Royal dancers accompanying the funerary urn at King Monivong's funeral in 1941.

April 24, 1941. Once again, French administrators seized the opportunity of a monarch's death to tighten their grip on Cambodia. Rather than appointing the king's son as the next monarch, Decoux made a fateful decision that the French would later regret. The French Governor-General decided that the king's eighteen-year-old grandson would be easier to control; on April 25 he selected Norodom Sihanouk to become the next King of Cambodia, with the coronation taking place in September.[102]

While Vichy continued to administrate Indochina, the Japanese were now the true masters of the region until the end of the war. A garrison of 8,000 troops remained stationed in Cambodia. On December 7, 1941 the Japanese staged a surprise attack against the United States at Pearl Harbor. The next day, they invaded Malaya and Thailand. By January 25, 1942, their control of Thailand was so absolute that the puppet Thai government declared war on the United States and the United Kingdom.

In Cambodia, life went on much as before. About a year after the coronation, Emperor Bảo Đại of Annam was invited for an official visit. By this time, the king's mother Princess Kossamak had devoted years to restoring the skills of the royal dancers. Now she would engage them to turn the occasion into a stunning victory for Cambodian prestige: "A flourishing troupe of royal dancers would clearly imply to Bảo Đại a strong monarchy in Cambodia...."[103] The French insisted that their favored troupe, run by Say Sangvann, would handle performances. But on November 22 the princess seized a strategic opportunity to present a special dance program for the Emperor and Empress at her son's twenty-first birthday celebration in the palace. As Cravath relates

> The performance was stunning and in that moment Kossamak gained a great victory on a small battlefield. For almost three subsequent decades the visible political activity of the Cambodian king would be identified with the art of his personal dancers, and, in that, Sihanouk gained an image of independence long before the political fact.
>
> ...it was Sihanouk — and his mother behind the throne — rather than the French, who appeared to all, including the neighboring Emperor, to be the sponsor and source of regality.[104]

George was probably pleased to see the country's precious dance once again restored to the service of the crown. But his true thoughts are

---

102. Details from *Wikipedia* sources: "Axis powers," "Franco-Thai War," "German–Japanese relations," "Invasion of French Indochina," "Jean Decoux" and "Tripartite Pact."
103. Cravath, *Earth in Flower*, 154.
104. Ibid., pp. 154-155.

Nichol's friend from their earlier voyage to Saigon together returned as Her Majesty Nam Phương, Imperial Princess of Annam, on November 20, 1942.

unknown. The family has no records for the final few years of his life and all his personal papers were lost in the ensuing confusion of the War.

One final manuscript did escape, but just barely. In 1942 George traveled to Saigon to hire publisher Albert Portail, to print his last book. Portail, who came to Saigon in 1905, issued dozens of specialized titles about Indochina including the works of Louis Finot, Henri Marchal and Roland Meyer. Unlike all George's earlier works, *Les Donneurs de Sang* (The Donors of Blood), is a psychological drama set in France. In it, he unfolds a tale about the owner of a modest radio-supply company, a man painfully aware of his own mediocrity. Intelligent orders placed by a retired doctor in the country attract his attention and he pays the customer a friendly visit. The doctor turns out to be the narrator's doppelgänger, a mysterious twin whose life instantly seems more appealing than his own. When he visits a second time he finds his twin dead, and spontaneously decides to adopt his identity. He quickly fakes his own death, assumes the doppelgänger's life, and thus becomes a "*donneur de sang et d'ame*" (a donor of blood and soul). George's creative diversion is as intriguing as the concept he presents.

In an ironic twist of fate one more book in George's name was released in his lifetime. With the military occupation of Cambodia an increasing number of Japanese tourists were discovering Angkor. In 1943, Shinkigensha press in Tokyo issued a translation of George's book on the topic; *Ankōru no iseki*. Two years later they would murder the author.

The D-Day invasion of June 6, 1944 marked the beginning of the end for the war in Europe. Paris was liberated by August 25 and Pétain's Vichy regime collapsed, both from allied attacks and French resistance. As Nicole relates

> ...my brother Bernard, he was a war hero! He fought fiercely against Nazis in southern France. He was a boy, not even eighteen, but he went to school by day and was out at night for sabotage with the resistance. He told me he once blew up a train! He fought with Charles de Gaulle and was with him when he entered Paris. Later, it was Bernard who came to Indochina to help with the liberation and he found me in Saigon.

Even as Vichy leaders fled to Germany for protection, Decoux tried to hold his control in Cambodia. As the War neared its conclusion in Europe the Japanese became more desperate. On March 9, 1945 Japanese troops overthrew the French colonial government, rallying support from the local population with the promise of autonomy. Four days later, with King Sihanouk as the new Head of State, Cambodia annulled the 1863 Treaty of the Protectorate and declared its independence from France and alignment with the Greater East Asian Co-Prosperity Sphere headed by Japan.[105]

French officials and citizens were immediately arrested and placed in guarded camps. Plans were put in place for a 5,000 man local volunteer army to assist the Japanese troops in preserving order, but the war ended before this action was implemented.[106]

Nicole relates what happened next:

> We were all herded to a concentration camp and forced to stay there, in that small camp. Men and women were separated. I did not see my father. I was alone. Many people in the camp became so ugly. Greedy. Mean. There were arguments over food, money and supplies. This bothered me so much. The nuns who I knew had set up a small hospital in the camp. I volunteered to help them

---

105. Edwards, *Cambodge*, p. 239-240.
106. Encyclopædia Britannica Online. 2010.

George's shortwave radio in March 4, 1933 with a map showing his global contacts. Perhaps the setup was even more sophisticated in 1945.

by bathing and feeding the sick. Keeping busy helped to stop my worries.

The Japanese had taken my father because they thought he was a spy. He was not a spy. He was a brave man, but the charges were false. When the war came to Cambodia my father had one of the only radios in Phnom Penh. He was a music lover. It was for listening to classical music. That is what he told me. The Japanese did not accept this. They tortured him but he had nothing to say.

> [On June 18] three days after my birthday I was called to the commander's office. I may have known there was something wrong but I can't remember now. I was taken to his office and he was sitting at his desk. He said nothing to me but gestured to a table. There were my father's glasses and a box with his ashes. His shoes were on the floor beneath. I picked them up and left. My God I was frightened and lonely that day.

As Nicole confirms, George had been a wireless radio enthusiast for many years, but his equipment and communications practices struck the Kempeitai, the Japanese secret police, as being much more than amateur. Was George working to liberate Cambodia? As a soldier in the First World War he faced a number of dangerous assignments as a balloonist, soldier and courier. His son Bernard was in France blowing up trains for the resistance. Is it likely that this man, who loved the culture of Cambodia so much, would sit idly while invaders threatened both the country of his birth and the country to which he passionately devoted his life? It seems more likely that this man of action would have acted, while shielding his daughter from the truth to protect her. Nicole retains the sealed records of her father's death that she received after the liberation. They remain sealed.

On August 28, 1945 — ten weeks and a day after George was killed — the Japanese occupation of Cambodia ended. Nicole's story of rescue is dramatic and I hope she will work with me to share it with readers in the future. She reunited with her brother Bernard in Saigon, where he finally arrived working on General Le Clair's staff. George's ashes were returned to France where they are interred today.

This concludes my brief biography of George Groslier. I hope this work inspires others to continue following his dream of nurturing the sacred Cambodian arts of sculpture, architecture, casting, weaving, carving, dance and music. May our shared goal be to help them flourish so that future generations will also know and appreciate the gifts and genius of the Khmer.

Le Khmérophile

On April 4, 1929, Suzanne, George, Gilbert and Bernard returned to their home in Phnom Penh while Nicole stayed in France to complete her confirmation.

The historic Groslier residence was also the home of museum director and Khmer scholar Madeleine Giteau. It is now at the corner of Preah Ang Makhak Vann (St 178) and Preah Ang Yukanthor (St 19). Hopefully this vital piece of Cambodian history will be preserved.

George Groslier
February 4, 1887 — June 18, 1945

George in his study with the family cat. This photo by Nicole is the last image of George in the family archives.

If there is a Frenchman whom destiny seems purposely to have selected to become a link between Cambodia and France — one of those bonds of mind and heart that no one, whatever his politics, can permit himself to denounce — that Frenchman's name is George Groslier.

Governor Penn Nouth of Phnom Penh
Inaugurating rue George Groslier
October 4, 1946

There is no longer a rue Groslier... but Nehru, Mao Zedong, and Tito figure in the urban legends provided on city maps. The palace and the arts school still grace the skyline.

Penny Edwards
Cambodge
2007

Of this absolute Beauty she is the sole pure expression, with no tyranny, war, or blood behind it... She is all the poetry, charm, and enchantment of this people, their most distinctive work.... Alone, she returns from the past to offer us her flower, while all else about her crumbles....

George Groslier
Danseuses Cambodgiennes
1912

Charles Gravelle
September 21, 1864 - October 20, 1929.
© Copyright 2010 Charles Gravelle Association.

Charles Gravelle:
Friend of Groslier - Patron of Cambodia
By Alain Gravelle and Kent Davis

The peaceful medieval town of Courtenay lies about 120 km southeast of Paris in the Loiret Department of France. It was there at 5AM on September 21, 1864 that Lucien Darnis-Gravelle and Marie-Marguerite Lechesne gave birth to a son they named Charles Jules Paul Darnis-Gravelle.

The history of his youth isn't clear. Records show that Charles Darnis-Gravelle studied law and registered as a lawyer in Paris. He never practiced and what happened within the family at that time is a bit of a mystery.

At this time, the family records indicate that the father exhausted his own wealth and that of his wife. Charles felt obligated to provide for the family's needs and decided to head to the French Colonies to earn a living. This is why he shortened his name to Charles Gravelle, with his brother Henri and sister Lucie following his example.

Throughout his life many close friends never knew his full name. By then in his early twenties, Charles received a fortuitous employment commitment from the Bank of Indochina (*Banque de l'Indochine*). This international venture was established ten years earlier, on January 21, 1875, to provide financial services in Cochin-china (South Vietnam) and Pondicherry (the French East Indies). Later that year the bank opened a branch in Saigon.[1]

The bank's objective was increasing monetary stability in French Indochina, which it accomplished through its authorization to create a local currency called the "piastre." Piastre notes and coins were valued on a silver standard until 1920, when they were pegged to the French franc. The coins were struck in Paris and England while notes were printed in Asia. The currency was in circulation from 1880 to 1952, replacing the French franc for commerce in Cambodia, the Thai *tikal* in Laos and the *dong* in Vietnam.

---

1. Pohl, Manfred, and Sabine Freitag. 1994. Handbook on the history of European banks. Aldershot, Hants, England: E. Elgar (ISBN 9781852789190).

One piastre coin struck in Paris, 1897.

Charles' new employer arranged passage to Cambodia by ship. The ship had just passed the tip of south India near Ceylon (now Sri Lanka) when he received a cable; the bank director in Pondicherry had died unexpectedly. Charles was directed to disembark to assume those responsibilities. His new position allowed Charles ample leisure time during which he began studying Hindu art. He also bought a high quality camera and began his lifelong passion for photography. He continued this independent research throughout his life publishing several books on art, finance and Asian culture.

It is uncertain exactly what year the Bank of Indochina transferred Charles from Pondicherry to a new position in Haiphong, Tonkin, in what is now northern Vietnam. What is certain is that the bank's Haiphong branch was established in 1885 followed by Hanoi in 1886. Charles had become involved in this venture at an ideal time; between 1885 and 1914 the bank opened 17 more branches throughout China and Southeast Asia. [2]

In fact, Charles' specific duties included establishing new bank branches to the south in Phnom Penh, Cambodia (1890) and Tourane (1891). One photo of Charles in his Haiphong apartment states that he is 27 years old which puts him there in 1891. Shortly thereafter, his base moved to Tourane (now called Danang). It was there that he was appointed head of the new bank branch in Phnom Penh, a position he held until his death. Initially, he commuted between Tourane and Phnom Penh but he finally established his permanent home in Cambodia where he started a family.

An energetic worker, Charles devoted business hours to bank duties while writing several books in his leisure time. He used his actual name for books relating to official functions, such as his 1915 work *La*

---

2. Ibid.

Valeur du Cambodge: étude économique, which was published in Phnom-Penh by the Protectorate Press. If the content held was in potential conflict with his bank duties, social position or family relations he published under different pseudonyms, primarily Paul Lechesne, which combined his middle name with his mother's maiden name. (See end of article for a list of works)

Appearing in various periodicals including the *Délégué de l'Alliance Française* and the journal of the EFEO *(Ecole Française d'Extrême-Orient)*, of which Charles was a member, his works demonstrated a deep understanding of Cambodian people, economy, politics and culture. His viewpoint, however, was decidedly outside the typically narrow colonial milieu, for which he had little regard. Charles focused on people and institutions that he respected within the Cambodian Protectorate, befriending those he held to be honest and whom he saw making positive contributions to the nation.

His views resonated with an organization founded in Paris in 1907 by Louis Delaporte, Louis Finot, Paul Doumer and others. It was called the Angkor Society for the Conservation of Ancient Monuments of Indochina (*la Société d'Angkor pour la conservation des monuments anciens d'Indochine*). In 1906, Cambodia attracted tremendous attention in France after the appearance of King Sisowath and the Royal Ballet at the Colonial Exposition in Marseilles. This interest prompted these prominent archaeologists, historians and explorers to join together in their effort to study and protect the Khmer legacy.

H.M. King Sisowath was the Society's patron in Cambodia, and Charles became a founding member. Base on their friendship, the king later helped Charles establish and operate his own educational foundation, the Society for the Protection of Children of Cambodia (*Société de Protection de l'Enfance du Cambodge*). Another early Society member was Jean Commaille, a painter and draftsman who originally came to Indochina with the French Foreign Legion. After he was discharged, Jean was painting at Angkor in 1898 when the Civil Service began hiring him for a series of jobs. In March 1908 he was officially appointed as Angkor's first conservator and he began the endless task of clearing brush and trees from hundreds of Khmer temples. In 1912, he published one of the area's first guidebooks, *Guide aux ruines d'Angkor*.[3]

---

3. Edwards, *Cambodge*, pp. 138-139.

In 1910, a new arrival named George Groslier came to Phnom Penh on an educational mission for the French government. The young man, then 23 years old, was actually returning to his birthplace: in 1887, he became the first Cambodian-born French child, but his mother quickly took him back to France in 1889 to escape the hot climate. George pursued his formal education in France aspiring to become an artist but, as fate turned out, he was destined to return to Cambodia. George joined the Society and admired the well-educated bank director who extended his friendship and guidance.

Charles encouraged George's passion for Cambodian culture and helped him meet the right people in Phnom Penh. The men also shared a fascination with Cambodian dance along with a third Society member, Roland Meyer, who later published his own historical novel relating to dance; *Saramani, danseuse Cambodgienne*. In 1910, George initiated his landmark study of Cambodian dance that was published in Paris in 1913 as *Danseuses Cambodgiennes anciennes et modernes*. In addition to penning the book's Foreword, Charles played a key role helping George with social, artistic and logistical arrangements. It seems logical that Charles' personal relationship with H.M. Sisowath and his position with the Bank of Indochina may have enhanced George's access to both palace dance events and even the priceless crowns and jewels he examined in making his sketches.

By 1911, Charles had become the Society's president in Cambodia, frequently traveling to Angkor with George, Roland and architect Henri Marchal to see fellow-member Jean at work clearing the temples. George completed his first Cambodian assignment in 1912 and returned to France where he also arranged publication of his first book, *Danseuses Cambodgiennes*. In April 1913, he returned to Cambodia for more adventures with Charles and his friend until June 1914 when World War I interrupted their camaraderie. George returned to France to serve in the balloon corps and didn't return to Cambodia until May 1917.

While George was in Europe, tragedy struck on April 30, 1916; Jean had set out from his home in Siem Reap to take the weekly payroll to laborers clearing brush at Angkor Thom. He was shot by robbers and died that day at the age of 48. His Khmer style crypt remains at the southwest corner of the Bayon.[4]

---

4. Ibid., p. 141.

Charles Gravelle with his portrait by George Groslier

Henri Marchal soon became the new conservator and the remaining Society members continued sharing their ideas and research. By the 1920s, Charles was well-known for his scholarship as well as his respect for Khmer culture and people. He was often called to accompany prestigious visitors to the country, for example when he accompanied Marshal Joffre on his journey to Angkor in 1922.

Based on explorations with his friends, Charles published four lectures on Angkor in 1921 titled *Quatre conférences sur Angkor, par Charles Gravelle*. These were reissued in 1923 to coincide with a conference of the French Alliance *(l'alliance française)* in which Charles was a delegate representing Cambodia. Despite his numerous publications many of his works and photos remain unpublished to this day.

Paintings of Gratitude and Love

As George completed his artistic study of the dance for *Danseuses Cambodgiennes anciennes et modernes* he expressed his gratitude to his friend Charles Gravelle with a near life-sized portrait dated August 1911. But it was "*Danseuse dorée (Rôle religieux)*" [5] — the dramatic painting appearing on the cover of this new edition — that revealed a most amazing story in 2010, nearly a century after George Groslier painted it.

In 1911, a 21-year-old girl dancing under the name Mali (which means Jasmine in Khmer) was a premiere ballerina with the royal troupe. Her actual name was Ratt Poss. Charles Gravelle had admired Cambodian ballet performances for many years, having even seen the troupe perform on their first visit to France in 1906. When George began his study of the dance Charles was happy to assist, apparently helping with the arrangements that allowed George to paint a full moon performance with Mali in the starring role.

George completed the canvas in 1911, taking it to France in 1912. The subject of the painting, however, was not recorded in the 1913 edition. From Groslier family archives, we see the painting in George's Paris studio in 1913 and once again in 1916, hanging on the wall of his family home in Marseille. Then, it disappeared from history — none of the Groslier family knew where it had gone.

---

5. "Golden dancer (Religious role)."

Danseuse dorée in George's Paris studio - 1913.

George's wife Suzanne and mother Angelina in the Groslier's Marseille salon in 1916 with *Danseuse dorée* at far right, behind a Buddha.

Gravelle family portrait, 1927. From the left: Monique Darnis-Gravelle, who became a nun in the order of the Sisters of Providence and is still living in France. Sharing her chair is Bernard (1924-1932). By his mother is Daniel (1920-1969), father of Alain Gravelle who is now director of the Charles Gravelle Association. Ratt Poss is seated with her newborn Denys (1927-1981). The young man standing at the right is Jean (1919-2000). Finally we have Charles with Thierry (1926-1948) in his lap, who would be killed by the Viet-Minh. Charles' sister Lucie and brother Henri are seen in the two paintings at the top of the photo.
© Copyright 2010 Charles Gravelle Association.

In April 2010, Charles' grandson, Alain Gravelle saw a draft of the cover of this new edition on the Internet and contacted editor Kent Davis with an amazing revelation: "My grandmother's picture is on the cover of your new book!" It seems that on January 24, 1923, Charles fulfilled more than a decade of admiration for this girl by marrying Ratt Poss in Phnom Penh.

As the photo shows, the Gravelle family grew quickly in the 1920's. Charles provided well for his own children and even started a

Charles Gravelle's tomb made from marble from *la montagne de marbre* in Danang, Vietnam near Charles' plantation. During the Khmer Rouge era, his grave — like those of most foreigners — was desecrated, looted and destroyed.
© Copyright 2010 Charles Gravelle Association.

foundation caring for abandoned children of mixed French-Cambodia descent. He continued managing a tea plantation in Tourane and bought a home in France at Talloires on Lake d'Annecy, Haute-Savoie. In the French home he supported his brother Henri and sister Lucie as they oversaw the studies of his children Jean and Daniel.

To the end of his life, Charles continued seeking new ways to open up international trade in Cambodia. On October 20, 1929, just a month after his 65th birthday, Charles died in Phnom Penh and was buried in the French cemetery.

Her love for her husband stayed with Ratt Poss throughout her life as a Buddhist. Towards the end she made a touching decision: she converted to Catholicism in order to "find Charles in the heaven." Ratt Poss, royal dancer, mother and loyal wife passed away on June 21, 1959. Instead of being cremated, as is the Cambodian custom, she chose to be buried in a Catholic ceremony like her husband, who died thirty years earlier.

Today, this book honors the sacred dance art Ratt Poss performed and it is poetically appropriate that her image graces its cover. As for the painting, George gave it to Charles and Ratt after World War I, perhaps on the occasion of their marriage. The painting remained in Cambodia until 1975, when it again returned to France. This painting is now owned by the children of Annette Darnis-Gravelle.

Charles Gravelle's life touched many of the greatest people who shaped Indochina. With the help of his friends, including King Sisowath and the *Sœurs de la Charité*, he founded the *Société de Protection de l'Enfance* and the *Fondation Charles Gravelle* to give care and hope to children abandoned in their own birth country. Today the work of Charles and Ratt continues through the efforts of the Charles Gravelle Foundation (www.fondation-charles-gravelle.org), dedicated to helping Cambodian children, and the Borann Foundation (www.borann.org) devoted to preserving and promoting Cambodian culture, especially classical dance.

Selected Works of Charles Gravelle

Published as Charles Gravelle:

Enquête sur la question des métis (1913).

Les métis et l'œuvre de la protection de l'enfance au Cambodge (1913).

Pondichéry et ses environs (1920).

Le Cambodge: Deux conférences (1921).

Quatre conférences sur Angkor (4 livrets - 1921).

Gingi, suprême solitude (1921).

Angkor. Les impressions de Monsieur Joseph Prudhomme (1921).

L'art Annamite (1925).

Published as Paul Lechesne:

Le devoir de la France en Indochine (1904), Bibliothèque de la Société des études coloniales et maritimes. France, s.n.

Notations lointaines; Indochine: réflexions (1905), *actualités* (1906), *possibilités économiques* (1906/1907). Paris: Librairie mondiale.

L'Annam, avril 1923 : agriculture, commerce ; le Laos assassin ; le crédit possible ; la question chinoise ; en parcourant le budget de 1923 ; dans l'ordre moral ; conclusion ; commentaire du rapport eéconomique de l'Annam pour 1923 ; recours aux statistiques ; le pétrole; le problème des étoffes. Quinhon (Annam): Imprimerie de Quinhon.

Loti revient à Angkor : Victor Hugo salue les ruines (1921). Quinhon (Annam): Impr. de Quinhon.

L'Indochine seconde: régions Moïs : Kontoum – Darlac (1924). Quinhon (Annam): Impr. de Quinhon.

Les Moïs du centre indochinois (1925). Quinhon (Annam): Impr. de Quinhon.

Timeline: Groslier Contemporaries in Khmer Studies

In the course of his life George Groslier associated with many individuals who shaped the art and culture of Cambodia. Some of the people below (all French, except as noted) were relevant to this study of Cambodian dance, while others are cited for connections to the author's life.

Note that this list is ordered by birth date. The "GG" column shows the birth year relative to George Groslier's in 1887: the goal is to give readers the perspective of understanding these people as the author's seniors, peers or juniors.

Portrait of George Groslier in his office by Martin Hürlimann, 1928.

NAME	LIFESPAN	GG	NOTES
Ernest Marie Louis Doudart de Lagrée	Mar 31, 1823 Mar 12, 1868	+64	Naval officer, explorer, French Rep. in Cambodge Apr 1863-July 1866.
Léon Feer	1830-1902	+57	Sanskrit & Pali linguist
Auguste Barth	May 22, 1834 Apr 15, 1916	+53	Sanskrit & Khmer specialist
HM King Norodom	1834-1904	+53	King of Cambodia 1860-1904
Henry Andre Groslier	1838-?	+49	GG's paternal grandfather
Abel Bergaigne	Aug 31, 1838 Aug 6, 1888	+49	Sanskrit scholar
Marie Joseph Francis Garnier	Jul 25, 1839 Dec 21, 1873	+48	Explorer
François-Auguste-René Rodin	Nov 12, 1840 Nov 17, 1917	+47	Artist
Louis Delaporte	Jan 11, 1842 May 3, 1925	+45	Explorer
HM Preah Bat Sisowath	Sep 7, 1840 Aug 9, 1927	+47	King of Cambodia 1904-1927

Marie Jeanne Eugenie Espirat	1843-1919	+44	GG's paternal grandmother
Étienne Aymonier	Jan 2, 1844 Jan 21, 1929	+43	Colonial officer, Khmer & Cham scholar
Albert Maignan	Oct 14, 1845 Sep 29, 1908	+42	Painter, historical illustrator & GG's art teacher
Pierre Loti	Jan 14, 1850 Jun 10, 1923	+37	Naval officer, writer
Son Diep	1855-1934	+32	Cambodian Statesman
Antoine George Groslier	April 16, 1856 Dec 14, 1928	+31	GG's father
Joseph Athanase Paul Doumer	Mar 22, 1857 May 7, 1932	+30	GGI 1897-1902, Statesman
Solomon Reinach	Aug 29, 1858 Nov 4, 1932	+29	Archeologist
Helen Churchill Candee	Oct 5, 1859 Aug 23, 1949	+28	American writer
Étienne-Edmond Lunet De Lajonquière	1861-?	+26	EFEO explorer
Thiounn Sambath	1864-1950	+23	Cambodian Statesman
Louis Finot	1864-1935	+23	Archaeologist, EFEO Director
Charles Gravelle	Sep 21, 1864 Oct 20, 1929	+23	Bank of Indochina Director, husband of royal dancer Ratt Poss
Angelina Sidonie Legrand	1865-1925	+22	GG's mother
Jean Commaille	1868 Apr 30, 1916	+19	Soldier, 1st Angkor conservator
Paul Claudel	Aug 6, 1868 Feb 23, 1955	+19	Poet, dramatist, diplomat
Charles Carpeaux	1870-1904	+17	Photographer
Pierre Mathieu Thédore Guesde	May 9, 1870 1955	+17	Colonial officer, father of author Makhali-Phal
Henri Parmentier	Jan 3, 1871 Feb 22, 1949	+17	Archaeologist
Albert Pierre Sarraut	Jul 28, 1872 Nov 26, 1962	+15	GGI 1912-1919, champion of Cambodia's national museum
Georges Maspero	Aug 21, 1872 Sep 21, 1942	+15	Colonial officer, EFEO member, Khmer linguist

HM Preah Bat Sisowath Monivong	Dec 27, 1875 Apr 24, 1941	+13	King of Cambodia 1927-41
Henri Marchal	Jun 24, 1876 Apr 12, 1970	+11	Architect, Angkor Conservator, father of Sappho Marchal
Lucille Sinclair Douglass	1878-1935	+9	American artist at Angkor, illustrator for Helen Candee
Auguste André Silice	Feb 11, 1880 Dec 1951	+7	Painter, GG successor as National Museum curator - 1935
Jean Despujols	Mar 19, 1886- Jan 26, 1965	+1	Prix de Rome-winning artist
George Cœdès	1886-1969	+1	Historian, Khmer Epigrapher, EFEO Director
GEORGE GROSLIER	**Feb 4, 1887 Jun 18, 1945**		**Artist, author, archaeologist & historian**
Jean Charles Jules Albert Stoeckel	Sept 12, 1888 ?	-2	GG friend & museum associate
Roland-Théodore-Emile Meyer	July 10, 1889 ?	-2	Author, Khmer & Lao linguist, historian
Ratt Poss	1890 Jun 21, 1959	-3	Royal dancer, married Charles Gravelle - 1923
Suzanne Karpeles	1890-1969	-3	Royal Library curator, Buddhist scholar
Suzanne Cecile Poujade	June 8, 1893 1979	-6	GG wife, wed May 27, 1916
Martin Hürlimann	Nov 12, 1897 Mar 4, 1984	-10	Swiss photographer
Makhali Phāl [Nelly-Pierette Guesde]	1898-1965	-11	Franco-Khmer author, daughter of Pierre Guesde
André Malraux	Nov 3, 1901 Nov 23, 1976	-14	Khmer temple looter, author, politician
Sappho Marchal	1904-1990?	-17	Artist, author
Bảo Đại	Oct 22, 1913 July 30, 1997	-26	Last ruler of Annam's Nguyễn Dynasty
Marguerite Duras	Apr 4, 1914 Mar 3, 1996	-27	Author
Madeleine Giteau	1918-2005	-31	Historian, museum director
Nicole Rea Groslier	June 15, 1918 Present	-31	GG's daughter
Gilbert Groslier	Sep 8, 1922 July 16, 2002	-35	GG's son
Norodom Sihanouk	Oct 31, 1922 Present	-37	King & leader of Cambodia
Bernard-Philippe Groslier	May 10, 1926 May 29, 1986	-39	GG's son

The Ernest Simon in Saigon from the Poujade family collection.

Groslier Family Voyages

The *Compagnie des Messageries Maritimes* began offering steamship transport to key French cargo and passenger destinations in 1835. In the age before air travel, its ships provided the only practical link between France and Indochina. Like other French residents in Asia, the Groslier family were frequent passengers on the roughly three-week-long route between Marseille and Saigon. The two World Wars disrupted travel and endangered lives. Here are the fates of a few ships that carried the Grosliers:

Angers: Awarded to France as WWI reparations.
Ernest Simon: Requisitioned as a WWI mail ship. Sunk in Mediterranean, 1917.
Magellan: Torpedoed, Dec 11, 1916.
Paul Lecat: Burned in Marseille, 1928.
General Metzinger: Bombed and sunk in Le Havre Roads, 1940.
Porthos: Sunk at Casablanca during allied landings, 1942.
D'Artagnan: Sunk by US submarine under Japanese flag, February 22, 1944.
Jean Laborde: Scuttled by retreating Germans in Marseille. 1944.

Route	Boat	Date	Details
Marseille Saigon	?	1885	Antoine & Angéline Groslier
Phnom Penh		1887, Feb 4	George Groslier born
Saigon Marseille	Shamrock	1889	George and his mother
Marseille		1906, Apr-Nov	Exposition coloniale
Marseille Saigon	Ernest Simon	1910	George
Saigon Marseille	Amazone	1912	George
Paris		1913	Danseuse Cambodgiennes published
Marseille Saigon	Paul Lecat	1913, April 1	George
Saigon Marseille	Magellan	1914, June	George
Marseille		1916, May 27	George & Suzanne wed
Brest Arkangelsk	Catherine II	1916, Oct 10 Oct 24	George
Murmansk-Oslo Liverpool	?	1917, Feb ? 1917, Mar 2	George
Marseille Saigon	Porthos	1917, April 29 May 24	George & Suzanne
Phnom Penh		1918, June 15	Nicole born
Saigon Marseille	Amazone	1920, Aug 27 Sep 25	George, Suzanne, Nicole, Sèk
Marseille Saigon	Paul Lecat	1921, April 30 May 30	George, Suzanne, Nicole, Sèk
Marseille		1922, Apr-Nov	Exposition nationale coloniale
Phnom Penh		1922, Sep 8	Gilbert born
Saigon Marseille	Porthos	1924, July 26 Aug 21	George, Suzanne (?), Nicole, Gilbert, Pok

Route	Boat	Date	Details
Marseille Saigon	Paul Lecat	1925, Feb 26 Mar 21	George, Suzanne, Nicole, Gilbert, Pok
Phnom Penh		*1926, May 10*	*Bernard-Philippe born*
Saigon Marseille	André Lebon	1928, May 1 May 27	Suzanne, Nicole, Gilbert, Bernard and Thi Sao
Saigon Marseille	Angers	1928, July 23 Aug 18	George (following the family)
Paris		*1929, Feb 14*	*George's Cambodian dance lecture at La Sorbonne*
Marseille Saigon	Athos II	1929, Mar 8 April 2	George, Suzanne, Nicole, Gilbert, Bernard & Thi Sao
Saigon Marseille	D'Artagnan	1929, Sep 17 Oct 12	Suzanne, Gilbert, Bernard and Ba
Phnom Penh		*1929, Oct 20*	*Charles Gravelle dies*
Saigon Marseille	D'Artagnan	1930, Dec 1 1931, Jan 9	George (following the family)
Paris		*1931, May-Nov*	*Exposition Coloniale Int'l*
Marseille Saigon	General Metzinger	1931, Oct 23 Nov 17	George & Ba return trip
Marseille, Aden, Penang, Saigon	André Lebon	1932, Aug 26 Sep 20	Suzanne, Nicole, Gilbert, Bernard
Saigon Marseille	D'Artagnan	1935, June 9 July 4	George, Suzanne, Nicole, Gilbert, Bernard
Marseille Saigon	Jean Laborde	1936, Aug 7 Sep 6	George
Marseille Saigon	D'Artagnan	1937, Nov 26 Dec 22	Suzanne, Nicole, Bernard
Saigon Marseille	D'Artagnan	1939, June July	Suzanne, Bernard
Phnom Penh		*1945, June 18*	*George executed by Japanese*
Phnom Penh		*1946, Oct 4*	*Mayor Penn Nouth dedicates Rue George Groslier*

The Works of George Groslier

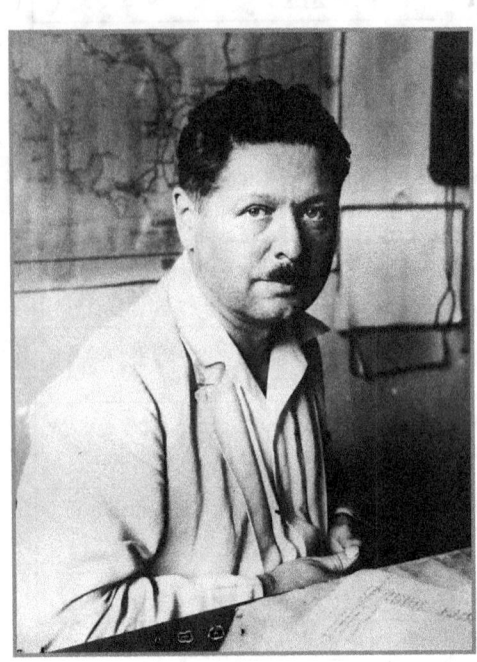

George Groslier in his office - 1928.
Photo Martin Hürlimann.

George Groslier was a passionate, creative and prolific artist with many talents. First trained as a fine artist under the master Albert Maignan in Paris, George returned to his Cambodian birthplace where he devoted his life to documenting, promoting, safeguarding and celebrating Khmer art, history and culture.

He expressed himself visually as a painter, imaginatively as a writer and intellectually as an archaeologist and essayist promoting the restoration and preservation of Khmer patrimony. He infused his works with a love, respect and sensitivity for his subjects that makes him a pleasure to read to this day.

Books

- *La Chanson d'un Jeune.* Self-published. 1904.
- *Danseuses cambodgiennes anciennes et modernes.* Paris : A. Challamel, 1913.
- *A l'ombre d'Angkor; notes et impressions sur les temples inconnus de l'ancien Cambodge, avec 16 photographies inédits d'après les clichés de l'auteur et une carte itinéraire.* Paris : A. Challamel, 1913.
- *Angkor...Ouvrage orné de 103 gravures et de 5 cartes et plans.* Paris: H. Laurens, 1924.
- *Directeur-fondateur et éditeur de Arts et Archéologie khmères, 2 vol.* Paris : A. Challamel, 1921-1926.
- *Recherches sur les Cambodgiens d'après les textes et les monuments depuis les premiers siècles de notre ère.* Paris : A. Challamel, 1921.
- *Arts et Archéologie Khmers. Revue des Recherches sur les Art, les Monuments et l'Ethnographie du Cambodge, depuis les Origines jusqu'à nos Jours.* Paris: Société d' Editions Géographiques, Maritimes et Coloniales, 1925.
- *La sculpture Khmère ancienne ; illustrée de 175 reproductions hors texte en similigravure.* Paris : G. Crès, 1925.
- *Les collections khmères du Musée Albert Sarraut à Phnom-Penh.* Paris: G. van Oest, 1931.
- *Eaux et lumières; journal de route sur le Mékong cambodgien.* Paris: Société d'éditions

- géographiques, maritimes et coloniales, 1931.
- *L'enseignement et la mise en pratique des arts indigènes au Cambodge (1918-1930)*. Paris: Sté d'éditions géographiques, maritimes et coloniales, 1931.
- *Angkor, with 103 illustrations, 5 maps and plans. Translated from the French by Paule Fercoq Du Leslay*. Evreux: impr. Hérissey, 1933.
- *Ankooru iseki*. Japanese translation of *Angkor*. Tokyo: Shinkigensha, 1943.

Novels
- *La Route du plus fort.* Paris, Emile-Paul frères, 1926. Reissued by Kailash in 1994 (ISBN 2-909052-52-4).
- *Le Retour à l'argile.* Paris : Emile-Paul frères, 1928. Reissued by Kailash in 1994 1994. (ISBN 2-909052-49-4).
- *Monsieur de la Garde, roi. Roman, inspiré des chroniques royales du Cambodge.* Paris: L'Illustration, 1934.
- *Les Donneurs de Sang, Phnom Penh et Saigon.* Saigon : Albert Portail, 1941.

Graphic Works
- *Les Ruines d'Angkor.* Indochine, 1911.

Archeological Publications
- "Objets anciens trouvés au Cambodge". *Revue archéologique*, 1916, 5e Série, vol. 4, pp. 129-139.
- "La batellerie cambodgienne du VIIIe au XIIIe siècles". *Revue archéologique*, 1917, 5e Série, vol. 5, pp. 198-204.
- "Objets cultuels en bronze dans l'ancien Cambodge." *Arts et Archéologie khmers*, 1921-3, vol. 1, fasc. 3, pp. 221-228.
- "Le temple de Phnom Chisor." Ibid, vol. 1, fasc. 1, p"p. 65-81.
- "Le temple de Ta Prohm (Ba Ti)". Ibid, vol. 1.. fasc. 2, pp. 139-148.
- "Le temple de Preah Vihear". Ibid, 1921-1922, vol. 1. fasc. 3, pp. 275-294.
- "Essai sur l'architecture classique khmère". *Arts et Archéologie khmers*, 1923, vol. 1, fasc. 3. pp. 229-273.
- "L'art khmèr". Paris, *Arts et Décoration*, août 1923. vol. 27. N° 260, pp. 34-40.
- "L'art du bronze au Cambodge". *Arts et Archéologie khmers*, 1923. vol. 1, fasc., pp. 413-423.
- "L'Art khmèr". Paris, *Arts et Décoration*, August 1923, vol. 1, pp. 413-423.
- "Amarendrapura dans Amoghapura". *Bulletin de l'Ecole Française d'Extrême-Orient*, Hanoï, 1924, vol. 24, pp. 359-372.
- *Angkor, Les Villes d'Art célèbres*. Paris, Laurens, 1924.
- *Catalogue du Musée de Phnom Penh*. Hanoï, IDEO, 1924.
- "La céramique dans l'ancien Cambodge". *Arts et Archéologie khmers*, 1924, vol. 2, fasc. 1, pp. 31-64.
- "La vie à Angkor au XIe siècle". Saigon, *Pages Indochinoises*, 15-1-1924, N.S., vol. 1, pp. 9-17.
- "Les empreintes du 'Pied du Buddha' d'Angkor Vat". *Arts et Archéologie khmers*, 1924, vol. 2, fasc. 2. pp. 65-80.
- "La région d'Angkor". *Arts et Archéologie khmers*, 1924, vol. 2, fasc. 2, pp. 113-130.

- "La région du Nord-Est du Cambodge et son art". Ibid., pp. 131-141.
- "L'Asram Maha Rosei" *Arts et Archéologie khmers*, 1924, vol. 2. fasc. 2. pp. 141-146.
- "L'Art hindou au Cambodge". *Arts et Archéologie khmers*, 1924. vol. 2, fasc. 1, pp. 81-93.
- "Essai sur le Buddha khmèr". Ibid, pp. 93-112.
- "Sur les origines de l'Art khmèr". *Mercure de France*, 1-xii-1924, vol. 176, N° 365, pp. 382-404.
- "Les influences grecques au Cambodge et l'art pré khmèr". Paris, *L'Art Vivant*, 1925.
- "Sur la route d'Angkor : le Prasat Phum Prasat". Saigon, *Extrême-Asie*, déc. 1925, N° 14, vol. 12, pp. 493-494.
- "Introduction à l'étude des arts khmèrs". *Arts et Archéologie khmers*, 1925, vol. 2. fasc. 2, pp. 167-234.
- "La femme dans la sculpture khmère ancienne". Paris, *Revue des Arts asiatiques*, 1925, vol. 2, fasc. 1, pp. 35-41.
- "La fin d'Angkor". Saigon, *Extrême-Asie*, Sept. 1925.
- "Note sur la sculpture khmère ancienne". Hanoï, *Études asiatiques*, *École Française d'Extrême-Orient*, 1925. vol. I, pp. 297-314.
- "A propos d'art hindou et d'art khmèr". *Arts et Archéologie khmers*, 1926, vol. 2, fasc. 3, pp. 329-348.
- "Les collections khmères du Musée Albert Sarraut". *Ars Asiatica*, XVI, Paris, G. Van Oest, 1931.
- "Les Temples inconnus du Cambodge". Paris, *Toute la terre*, June 1931.
- *Angkor, Les Villes d'Art célèbres*. Paris. Laurens, 1932 (English translation).
- "Troisième recherche sur les Cambodgiens". *Bulletin de l'Ecole Française d'Extrême-Orient*, Hanoi, 1935, vol. 35, pp. 159-206.
- "Une merveilleuse cité khmère. Banteai Chhma, ville ancienne du Cambodge". Paris, *L'Illustration*, April 3, 1937, N° 4909, pp. 352-357.
- "Les Monuments khmers sont-ils des tombeaux?" Saigon. Bulletin de la Société des Eudes Indochinoises.1941, N.S., vol. 16. N°1 pp. 121-126.

Publications on the Indigenous Arts of Cambodia

- "La Convalescence des Arts cambodgiens". Hanoï, *Revue Indochinoise*, Imprimerie d'Extrême-Orient, 2e sem. 1918, p. 207; 1er sem. 1919, pp. 871-890, 22 p. ill. p. 16, fig. 21.
- "L'agonie des Arts cambodgiens". Hanoï, *Revue Indochinoise*, 2e sem. 1918, p.207.
- "Question d'art indigène". Hué, *Bulletin des Amis du Vieux-Hué*, Oct.-Dec. déc. 1920, pp. 444-452.
- "Étude sur la psychologie de l'artisan cambodgien". *Arts et Archéologie khmers*, 1921, vol. 1, fasc. 2, pp. 125-137.
- "Seconde étude sur la psychologie de l'artisan cambodgien". *Arts et Archéologie khmers*, 1921, vol. 1. fasc. 2, pp. 205-220.
- "Royal Dancers of Cambodia". *Asia*, 1922, vol. 22, N° 1, pp. 47-55, 74-75.
- "Soixante-seize dessins cambodgiens tracés par l'oknha Tep Nimit Mak et l'oknha Reachna Prasor Mao, Arts et Archéologie khmers". Paris: *Société d'Edition Géographique, Maritime et Coloniale*, 1923. 331-386 p.
- "The Oldest Living Monarch". *Asia*, 1923. vol. 23. pp. 587-589.
- "La reprise des arts khmèrs". *La Revue de Paris*, Nov. 15, 1925. pp. 395-422.

- "Avec les danseuses royales du Cambodge". Mercure de France, May 1, 1928, pp. 536-565.
- "La mort de S.M. Sisowath". *L'Illustration*, Oct. 1927.
- "Les cérémonies d'incinérations de S.M. Sisowath". *L'Illustration*, April 1928. 86è année, n°4443. Samedi 28 Avril 1928. pp. 410-415.
- "Die Kunst der Kambodschanischen tànzerinn". Munich, *Atlantis*, Jan.-Mar. 1929, vol. 1, pp. 10-16.
- "Die Tanzerinnen des Konigs". [Miscellanea], p 16. 2 plates (1 col.) *Atlantis*, Jan 1929.
- "Le théâtre et la danse au Cambodge". Paris, *Journal Asiatique*, Jan.-Mar. 1929. vol. 214, pp. 125-143. (See Appendix for English translation)
- "Contemporary Cambodian art studied in the Light of the Past Forms". Boston, *Eastern Art*, 1930. vol. 2, pp. 127-141.
- "La Direction des Arts cambodgiens et l'École des Arts cambodgiens". Saigon, *Extrême-Asie*, March 1930, N° 45, pp. 119-127.
- "La fin d'un art". Paris, *Revue des Arts Asiatiques*, 1929-1930, vol. 6, fasc. 3., pp. 176-186; p. 184 et 251, fasc. 4, pp. 244-254.
- "La fin d'une tradition d'art : les pagodes cambodgiennes et le ciment armé". *L'Illustration*, January 11, 1930, vol. 175, pp. 50-53.
- "De Pagode en Pagode". Paris. *Toute la Terre*, July 1931.
- "L'Orfèvrerie cambodgienne à l'Exposition Coloniale". Paris, *La Perle*, 1931.
- "Rapport sur les arts indigènes au Cambodge". Congrès International et Intercolonial de la Société Indigène, Paris. 1931.
- "L'Enseignement et la mise en pratique des Arts indigènes au Cambodge". *Bulletin de Académie des Sciences Coloniales*, Paris, 1931.
- "Les Arts indigènes au Cambodge". *Exp. int. des Arts et Techniques*, Indochine Française, Paris, 1937.
- "Les Arts indigènes au Cambodge". 10th *Congress of the Far-Eastern Association of Tropical Medicine*, Hanoi, 1938, pp. 161-181.

Narratives
- "Propos sur la maison coloniale". Saigon, *Extrême-Asie*, 3° trim. 1926, pp. 2-10; March 1927, pp. 307-366.
- "Le Singe qui montre la Lanterne magique". Saigon, *Extrême-Asie*, Feb. 1928, pp. 347-366; mars 1928, pp. 435-450; avril 1928, pp. 499-505; mai 1928, pp. 546-554.
- "C'est une idylle...". Paris, *Mercure de France*, July 1929.
- *La Mode masculine aux colonies*. Paris : Adam, 1931.
- "Nos boys". Saigon, *Extrême-Asie*, August 1931, N° 55, pp. 69-76.

Two Cambodian dancers portray female and male roles in Marseille, 1906.

Appendix II

The Cambodian Dancers in France
George Bois
Hanoi–Haiphong — 1913
Imprimerie D'Extrême Orient

The die is cast. In 1916 Marseille will hold a Colonial Exposition. How can the announcement not recall the splendor of the 1906 Exposition, where Indochina triumphed? But these are past splendors, for the ancient Phocaean city will never again host such a showing from our colony. True, the riches and art will be still be on display, but the thing that put a smile on every face last time — namely, the light grace of the Cambodian dancers — will be missing. Before the new show eclipses the previous one, let me evoke the memory of these dancers' charming and triumphant tour of France.

This journey of theirs was a smashing success as an artistic curiosity, and it gives me infinite pleasure to say that it was my idea.

In Cambodia, talk of such a journey delighted the upper echelons of the Administration. As Head of Fine Arts and chief organizer of Indochina attractions for the Colonial Exposition of Marseille, I arrived at Phnom Penh in December 1904, spellbound by the enchanting idea of a light schooner carrying the troupe of

Before the exotic Cambodian dancers ever set foot in France postcards like this 1905 example, piqued public curiosity.

graceful ballerinas to the coasts of Provence. Moving the very hill of Phnom's public garden, complete with peaked pagoda guarded by the stone giants, seemed no bolder a proposition.

"Don't even think of it!" exclaimed Mr. Morel, Resident Superior of Cambodia. "Your idea is insane! The dancers all are daughters of governors, of high dignitaries, offered to the King out of a desire to please him and, especially, to obtain favors.... Who would escort them to France? The King wouldn't entrust them to anyone. Their dances are part of all the age-old rituals of the Court and are as essential to royal ceremonies as the Throne itself. And where would you find the considerable sum needed for such an enterprise? The appropriations of Cambodia for the Exposition of Marseille are insignificant, and the coffers of King Sisowath forbid any such munificence."

But none of these very reasonable observations could dampen my hopes. I trusted the broad mind and refined artistic sense of Mr. Beau, the Governor General. "Still," added the Superior Resident, shaken by my firmness, "far be it from me to set up obstacles. Try!" And I tried.

I went to find the Minister of the Palace, Mr. Thiounn,[1] spokesman of King Sisowath, whose knowledge of the smallest nuances of

---

1. Oknka Veâng

Cambodian protocol was in no way inferior to that of President Fallières's spokesman, and whose tact and eager friendliness would win over many hearts in Marseille and Paris.

Mr. Thiounn — who Mr. Morel said would be aghast at my proposal — flashed his fine, phlegmatic smile and replied: "For the dancers of the Palace, it is impossible, but the Minister of the Navy, Col de Monteiro, has a personal troupe. At three o'clock, I shall accompany him to the Palace of Justice. Join me there, and we will discuss your idea." Mischievously, he added: "You shall hint that he could accompany his dancers to France!"

I did not miss my appointment. Several ministers seated around a large table on a green carpet were listening attentively to a Cambodian, who was standing with an air of humility and contrition. His Excellency Col de Monteiro had a European face, recalling his Portuguese origin, and a sharp eye. On seeing me, he excused himself, as did his colleague Thiounn. We all went into a small office, and the doors were carefully closed. The thought of going to France made the old minister's eyes sparkle, and the face of the Minister of the Palace soon showed similar enthusiasm. Perhaps he too was hoping for a berth on the voyage.

Col de Monteiro had twenty dancers. "Twenty dancers! We need more!" objected Dr. Hahn, mayor of Phnom Penh and faithful friend to Norodom, who had persuaded the king to request protectorate status for Cambodia from France.

Norodom had earned considerable interest off a life annuity for buildings relinquished to France. On Norodom's death, his successor, Sisowath, had no income other than his annual government pay of 450,000 piastres. Despite his generosity, he could not support the entire troupe of dancers and had dismissed a great number, many of whom had immediately been imprisoned over debts.

On the advice of Doctor Hahn, I hastened to the prison. A militiaman on guard duty, dressed in khaki and sporting the beret of our Alpine Hunters, presented his weapon. Upstairs in the first building on the street, Oknha Réach Rong Muoug Râth, warden of the Cambodian prison, sat in the center of the room on a mat, surrounded by five or six squatting women, all smoking cigarettes. At my first proposals, Râth's old wrinkled face lit up. He promised to have a troupe roster for me that very evening, but on one irrevocable condition. We had to take him on as impresario. The warden of the Cambodian prison as impresario of a dance troupe made up of his prisoners! Could this perhaps satisfy the apparently insatiable Parisian appetite for oddities?

Leaving the prison, I scanned the courtyard, where prisoners were milling about. I saw men young and old, in sordid clothes, squatting, weighed down by chains riveted to the ground, eating rice from large communal jars. Unattended children, no doubt the prisoners' own, came to peck from the jars, like sweet little scavenging birds. A tall young man with fine features and sad eyes begged me to ask for his pardon. He had committed theft and was swearing, with persuasive gestures, never to do it again. I was touched and promised.

I had hardly returned to my home when the roster arrived, through an intermediary of the Minister of the Palace. It had been drawn up by Dr. Hahn and in France could have conveyed a rather accurate idea of the royal dances of Cambodia, but it was later abandoned.

Typical corps de ballet:[2]
    1 Krôur Lokhon (directress)
    2 Néai rongs (playing kings, princes, or chiefs)
    4 Sèna (playing army lieutenants or commanders)
    4 Philiengs (playing governors of princes)
    2 Yaks Ek (giants of the first order)
    2 Sèna Yeak Ek (lieutenants of giants of the first order)
    2 Sèna Yeak To (lieutenants of giants of the second order)

---

2. Editor's Note - While Khmer terms are used for the orchestra the actresses and chorus include many Siamese terms, substantiating the influence of Siamese instructors on the Cambodian Royal Court dance in the early 19th century.

2 Sva (monkeys)
   2 Néang Ek (queens, princesses, or women of the first order)
   4 Philiengs (governesses)
   4 Néang Komnan (followers)
   12 Khons (standard bearers and soldiers)

Chorus:
   1 Bok Krang, reader
   2 Dœum bât, principal singers
   10 Kon Krap, singers and bamboo-stick timekeepers
   6 Puoc Têng (costumers)

In total, 60 women accompanied by 10 musicians and 2 clowns.

Orchestra:
   1 Orchestra leader
   1 Skor thom (tambour)
   1 Sampho (tambourine)
   1 Ronéat Ek (a boat-shaped bamboo xylophone)
   1 Ronéat Thung (... d°...)
   1 Ronéat dèk (a boat-shaped xylophone with metal bars)
   1 Kong thom (large gong)
   1 Kong toch (small gong)
   1 Sralay nâc (high-pitched flute)
   1 Sralay nay (mid-pitched flute)

The Resident Superior, a decisive, trenchant man, rightly thought that before we proceeded we should seek the Governor General's opinion. He telegraphed Mr. Beau, now in Hanoi: "Mr. Bois, Delegate Fine Arts for Marseille Exposition, says attraction impossible without Cambodian dancers. Money short." We didn't have to wait long for the answer: Mr. Beau, who figured that the dancers would be putting on the colony's sole artistic performance, recommended finding a financial solution.

At this point Mr. Baudoin, French Resident in Kompong Cham, a province close to Phnom Penh, was named Cambodian Commissioner to the Marseille Exposition. Long known for his initiative, taste, and industry, Mr. Baudoin was the best man for the job. He was studying the question when the way was opened to a solution by the King himself. His Majesty Sisowath — like Col de Monteiro, like the prison warden — offered his corps de ballet as long as he could come along! What a coup

H. M. King Sisowath (1840-1927)

for Indochina in Marseille: the King of Cambodia with his dancers! Enthusiasm spread, and the King, with his natural expansiveness and generosity, offered to lend the gold of his coffers and his splendid jewels for display in the Cambodian pavilion's showcases at the Exposition.

The Governor General and the Minister of Colonies discussed the matter. Mr. Baudoin presented Mr. Beau with a clear and clever report laying out the expenses for such an undertaking. And one beautiful morning the elated press in Marseille announced the voyage of King Sisowath and his dancers.

A special ship carried the King, two of his Ministers (Thiounn, Minister of the Palace, Col de Monteiro, Minister of the Navy), his sons, one of Norodom's sons (Prince Sontaroth), Princess Sounpady with her oldest daughter, and the Secretary Minister (Son-Diep) to Marseille. The last two were charged specially with directing the dancers.

The troupe was composed of 42 dancers, 8 time-keepers, 8 costumers, 12 musicians, 8 readers, 2 jewelers: 80 people in total.

On the day of arrival, all of Marseille was merry. Its population was flooding Canebière[3] and the old port, feverishly awaiting the royal procession. It had been a calm voyage, but whenever the boat had listed abruptly the King had summoned the captain for a sharp reproach. He could not understand why we weren't hugging the coast the whole way.

---

3. La Canebière is the historic high street in the old quarter of Marseille. About a kilometer long, it runs from the Vieux-Port ("old port") to the Réformés quarter.

King Sisowath's procession into the town of Marseille, 1906.

In Marseille, Sisowath took up residence at the Prefecture, in the "Emperor's apartment," on the first floor. He was disappointed not to be able to keep his pretty flock of ballerinas under the same roof, as in his Palace in Phnom Penh. He was, however, reassured to learn that the Princess and her faithful secretary, Son-Diep, would stay with them and live at their side.

The staircase and the anterooms of the royal apartment saw a steady stream of suppliers, reporters, visitors, and painters, of people seeking honors or even money.

Among the Indochina pavilions of the colonial Exposition a Cambodian-style theater had been set up to receive the royal dancers, but it was soon deemed insufficient to contain the throng seeking an early peek at the sensational exhibition.

Performances took place in the evening at the Exposition's music hall. The first three nights attracted such crowds that subsequent performances were held in the open, on the terrace of the Grand Palace, overlooking the basin and the lighted fountains.

Every evening more than thirty thousand people crowded around the stage to watch the marvelous dolls, with their perfect figures, undulate, shimmering with rivulets of gold and precious stones, in the dazzle of electric lights.

It was crazy. Cambodia, its King, and his dancers dominated every conversation. Photographers swarmed the city like famished locusts. The newspapers of Paris and Marseille vied to snap the most seductive picture.

As promised, the King placed his most beautiful jewels under the protection of the Commissioner of Cambodia , whom he trusted. The diadems, bracelets, rings, chains, and cups, enriched with diamonds and precious stones, the diplomatic gifts, and the rest were worth an estimated eight hundred thousand francs.

The curious could stare in wonder at this treasure of astonishing artistic originality through a cage, which contained the showcase, which contained the jewels. The cage was closed at night and guarded by several watchmen. This was perhaps the only time in the history of the Expositions that every precious object was accounted for. Every one returned safely to Phnom Penh and the coffers of the Royal palace.

An impresario offered 200,000 francs to the Commissioner of Cambodia for 20 performances, with 30 dancers, in the capitals of Europe. Loie Fuller,[4] the great and likeable artist, also desperately wanted to exhibit some of them under the aegis of her

---

4. Loie Fuller (January 15, 1862–January 1, 1928) was an American pioneer of modern dance and theatrical lighting techniques. She achieved fame in France for performances in Paris and throughout Europe.

famous name. But they belonged to the King. They had come with him, and with him they would return. The Minister of Colonies, Mr. Georges Leygues, was luckier. He had only to say the word, and all those delicious living statuettes — so unsettling to Rodin, who saw them as animated antiquities — were piled into two coaches on the express to Paris. Mr. Leygues was too Parisian and too poetic to deprive the capital's intellectual and artistic elite of this unique spectacle. The King preceded his dancers to Paris. Nothing could shock the dancers. Neither the whistling locomotive nor its long ribbon of coaches could elicit the slightest exclamation of surprise. They dashed into the compartments like seasoned rail travelers, poked their gentle faces out the windows, and smiled placidly to friends and onlookers come to see them off.

Several of them hoisted their slender bodies into the net used for parcels and went to sleep as if in a hammock.

In Paris, they stayed in a private residence, on Avenue Malakoff, opposite the one housing the King, who was always eager to have them nearby. There was a large garden in front, amid whose thick mass of foliage sprang a fountain in a large basin, to the dancers' delight. At certain times of day they went there, in groups of four or five, to plunge their curvy figures into the crystalline water.

The residence was besieged by curiosity seekers. There were more than in Marseille, and most were officials or Parisian celebrities.

One day, the Minister of Colonies arrived unannounced. He was delighted by the mad gaiety of the pensioners, chirping like birds in an aviary, and was smitten by the beauty of some. But ministerial austerity kept him from remaining incognito very long and soon restored the dignity of his visit.

At the Elysée Palace, the dancers had only one wish, to see the President of the Republic. They scanned the room and had him pointed out.

One evening, the Minister of Colonies had the idea to exhibit the Cambodian dancers in the open air.

An open-air theater with twelve hundred seats was arranged at the Pré Catelan, a botanical garden in the Bois de Boulogne.

The Cambodian dancers performing at the Bois de Boulogne on July 10, 1906.

Imprudently, five thousand invitations were sent out. Mr. Leygues and Mr. Baudoin directed rehearsals, with the Minister himself adjusting the electric lighting and selecting the gels.[5]

On the agreed evening, all the happy ticket holders gathered at the Pré Catelan, meeting in a crush of people that was driven back by the municipal guards. The Ambassador of England was jostled. Ladies had their jewels torn off and their ensembles ripped. Those lucky enough to get in stoked the jealousy of the irritated crowd outside. Protests, catcalls, and animal cries burst out all over, drowning out the treble of the Cambodian orchestra.

Greek dances, under the direction of Mr. Gaillard from the Opéra, preceded the Cambodian dances. Meanwhile, Princess Sounpady, ignorant of protocol, naively went to shake hands with the President. An angry Mr. Mellard complained to Mr. Baudoin, who cheerfully replied that he had no control over the behavior of the fantastic and authoritative princess.

During the performance, it was Princess Sounpady's turn to be indisposed. Led to the buffet, she had a Bordeaux wine glass filled with Picon bitters[6] and downed it all in a gulp, to the amazement of the

---

5. A sheet of colored gelatin used to add color to theatrical spotlights.
6. Picon is a 78-proof (39% alcohol) caramel-colored, bitter apéritif popular in the east and north of France.

maîtres d'hôtel. Her discomfort diminished after a few moments.

She had tasted and enjoyed Picon bitters at the company's tasting stand, some fifty meters from the Cambodian pavilion at the Marseille Exposition. They had sent her a few bottles, then a few cases, which she would later carry back to Cambodia.

Once the program was over, the Minister tried to calm tempers and put an end to the outcry outside. He charged the skilful and persuasive Commissioner of Cambodia with approaching the princess and requesting a second performance, to take place immediately. She grudgingly agreed.

At midnight, their clothes in tatters, their hair a mussed up, fifteen hundred people could finally watch for themselves the show that had all Marseille and now all Paris atwitter. But how many went home disappointed!

Large carriages took the dancers to the Eiffel tower. The princess was determined to climb to the top. She descended with a pout.

The dancers returned to spend a few days in Marseille, unaware of their triumph and by no means dazzled by what they had seen. They poured out onto the train-station platform like a bevy of sparrows, their arms laden with dolls and animals of painted cardboard. Their Parisian admirers had loaded them with gifts, especially toys, which they preferred. Large horse-drawn carriages, covered with ads for mustard or elixirs, had taken them from the villa to the Exposition for their evening shows. The same carriages now returned them at top speed to the far end of the Prado, on the route de Mazargues, to the Villa des Glycines, henceforth famed as the "villa of the Cambodian dancers."

It was a modest house with one upper floor, surrounded by a high wall with a gate on the avenue, and guarded by two policemen. It had been chosen for its proximity to the Exposition and its distance from the city, so as to avoid nuisances. All for naught. Neither sentinel was any Cerberus. Both yielded to pleas or intimidation. The most famous and impassioned of the dancers' visitors was Rodin, who had seen them in Paris and followed them in a state of fascination to Marseille. He had even taken the same train and accompanied them to the Villa des Glycines.

The Cambodian pavilion at Exposition Coloniale in Marseille.

Students and admirers watching Michelangelo at work were never more awestruck than I was watching our great Rodin amid those petite Cambodian women, his eyes sparkling, his hand busily sketching their revelatory gestures on a broad white paper.

He had two favorite models, Sâp and Soun, both grace incarnate, whose obedience he had obtained through small gifts. Soun, moreover, was amusingly mischievousness, and had earned herself a number of French friends.

Sometimes a model would tire quickly, driving Rodin to despair. His time was running out. Tense, short of breath, he seemed to bury his hands in the treasure before him, drawing it out in great handfuls while he still could. The Admiral Ponty, the ship that was to take the King and his dancers back to Cambodia, was already building up steam.

They fidgeted constantly, while Rodin struggled to capture a movement, a line: "Stop moving!" he exclaimed, his voice trembling with emotion, his pencil scribbling feverishly. Drawing behind the master, sketching his finds, was Noël Dorville, caricaturist for the magazine

Illustration, sent to the Villa des Glycines by the Minister of Colonies.

Before their departure from Marseille, the Minister of Colonies had ordered the dancers photographed in costume. Dressing them is quite a long process, taking all day for some. The gold-embroidered tunics, sparkling with precious stones, are sewed onto the body. Hair, make-up, and tiara placement are all extremely complicated.

One morning, then, they were asked to prepare themselves. Mr. Baudoin had obtained authorization to take them to a chateau near the Villa des Glycines, an old royal hunting lodge. There, on the steps of a monumental staircase, under the shade of centennial trees, they were to form a fairy-tale tableaux. But the sun was already setting, and the photographer waited anxiously as the rowdy, giggling dancers took up their positions before the camera, accompanied by the princess.

The dreaded day finally arrived. The Villa des Glycines was calm and melancholic, like an aviary at the approach of a storm. On the ground floor, desolation reined in the small, ground-floor living room, expanded by a veranda that Secretary Minister Son-Diêp used as his apartment. Mrs. Noël Dorville hugged the gentle Soun, and great tears rolled down their cheeks in their silent despair. A few steps away an equally silent Rodin worked with an ardor to match the mood of the moment. When he looked up to capture a gesture, a contour, one could see the glint of moist eyelids behind the sparkle of his spectacles.

"Is this weeping?" I exclaimed.

"We're all weeping!" Rodin answered.

The time came to say goodbye. A long, fantastic procession made its way through the streets of Marseille to the pier. First went trucks loaded with innumerable trunks, covered with long addresses in the name of the King of Cambodia, stuffed with every item that had caught the fancy of these extraordinary visitors and with gifts of all kinds from the Exposition Administration. Next came the horse-drawn carriages of the dancers themselves, followed by the carriages of the princess and her entourage.

The artist Rodin hurriedly sketching the dancer "Little Sap."

The dancers devoted their last moments in Marseille to shopping at the city's stores and bazaars. Gay as a flock of birds, their colors cutting a swath of color amid the monotony of European suits, they plundered the displays one last time. Princess Sounpady set the example, astounding Mr. Baudoin, who held the keys to the coffer, with her exorbitant purchases. A few hours before departure, she ordered sixty pairs of gloves, a hundred pairs of silk stockings, fifty boleros, and remnants of all sorts of fabrics, and then neglected to pay the bill delivered to the ship.

The French budget for Indochina was gallant to the end!

In Phnom Penh, where they were maintained by the King, the royal dancers were not paid. For their trip to France, however, each received an allowance. Those with starring roles received two hundred francs per month; those with secondary roles, a hundred francs; those with small roles, sixty francs.

Preliminary expenditures in Phnom Penh, before the departure for France	50,000 francs.
Transport for the troupe from Saigon to Marseille (round trip)	30,000 francs.
Stay in Paris	45,000 francs.
Stay in Marseille	20,000 francs.

Enthusiasts and the faithful insisted on remaining aboard the ship with their little friends until the last peal of the bell. All the dancers turned teary eyed to gaze at France, generous and magnificent. They seemed already to mourn their loss, bidding it an eternal adieu. All the joys and marvels of the past few weeks were about to slip away, leaving a hole in their hearts that would only deepen on their return to the monotonous, silent palace of Phnom Penh.

The King had arranged a few hours' delay in the ship's departure. Sisowath did not hide his sorrow over leaving France. Friends and onlookers alike could see his tears.

Rodin, whom we sought in vain in the cabins of his beloved models, had been unable to come. He was ill, and we could imagine the blow to him his forced absence must have been. Presently a store deliveryman delivered a box to Noël Dorville. The inscription was in the master's hand:

"To Noël Dorville, for little Sâp, who sings the Marseillaise."

On the corner of the paper: 15 FR. 50.

In the box was the pair of pumps that Rodin had promised Sâp the day before but had been unable to bring himself! We were deeply moved by this delicate, paternal gesture, from a man whom everyone thought as hard as the marble in which he chiseled his masterpieces.

"For little Sâp, who sings the Marseillaise!" Sâp, who was quite intelligent, had returned from Paris singing a verse of the national anthem. Many of her companions had learned a few words and typical phrases in our language. We used them, rather than their names, to identify them. Soun would stretch her arms out to the side, palms up, shrug, and articulately and comically intone: "None left!" She could have learned French easily and made an excellent little actress.

The bell pealed its last! … and the ship's deck was a sea of hugs.

The crowd gathered on the docks applauded and yelled out many a sincere au revoir. The King, accompanied by his Minister of the Palace, approached the rail. Everyone removed his hat, and in the religious silence that reined Mr. Thiounn said, "Goodbye. We are very grateful to you. You are our friends, our family, and we shall never forget you!"

Cambodian music played on the bridge, with a lighted candle on each instrument. Noël Dorville was intrigued by this mystical peculiarity and questioned a musician, who answered: "It is for friends whom we have met and shall never meet again."

The ship turned around ever so slowly and sailed off towards the horizon, over which it disappeared, handkerchiefs still waving as flashing points of white.

Why hadn't Rodin come to the ship? We found him in his room at the hotel, physically broken but increasingly enthusiastic, drunk on the artistic urges raging within him for the previous three days at the Villa des Glycines. He now had an obsession: to travel to Cambodia! In a flight of passion, he let loose with his impressions. It was a regular torrent, which I collected, and which was published in Illustration, with a few quick sketches — notes on line and movement — to the amusement of the uninitiated, who failed to understand.

"The dancers of the King of Cambodia," noted Illustration, "did more in France than achieve success as a curiosity. They truly piqued the interest of several artists, among them the celebrated sculptor Rodin. He showed particular enthusiasm when they left Paris by following them to Marseille, so as to prolong and refine in person his study of their poses and their gestures.

"We have obtained permission to reproduce some of his innumerable sketches of the Asian ballerinas. To the layman they will perhaps appear rough and strange, but not so to his admirers. To them nothing from the sculptor of The Thinker, Balzac, and The Door of Hell is indifferent, even if he abandons the chisel for a simple pencil or a coarse brush. We leave it to one of his most enthusiastic admirers, Mr. George Bois, inspector of Vocational Education in Indochina and of Fine Arts for the Marseille Colonial Exposition, to comment on and explain the drawings that the Cambodian dancers inspired from Mr. Rodin:

" 'Like a flight of marvelous birds that strayed momentarily into our gray skies, the little Cambodian dancing girls are gone, never to return!' "

The crowd saw in their dances only a delicious but futile shimmering of precious stones in the slow rhythm of monotonous movements. Their disconcerted ears quickly tired of the bright, clattering music. Only an artist of Rodin's genius could understand such perfection of beauty, a perfection always dreamed of, always sought, and suddenly right in front of him. When King Sisowath's dancers flitted away from the Pré Catelan to return to their Villa des Glycines in Marseille, Rodin became feverish. The rush of enthusiasm made him look thirty years younger. He followed them south and set to work in their midst, paper on lap and pencil in hand.

In 1906, King Sisowath and his royal dancers caused a sensation during their first appearance in France, beginning at the Exposition Coloniale in Marseille.

Often a model would suddenly get bored, break her pose, and pout. Rodin would get up and make a purchase from the basket of the merchant who was always at the villa. In exchange for the small gift, he would persuade the rebel to take up her pose again. Moments later she would want to flee anew, but the master would remain calm, sweet, patient, and careful not to waste the little time that remained before the royal ship's departure. He would continue to suffer the demands of his model. One day Rodin spread a blank sheet over his knee, said to little Sâp, "Place your foot there," and traced the contour with his pencil, adding: "It is agreed. Tomorrow you shall have your shoes, but pose for me a little longer!" Tired of perfume atomizers and cardboard cats, Sâp had asked her "Papa" for a pair of pumps!

Every evening, sketches in hand, eyes ablaze, Rodin would return to his hotel for a rest. Despite his exhaustion, he would be delirious with artistic joy. I am happy and quite proud to have recorded his impressions, which he delivered in spurts. I have transcribed some of them here, verbatim:

"There are stones so ancient that you can no longer date them. When you see them, you think of millennia, and here life, living nature, is producing the same effect. These Cambodians have given us everything that antiquity can contain, their own antiquity, which is just as valuable as ours. We have lived three days from three thousand years ago. It is impossible to see the human being brought to such perfection. Only they and the Greeks have done it. They have even discovered a new movement, one that I didn't know: a jolting of the body and the jolt with which the body descends. And then there's the great wellspring, their permanent bending of the legs, a reservoir of leaps, which they can then shape as they like, and which allow them to rise, to enlarge themselves, at certain times.

"Another motion of theirs, unknown to the ancients as well as to us: they spread their arms wide in a cross and produce an undulation from one hand to the other, through the shoulder blades. That motion belongs to the Far East. It is unknown, hitherto unseen. That's to say, the left arm moves in a concave arc while the right arm moves in a convex arc. With the play of their arms, the movement flashes through the shoulder blades.

"The bent-knee motion belongs to them. The bent knees are a wellspring of expressions. From time to time they can lift the body, with the rhythm of the music. And the finger joints, which can extend the fingers with considerable flexibility, all while retaining the ability to tremble! Single fingers have their own movements. The pulleys in their joints are greatly extended, for repetitive motions. They are put to use at a tender age.

"These dances are religious. I have always confused religious art with art. When religion is lost, so too is art. All the masterpieces, be they Greek, Roman, or ours, are religious. The princess, who seems so mean, and the king must be great artists, for without them all of this would disappear. The princess is absolutely absorbed in her dances. There so many who demand beauty and contribute none. Well, the King of

Cambodia delivers it. I am like Saul, dazzled by an unknown light, the light that I study so diligently in antiquity.

"From the point of view of forms, all of these women are remarkably beautiful. Their steps astonish us. They recall our Italian models. There have a simplicity that also recalls Egyptian granites. You could make them in granite, well polished, as pure as marble. Marble wouldn't render their forms as well.

"The masks are not grotesque. They wear them wonderfully well. Their costume is beauty itself. It hides no line…. A mass of complications that is in no way complicated and lets you see the naked line.

"The music too is wonderful. No other music could accompany these dances. And the singer, her thin voice rising to one tone and staying there, suspended like a little lark, with accents from the dull tom-tom as it scans the measures!

"These dancers understand, I'm sure of it, and are incapable of descending from this superior art. There are great artists among the dance mistresses. Even the children are great artists. It's frightening!"

Review by Henri PARMENTIER

Bulletin de l'École Française d'Extrême-Orient,
1914, Volume 14, Number 1 pp. 54–57

— Cambodian Dancers - Ancient and Modern — Georges GROSLIER

Paris, Challamel, 1913: 1 vol. in 4°, 179 pp., illustrated.

M. Parmentier's page references have been adjusted for this edition

Mr. G. Groslier is a painter, but here, despite his denial (p. 108), he has sought to combine the work of an artist with that of a historian. His work has led him to it. Indeed, none of modern-day Cambodia is comprehensible without continuous reference to old Cambodia. Mr. G's genuinely interesting study, arriving just in time to preserve the memory of an exquisite and all but extinct art, has three parts: a series of sketches and drawings of the dancers in Phnom Penh's Royal Palace, along with their essential accoutrements; a description of their life, recruitment, and costumes; and, finally, a study reconnecting this art with the glorious past of Angkor.

The parts are of unequal value. The illustrations — surely the artist in Mr. G will take no offense at a fellow artist's observation — make up the most important part by far. Mr. G shows remarkable understanding of movements and poses, and some of his figures, executed in a few bold strokes, acutely convey the astounding squatting walk of these dances. For those who have seen and enjoyed these performances, many of his images will strikingly evoke the exquisite sum of the parts, not to mention its wonderful rhythm, with the strange musical accompaniment and the percussive clatter that underscores it. The evocation is complete. Unfortunately, it will perhaps elude a European reader who, unlike some of us, has not enjoyed any such performances as the indissociable wholes they are meant to be.

Mr. G has a real talent for expressing the subtlest movements in a few strokes. His drawings might sometimes be a little loose, but they are always vibrant. Curiously, the artist succeeds at the

Henri Parmentier - 1871-1949.

most difficult task, capturing the figure — figures utterly different in spirit, and even in anatomical form, from those one learns to draw in France — while struggling with the altogether easier task of rendering sculpture and especially objects. The reason, I think, lies in that very simplicity.

Though he grasps fleeting gestures instantly, Mr. G lacks the perseverance of a seeker, the patience to chisel out an inanimate contour. And so, despite his good intentions, his work falls short as a documentary effort. I praise his method for providing us with the patterns of certain costumes (p. 65) and for detailing the most important parts of the set (pp. 63, 70). But I must note that his drawings, focused as they are on effect, inadequately convey the motifs. In works like this, sketches should be sufficiently clear and precise for a jeweler to duplicate the jewelry depicted.

My criticism of the second part, on the dances and the dancers, is analogous. It is more of a poetic account than a study. Distilled from the rest of the document, the actual information imparted amounts to very little.

It is perhaps unfair of me to criticize the artist and poet too harshly for getting carried away with his admiration, but I have the right and duty to be harder on the author in the third section, though I share most of Mr. G's opinions and my observations concern only minor details.

Let me first get the main criticism out of the way. May the author permit me to point out what amounts to a serious flaw for a work aspiring to the status of archeological study: namely, the nearly complete absence of references. He cites an opinion of Mr. de Bellouène's (p. 117) without mentioning the page or even the work where it might be found. He provides fragments of inscriptions (pp. 124, 144, etc.) with no information to lead those unfamiliar with them to the complete texts.

Mr. G has a passion for Khmer ruins and great interest in the work of the Société d'Angkor, and he promotes the beautiful collection of photographs that the society sells, with proceeds going to the ruins. But without a footnote, rather embarrassingly — and, of course, unintentionally — it takes on the appearance of a simple and naïve advertisement.

The same sort of imprecision, in the service of his cause, leads him to accept uncorroborated dates without question. He dates the monuments of Preah Khan[1] and Wat Nokor to the 8th century. That

---

1. Mr. G does not clearly indicate if he is speaking of the Preah Khan of Angkor or of Kompong Svay.

seems a bit too early for the former and is simply incorrect for the latter, which in certain details seems more recent than a good number of Angkor monuments.²

This is, however, an entirely personal impression, cautiously advanced. I wish only to point out the danger of confident assertions with the present state of scholarship. Caution must be the order of the day in examining a civilization whose peak was first dated to the remote time of the Assyrian kings and then, after a reading of the inscriptions, pushed up almost into modern times.

In the same way, given the lack of references or more specific information, we must credit the author with the parallel drawn between *mokot* (*mukuta*) and Mount Meru (p. 81). It more likely emanated from the overheated mind of some over-educated Cambodian. Furthermore, why does Mr. G so easily accept the idea that ancient Khmers burned sticks of incense (p. 123)? It is possible, though the custom seems mainly Chinese, but is there a single image in the bas-reliefs, a single detail in the construction of the temples, to corroborate the assertion?

In addition, what is the evidence for the symbolic meaning attributed to the white make-up (p. 51)? Mr. G asserts that the Hindus, to which I would add the Javanese, cover their dancers only in saffron or turmeric. He claims a probable Chinese origin for the white. He identifies, rightly, all Cambodian religious thought as stemming from India. If so, then it seems highly unlikely that the symbolism in question would come into existence over so brief a time in a country that today seems rather resistant to subtle hypotheses.

Not that we've dispensed with the observations of fact and principle, let us briefly state Mr. G's thesis. I shall not follow up on his quest for the "metaphysical" meaning (p. 111) of the gesture in which a dancer offers an imaginary flower. It's a rather grand word for a pretty movement. I observe with the author that the female figures of Angkor strike the same pose, and the similarity is enough for me to

---

2. Editor's Note: These dates, and most French dates for Khmer monuments determined at the beginning of the 20th century, were indeed quite wrong. Because of their poor condition, Preah Khan and other Angkor Thom monuments of Jayavarman VII were thought to predate Angkor Wat (ca. 1116 AD-1150 AD). In fact, the main image of Preah Khan was not dedicated until 1191 AD. Wat Nokor is now dated to the 11th century.

accept his starting point. According to Mr. G, what the Royal Dancers do is evoke, while clothed in costumes revised by Siamese influence, extremely ancient dances (p. 117), dances that in the past would have been purely religious.

The dancers depicted at Wat Nokor and Preah Khan in the 8th century[3], and then at Angkor Thom[4] in the 9th (p. 131), conform to an original Hindu type; once the civilizing element had spread to the mass of the aboriginal people, the last model depicted would be a pure Cambodian type. The tradition of these dances would have been preserved and transformed — Mr. G does not explain why — in theatrical performances, true pantomimes retelling ancient legends. The author correctly points out another too-often neglected change: that of the costumes (p. 135). In his view, the nude torsos of the ancient dancers were an entirely Hindu custom, and the Khmers, who had grudgingly gone along, rid themselves of it when the Thais subjugated the country.

While in agreement with him nearly everywhere else, I cannot agree with Mr. G here. The modesty of present-day Cambodian women with regard to their breasts doesn't seem to me to prove very much. The object of modesty is a matter of fashion and quickly learned. A good many women — Laotian, Khmer, Javanese or Moi, to cite only the Far Eastern populations that I know — seem unfazed by their bare-breasted lives, whereas Annamite women almost never remove the fabric square that serves to hide their breasts. Moreover, we know from Zhou Daguan that in the glory days of Angkor Cambodian women, even the wealthiest among them, left their breasts uncovered.

The same opposition exists in Java. I remember attending dances at the residence of the Sultan of Jakarta in 1904 and noting the amusing contrast between the hundreds of bare-breasted women seated in the audience and the dancers whom they surrounded, dancers squeezed even more tightly into high-riding costumes than their Cambodian counterparts. In my view, modesty has nothing to do with it. This kind of dance, whether sacred ritual, simple ballet, or pantomime, seems in no way intended to excite the senses. Its costumes are, above all, a means

---

3. I have already expressed my reservations over these dates. It's too bad that Mr. G. did not provide a sketch of the figures that he finds so interesting.
4. See footnote 2.

of expression. The prettiest dancer does not hesitate to hide her features under a grotesque but recognizable mask, so she covers herself completely with a more or less sumptuous costume that defines her character.

Modern dancers dress like ancient princes and heroines,[5] whom they portray. The dancers of Angkor have bare torsos because such was the custom of the time. There was nothing shocking about it. Gods and goddesses are no better covered. The Thais came from the northernmost areas, and no doubt thus adopted out of necessity the practice of using full costumes, substituting them for the partial nudity appropriate to the climate of southern India and Cambodia.

Except on this single point, I believe Mr. G's entire system correct. The comparison between modern dances and the illustrated dances shines considerable light on the subject. It allows for very interesting recreations of ancient dancers on the basis of the bas-reliefs: for example, in the plates on pp. 118 and 146. But why did the author of the first plate's beautiful figure (p. 119) transform the second plate's two fine *devata* (p. 156) into bizarre macrocephalous dwarves?

Such as it is, with its many qualities and its defects, the work bodes well for "Khmer Decoration," which the author is now preparing. If Mr. G tightens up his drawings and substitutes more precise documentation for his poetic but often uninstructive outpourings, then his new work has every hope of achieving excellence.

H. Parmentier

---

5. But from where or what era remains an open question.

Portrait of a royal Cambodian dancer - 1907.

Theater and Dance in Cambodia

George GROSLIER

Conference held at the Sorbonne on February 4, 1929

(Friends of the University)

LADIES AND GENTLEMEN.

Cambodian theater! No other art in Cambodia, and perhaps even in all the Far East, seems to offer such riches. It is nearly unknown in France, though its actresses, whom we call *danseuses Cambodgiennes*, enjoy a pleasant prestige here. They visited us in 1922, performing once at the Opéra, in a program designed to appeal to the general public. The press was so favorable, and cast their lives in such mysterious light, that these young women, with their slow, slow gestures, became sacred priestesses in the public imagination. Tonight, let us try to discover what they really are and discern their true merit. Their art is sufficiently beautiful and complete to dispense with any embellishment.

There are several kinds of theaters in Cambodia. We will limit our focus to the classical theater, now performed only in the royal court, with women playing all the roles. Over the centuries it has remained exemplary and been raised to a state of perfection. It is Cambodia's classical theater, and corresponds fairly well to our French *théâtre classique*.

In general, the plays unfold in time and space. Burlesque meets tragedy, reality meets fantasy. Don César de Bazan[1] rubs elbows with Britannicus.[2] Warriors act out an epic battle, assuming the poses of a bas-relief frieze[3] and moving about in ways strictly determined by convention.

---

1. A romantic opera by Jules Massenet, based on Victor Hugo's play *Ruy Blas*. First performed at the Opéra Comique in Paris on November 30, 1872.
2. First performed in 1669, a tragic play about royal choice in Roman times by French playwright Jean Racine.
3. Pictorial versions of Cambodian history are inscribed in bas-relief panels that appear in many of the ancient temples.

But moments later they are drunk, rolling on the floor with the most daring realism. Ultimately, this sort of theater establishes nothing and comes to no end. Indeed, my attempt to point out that it is limitless succeeds only in imposing a limit.

As soon as we start looking into things, we stumble upon a surprise: the monotony, the paucity, of the written repertoire. The archives of the Royal Palace preserve a scant thirty plays, and incomplete plays at that, in which you'd be hard pressed to glean more than ten different themes. A beautiful princess is kidnapped. Giants intervene to take part in or thwart the kidnapping. The princess's father or the outraged husband gives chase. Scenes of seduction, pitched battles, hand-to-hand combat. The ugliest of heroes transformed into a radiant adolescent. Metamorphosis of animals. A god appears to restore order, or to upset it. We could go on forever listing episodes, each essentially the same as the last, whatever its dramatic means.

But let's not draw hasty conclusions, for the charms of Khmer theater might yet lie elsewhere. Perhaps the authors don't rely on the text to achieve their desired effect. Perhaps the unlikeliest episode is basis enough for the ballet mistress to erect her edifice of beauty and craft.

How will the episode unfold before the spectator? As an intimate and complicated assembly of literature, music (orchestra and chorus), pantomime, dance, and dialog. Line by line, a narrator reads the play (generally written in verses of seven syllables). The chorus repeats each phrase with a set melody. The actress mimes the actions or feelings declaimed. Time-keepers set the rhythm by clapping wooden sticks together. Sometimes the orchestra and chorus stop and the actresses onstage engage in a sort of repartee among themselves.

The mime maneuvers within this framework. Her gestures are designed and learned in advance, since every plastic phrase that she executes has a necessary duration and development, set by the musical phrase in the orchestra or chorus.

Perceive this connection, and you immediately glimpse difficulties of all kinds. Now, I could tell you how such-and-such melody may in practice be drawn out or shortened, but the result should nevertheless

Dancers at the Royal Palace in Phnom Penh - 1923.

be a whole that resists distortion. Because it is prepared, coolly studied, refined over time and by generations of ballet mistresses, it can achieve a supreme logic — indeed, perfection — and it is my aim in the course of this talk to convey some idea of it to you.

It is commonly believed that the actress wears a dance costume whose chief characteristic is a pointed headdress. In truth, the headdress is the divine and royal crown, worn exclusively by an actress playing a prince, a king, or a god. Headdresses and costumes vary with the characters onstage, as they do in our theater. Moreover, masks of colored skins signal fantastical characters. Costumes and accessories are traditional and invariable, down to the smallest detail.

Rama, a princess, Ravana — as soon as they hit the stage the thousand Cambodians in attendance recognize them. No surprises. Nothing could be simpler. The director makes no effort to vary the wardrobe of his troupe. Costumes and jewelry are well known in advance, as well known as the episodes stitched together by the author.

In fact, the director is a most fortunate man! Khmer theater plays without a set — or, more accurately, with an unchanging set.

The hall consists of a roof supported by columns. The audience sits all around, as in a circus, though with a rectangular ring. The king and dignitaries sit on one long side of the rectangle. Facing them is the chorus. At one short side is the orchestra, across from which the actresses enter by one door and leave by another. Two low tables face each other onstage. When the action calls for a prop — a small mirror, an offering, a bow, a cushion, a magic box — a female servant quite openly brings it onstage and comes to fetch it when it is no longer needed. The costumer makes no bones about coming onstage mid-play to adjust a belt or rearrange the costume of an actress in motion. There is thus really nothing for a director to do. Again, nothing could be simpler, or less theatrical. Certainly no effort goes into maintaining any illusion or capturing the audience's imagination by material means.

Of what, then, does this theater consist? What are these riches that I proclaimed early on? After all, I've pointed out the meagerness of the texts, the fixity of the sets and costumes. Suppose we were Cambodians. What would we seek at the theater, since we practically know the scenes and the chants by heart and could sketch out the costumes for ourselves?

If you're asking yourself these questions, it's because I wanted you to grasp something straight off: that the efforts of the Cambodian actress are in no way dispersed. There's nothing remarkable going on around her, so her performance becomes the focus. This performance *is* the language, the sufficient language, of Cambodian theater.

What does the actress need with a painted backdrop representing a forest? Her gestures show us that she is advancing through one, drawing aside branches, picking flowers. What does she need with a machine to lift her into the air? Her plastic vocabulary contains some ten poses of such lightness, of such detachment from the ground, that you will fail to see her as being anchored anywhere. Why worry about the placement of torches and the variety of lights? This mime is clothed not in tinsel but in splendid fabrics, with pure gold and real gems. Touch them, weigh them: fifteen necklaces, ten rings, collars and armbands, the oval belt buckle. It's all in precious materials. No need for any artifice to make it seem real. Look at my costume, with its impeccable cut, shape, color, and composition. You know these qualities when you see them? Then see for yourself! There's no illusion, no need for me to appear as what I am not! I am! I am the perfection that you have conceived over centuries. I have perfected myself over time to match your evolving aspirations.

The actress is thus everything the spectator could wish for. She is, in a very real sense, a reality that has matched a fiction. Through jewels and costumes and the very role she plays, her actual value is equal to her suggested value. For the wretched spectator, in other words, is the richness of this finery not even more unattainable, even more stupefying, than the fleeting, artificial luster of stage rags?

I insist on this point because I believe it to be the very symbol of all Cambodian theater. It abhors falsity, all that is facile and secondary. It has pared itself down, that its riches might shine forth unhindered. It has chosen the rarest of methods to make itself manifest. To achieve its effect, it keeps its episodes simple, using ancient fables known to all, and thus ensures that the audience rises to the occasion. Such is the audience's role, the link between them and the play. The audience does not come to the theater to learn, discover, or discuss. That's the last thing on their minds! They come to verify and observe, to see in the flesh what they have hitherto but dimly conceived in their minds. Thus the play, the miracle, begins. Filling the space between the audience's own murky imaginings and the indisputable precision, the insuperable perfection, now offered them is the ten years of rigorous training undergone by the average actress, as well as the ballet mistress's craft, inherited from years past.

How hard is that training, and in what way? Let us see.

As we have already said, no gesture of the actress has its own rhythm. It has no movement or even activity that is proper to it. These are conferred on the gesture by a chanted phrase. The gesture is thus stripped of its humanity and life, of its usual purpose. It is plastic and "new" insofar as its slowness allows us to follow and evaluate it as it unfolds. Nothing is spontaneous. Rather, everything is deliberate.

In fact, if we were to immobilize the actress at any stage of her gesture she would appear to us as a finished, perfectly balanced statue. The performance is carried so far that we could walk all around her and see the same qualities of composition from every angle.

That's why Khmer theater is not played on a stage, with a backdrop, but in the round. The actress can then face in any direction, as dictated by the logic of her gestures and the dynamic sequence of her poses. She needn't play to spectators and lighting massed arbitrarily on one side.

An even closer look reveals that the actress does not express actions and feelings directly. She is impassive, impersonal. (I will tell you later what this illiterate and detached young girl truly is.) She uses a vocabulary of gestures and poses. Some, functioning on a spiritual plane, convey sadness, anger, or love. Others, on a physical plane, depict dressing, springing into the air, or drawing a bowstring. These are invariable signs, whose meaning is clear on execution, regardless of the actress's intention. She need focus only on accurately tracing them out with her limbs. She is a calligrapher.

Let's cite some examples. Take the "gesture-words" for sadness and dressing.

Sadness: one hand supports the inclined forehead for 6,8,10 measures. The other hand is draped over the belt. Of course, each hand will have a precise location, be opened to an unvarying extent, and form time-tested angles with the arms. You will see the ballet mistress apply a firm finger to an actress's insufficiently open elbow. The rest of the actress's body and the legs, meanwhile, are subject to the same precision of composition, in harmony with the arms.

Whether she's the *première danseuse* or a student, whether she's playing the wretched Princess Sorincha, driven from the palace, or the brilliant Prince Soryavong, overwhelmed by misfortune, every actress will express sadness in the same way and trace the same signs.

Dressing! She simulates putting on a belt, closing the buckle, tossing a scarf over her shoulders, and adding imaginary rings to her fingers.

Dancers at the Royal Palace in Phnom Penh - 1923.

These gestures — these, in a word, sculptural gestures — are more than broken down, delimited by a musical phrase, carefully combined with the rest of the body. They are transformed through the judicious addition of details absent from the text.

A weeping princess will collect each tear on her fingertip and fling it away. Having slipped on his rings, the prince will stretch out his arms and wiggle his hands, to produce a play of light on the gems. Thus does the Khmer genius add adjectives to the gesture-words for "sadness" or "dressing up."

I have given you two examples of gestures, translating feeling and action. Their meaning is clear. Follow them attentively, and you will understand. The text presents the following scene, free of commentary: The princess and two maidservants are strolling in a garden. The princess sees a flower, stops, points it out. How beautiful it is! A maidservant advances, picks the flower, and gives it to the princess. So chants the chorus. But look again! Look closely at the details added by the ballet mistress. What realism in the stylization! What subtle observations beneath all the conventions!

Grasping the flower means drawing aside the branches, isolating the fragile stem with one hand, using the other to take hold (with what care!) of the blossom, plucking it, shaking away the pollen, bowing to the princess before she takes the offering and again afterwards. Note how the maidservant crossed the three meters separating her from the invisible blooming bush. Did you count the steps? Did you realize that they corresponded to six measures of music from the orchestra? Did you notice how the maidservant rubbed her arms before plucking the flower? Why? Ah, you are outsiders! You don't know how to look at images! You see, the blooming bush was covered with ants, which fell onto the young girl's bare arms.

If now you are reaching a point where my definitions conjure up for you a rigid, inviolable system, a theatrical conception that you feel could not possibly be more monotonous and narrow, permit me to stop you right there. Let me show you a single example of the flexibility and infinite variety that a Cambodian derives from it. Today it's the ants. In another role it will be dew hindering the flower-picking. Here, one maidservant does it all. A little later, two maidservants will work together. Another time, four women will take part, each bringing a flower to the princess, or each passing the same flower to the next maidservant. The flower may be almost out of reach and plucked from on high. Otherwise, it may be plucked from the ground, with a new movement, completely different from the preceding, substituting lowered bodies for bodies stretched out.

With this in mind, think about all the possible gestures, all the ways to break them down and reassemble them, all the possible sequences of ideas and acts. This still doesn't cover it. Pantomime takes up only half the performance. The other half is dance, which can mix with the pantomime, blend into it, or succeed it, with no apparent connection. The maidservant's steps as she gathers the flower were dance steps. The trio's stroll before the flower-picking was dance. Poses always follow poses, because, even when pantomiming nothing and bound by no text, the actress simply will not move like a human being, in step with the rhythm of vulgar everyday life. Her body must always yield to a higher purpose, which never goes unheeded, and which has determined that nothing unpurified by time and successive generations is worthy of expression.

We should devote a few moments to these dance postures that mean nothing in particular. In a sense, they are the letters composing the gesture-words that I have just described. Moreover, to be understood, such-and-such pantomime gesture does not need the right hand to be in such-and-such position, where we see that it fits well and contributes to the whole. These gestures are therefore like etymological letters. They are remnants dating back to the very origins of the theater, when it was exclusively a religious dance. There are only a very few, but we see them again and again.

They are visible on bas-reliefs of the 8th to the 13th centuries, where representations of dancers abound. The overturned hand, the open hand, hands joined in the *anjali*[4] — surely you recognize them. No need for me to insist. Ponder the foregoing allusion for a while, and it will be easy for you to see the industry and patient imagination of the ballet mistresses. Following one another for centuries on the Khmer stage, they have taken the few letters that we have just spelled and managed to compile a dictionary. The maidservant now need only draw from it to pick a flower and offer it to her mistress.

This plastic repertory is manifest only in space and in the memory of a few old women. We have tried to catalog it photographically, and our initial inventory has logged some 1,165 principal poses. These are something like the root words of a glossary at the end of a book. Indeed, each has a name. Many of the names are curious and hold a number of philological surprises:

Some have clear meanings: raise the arm, bend the arm.

Others determine an act: crying, sleeping.

Others are mysterious: for example, hold the ball. What does that mean? The gesture is symbolic: the hand seems to hold a small ball between the middle finger and the palm. For twenty centuries thousands of statues in India and China have made this very sign, so we can hazard a few hypotheses.

---

4. *Anjali* is a Sanskrit word meaning divine offering. The Añjali Mudrā is a Buddhist or Hindu gesture of greeting in which the palms are joined together in front of the chest.

Still other names evoke by analogy. For example, the amorous prince who presents himself to his paramour strikes an advantageous pose. He extends his arms and quivers on his legs. This pose is "the peacock spreading its tail." The allusion is clear. But it's a subtle mind indeed that can divine the origin or the analogy behind "the fish that grazes on the riverbank," a pose on folded legs, with arms open.

Finally, there are untranslatable names meaning nothing, alluding to nothing. Let's leave them aside!

To finish with the matter of plasticity in Khmer theater, let us note that movement is only a means to building a pose, a fleeting immobility in which the entire body finds a balance. An actress striving to suggest the idea of taking flight therefore immobilizes herself, taking an approach more or less diametrically opposite to a Western dancer's. To create the illusion, she relies on a symbolic position, which is independent of the meaning of preceding gestures — independent, if you will, of the context. She works her body into an utterly unexpected pose, jarringly different from the dictates of the spectator's logic, and incompatible with the immobility that nevertheless results. For the spectator, the sensation that the actress no longer rests on anything, has detached herself from the ground, overcomes reality.

The same dynamic underlies the hyperextension and hyperflexion of joints. Note that there is no dislocation, nothing anatomically abnormal, like the *pointes*[5] in European ballet. Instead, the gesture only slightly exceeds the usual limits. Consequently, it eliminates any suggestion of stopping and seems immaterial.

Now let us move on to the actual technique of the Cambodian theater. First of all, just what is the actress on whom this art places such demands, and on whom it ultimately depends for everything?

At the age of six or seven years, she begins, engaging in group exercises, understanding absolutely nothing. Little by little she learns such-and-such pose goes with such-and-such melody, that it follows from another, that the foot must be here and the hand there and only there.

---

5. Ballerinas often dance *en pointe*: that is, on the tips of their toes.

Don't go thinking that ballet mistresses go in for speeches and explanations of why! "Wait a moment, my child! You're not arching enough." A little pinch. "I've told you three times to raise your hand to the height of your eyebrows, and it's still not there!" Wham! Slap! An arm yanked up. A finger thrust into the hip, right in the sensitive spot. Between sessions, our little actress runs some errands for her elders, sweeps the bedroom, fetches the water. And if she's a good little girl she starts up again on the morrow.

Group exercises are held daily, by category, in accordance with the four fundamental roles of the theater: princes, princesses, giants, and monkeys. Each exercise lasts thirty minutes without a break. Sweat literally streams down faces and napes. Hard labor and hard training go into this performing sculpture. This whole conference can give only an incomplete summary of the method.

At age twelve, our little actress knows all her exercises in order. She doesn't execute them very well, but with a few more wallops, and a little maturity, she'll soon be satisfactory. Satisfactory, and nothing more. This is a terrible word on the lips of a ballet mistress. By sixteen, the average pupil is adequate. That's it. There's your actress. She is illiterate. Of the seventy-five actresses in the royal troupe in 1927, four could read. Of those four, two could write, with difficulty. Of the eleven ballet mistresses, only one could read and write. That's the way it is. Our actress, then, is ready.

Let's call her Suon, to make things easier. She is an unknown girl, maidservant and concubine to the master of the troop, who is a king, prince, or high mandarin. She has an average physique and average intelligence. She is flexible, for reasons we've already seen. Through her lengthy apprenticeship, however, she has developed two things to an extraordinary degree: memory and pride. Now, at the beginning of her career, memory will substitute for intelligence and pride will serve as motivation. If, however, she is pretty and clever, doors will open faster for her, here as in all the countries of the world. Finally, if as a pretty and clever actress she increases her flexibility and cultivates her memory, she will become a star or a favorite, or even a favorite that everyone considers a star.

Dancers in costume - 1908.

But young Suon is neither one nor the other yet. She has never performed. The play Chantalivong is announced, and Suon is chosen to play the beautiful Sovann Macha. She doesn't know the role. She can't read it. No one will explain it to her. She sits in a corner, and the rehearsal begins without further ado. The scene where Sovann Macha appears finally comes along. "Suon! Come here… and hurry it up!"

The ballet teacher comes before her and plays the role. Suon, like a mirror image of the mistress, imitates the model. The orchestra plays; the chorus sings. The young actress keeps up as best she can, stumbles, loses the thread, gets lost. The ballet mistress stops the chorus and orchestra, calls her an idiot, and takes up the sequence again. And off they go. Beginning to end, for hours. Night falls. More of the same the next day.

But by the third rehearsal Suon has stored away the thousand details of her role and ordered in correct sequence the hundred poses learned during her training. A role lasting several hours is thus learned by a eighteen-year-old actress in four or five rehearsals. It is stamped in her memory. If she needs to play it two years on, one rehearsal will suffice.

Dancers at ease in the palace - 1908.

Witness the startling contrast between the grandeur of this theater, its extraordinary demands, and the weakness, the mediocrity, of the actress. As we now know, this theater eschews all artifice and *mise-en-scène*. It uses no sets and only the most commonplace texts. It seizes on the actress, needing only a little flesh and some young limbs, too confident to rely on individual idiosyncrasies. A theatrical troupe is just human equipment, clockwork.

The actress is remarkable not for the beauty that she creates or a gesture that she invents but for the beauty in which she is clothed, epitomized by gestures studied and refined by preceding generations. Gradually she is molded and stimulated, and learns her craft, adding one role after another, advancing from that of maidservant to that of confidante, and finally to that of queen.

She advances in the hierarchy and grows rich, not through successive creations but through the increasingly complete absorption of the sterile vocabulary. Soon she will have exceeded the level to which the intelligence and temperament of an average woman could have taken her. The past in its entirety enters into her performance. She recreates it every time.

Princess Wongat Say Sangvann's troupe at Angkor Wat, circa 1935. Shortly after George Groslier's lecture the Royal Ballet was so depleted that when invited to perform at the 1931 Colonial Exhibition the king declined. While dance presentations had become important to French priorities the king had no desire to accommodate them. At that time Princess Say Sangvann, who had her own troupe of dancers, left the court over a disagreement. The French were happy to use her dancers in place of the royal troupe and she performed through the 1930s. Source: *Earth in Flower* by Paul Cravath, 2008.

I cannot overemphasize this point: the plasticity of Khmer theatre is flagrant, so much so that it can make do with this unimportant, common young girl, who five minutes ago was joking and cackling with her peers. She is enough, I tell you, even without her spangled velvet and heavy jewels. In her simple rehearsal costume, she can achieve her transformation simply by planting herself on the floor, bending her legs, and opening her arms while the orchestra plays. Her face, suddenly serious and blank, becomes ageless. Her gestures, which are nothing but stylization, strip away the last of her humanity. All at once this mediocre soul is transformed. Quickened, as if stepping out of a shadow, this little, insignificant woman begins to move on a supernatural plane. What we see of her now is only legend, art, and translation.

I trust you haven't forgotten that we're still just talking about Suon, our adequate actress. Now imagine a haughty actress with a beautiful face. Instead of a subject who applies herself, imagine a subject who moves with ease. After all, there is flexibility and there is flexibility. One is always tense, the other abandons itself. There are vulgar hands and hands that are miracles of finesse. Such are the nuances that will distinguish the approximately twenty actresses, impersonal actresses, who will perform this evening — nuances that aficionados will quickly seize upon. We needn't go into detail.

Since the actress is an automaton, who should get credit for all the craft and art that goes into a performance? The ballet mistress.

Is she some kind of genius? Not at all. But she is an old actress, who has played all the roles, played all the plays, seen generation after generation of ballerinas pass! She is a living lexicon. She is thus free to arrange the phrases, adjust their duration, stitch together the episodes. There is yet another tradition for such adjustments and stitching, but there's enough leeway here and there for a nudge in the right direction. And the nudge comes from the ballet mistress. Let's see how it works.

Suon is playing the role of the beautiful Sovann Macha. During one scene, she must leave her palace at night, while her parents and maidservants are sleeping, and meet her lover. Nothing more, nothing less. The script doesn't say anything else. Traditionally, the princess begins on her bed, with four maidservants asleep at her feet. Descending from the bed, she is supposed to cross the space separating her from her seducer in a twenty-measure dance. Nothing more, nothing less.

A scholar, prince, or king attending the rehearsal finds this exit banal and tells the ballet mistress. This is the 18th century. The ballet mistress thinks for a moment and then orders the orchestra to play its theme for forty measures instead of twenty. She takes Suon's place. She wakes up, rises, and moves towards the exit, but instead of continuing, she bumps a sleeping maidservant with her foot, takes fright, and runs back to bed. The original scene is transformed, its drama heightened. Suon will learn the new version and play it from now on, changing nothing.

A century later, an even more demanding critic will come along. The ballet mistress, a student of Suon's, will bump the maidservant with her foot and have the maidservant feel around her. Thus the scene will improve over time. Are you convinced that this theater is not immobile? It does have sacred, immutable, and inert elements, but they are in the service of a slow transformation. They are incorporated in ever-different combinations, but only by artists who possess the complete vocabulary. Only they can evaluate the need for a change, as well as the possibility and opportunity to make it.

Let us attend a traditional performance. It generally takes place at night. At about two in the afternoon, costumes are donned. Our actress is sewn into her clothing. Why? Because today Suon is playing the prince, but tomorrow it will be one of her colleagues. The two young women do not have the same figures, and a sewn-on garment can be adjusted to either of them. After costuming comes the make-up, covering every side, like that of a Pierrot.[6] The application lasts about two hours. Each actress is responsible for the jewels she wears. She returns them after each performance. Two hours before the overture, the troupe is ready and waiting.

The traditional performance starts with a ballet, "Chap Robam," which can accurately be translated as "Opening Ballet." In a moment you will see a three-minute film showing a few steps, as performed by the royal troupe. The whole thing lasts fifty-five minutes, without a

---

6. A clown, based on a character from French pantomime with a whitened face.

break, and consists of five reprises with four grand salutes in between. The actresses go in pairs, and the theme is a romantic stroll.

The featured play starts immediately afterwards. There are no breaks, no intermissions. As the characters of a finished scene exit, the characters of the following scene enter. So it goes until dawn, except during certain festivals, when it goes on for several successive nights.

The prince takes leave of an old hermit, his teacher, to return to the palace of the king, his father. He is accompanied by a giant, whose duty is protect the prince during the journey. That's the first episode. The hermit remains seated on the low table until his disciple completes his leave-taking. Then he exits, and the young prince, followed by the giant, goes round and round the stage, simulating his journey through forests and plains. Finally, the travelers disappear through the exit door.

A king and queen enter and sit on the mat. Two maidservants kneel, one on each side. The princess, escorted by four maidservants, comes before her parents and asks their permission to stroll in the nearby forest. They consent. Since granting permission is their only function, they promptly exit. So concludes the second scene.

Third scene. The princess's stroll.

Fourth scene. You guessed it. The prince and his giant pass by, see the women on their stroll. Let me intervene here with a warning, for surely you cannot predict what's going to happen! The prince, you see, falls in love with the princess! They meet. The prince advances, bewitched. The princess retreats, confused. He declares his love. She demurs. This theme opens the way to more than thirty traditional motifs, each more charming than the last.

Fourth, fifth, tenth scene. The difficulties of the fresh-blooming idyll begin and persist. Learning of the forest encounter, the parents of the princess dispatch warriors to capture the prince. But the giant intervenes.

Eleventh scene. An incident. Actresses who until now have remained mute speak and engage briefly in some repartee. A comic, even grotesque, and often satirical, episode unfolds. The giant chases the warriors. They stagger and tremble, their hands joined, while the chief covers their retreat. Suddenly, they stop. They see something, something disturbing.

"What is it?" asks the chief.

"There!" says the head soldier, pointing ahead into the distance.

The troops flee, only to be brought back by the chief. They stop again, show the same terror, ask the same question, get the same answer, and turn tail again. The scene plays three times, repetition bringing out its comedy.

Finally the chief makes his stand. With his fear showing plainly through his courage, he goes to confront the danger. He advances, trembling, to the spot and finds … a puddle reflecting their image!

The hitherto vanquished soldiers are suddenly bragging old warhorses. "Forward!" they cry, brandishing terrible weapons, adjusting their equipment, slapping one another on the back. Nothing can stop them now! In passing the puddle, each in turn puffs himself up with bravado, kneels, and takes a sip!

Twentieth scene. With the farce complete, the play takes up where it left off. The princess yields to her seducer, and her father disowns her. There follows an extraordinary performance. Wretched, pathetic, she drags herself along on her knees, crawls after her intractable, merciless father. She caresses his feet, implores him with open arms. She sags, as if in the throes of death, and finally staggers off. Five minutes of poignant pantomime, utterly human yet utterly precise. So technically daunting, so pure is this scene that I don't think there's anything to match it in all our classical theater.

Thirtieth scene.

It is three o'clock in the morning, and the play still isn't over! But let's stop here. Over the past five hours, you have watched about twenty young women play princes, princesses, giants, attendants, and warriors. They have worn costumes and jewels of age-old design. They have run, loved, worshipped, battled, passed from the heavens to the earth. They have brimmed with every human passion, wielded every divine power. Their faces have remained impassive and their eyes glazed over while their bodies undulated, showing no fatigue. They have glided about, intertwining, following one another in necessary order, carried along by an orchestra and chorus, all locked in rhythm. You have seen a thousand poses, all devised in advance, each with its own name, each adapted to the purpose at hand. They have been arranged as needed like so many impressions in stone, preserved in an atmosphere of history. In attending this performance, you have witnessed the flowering of one of the world's most beautiful living traditions.

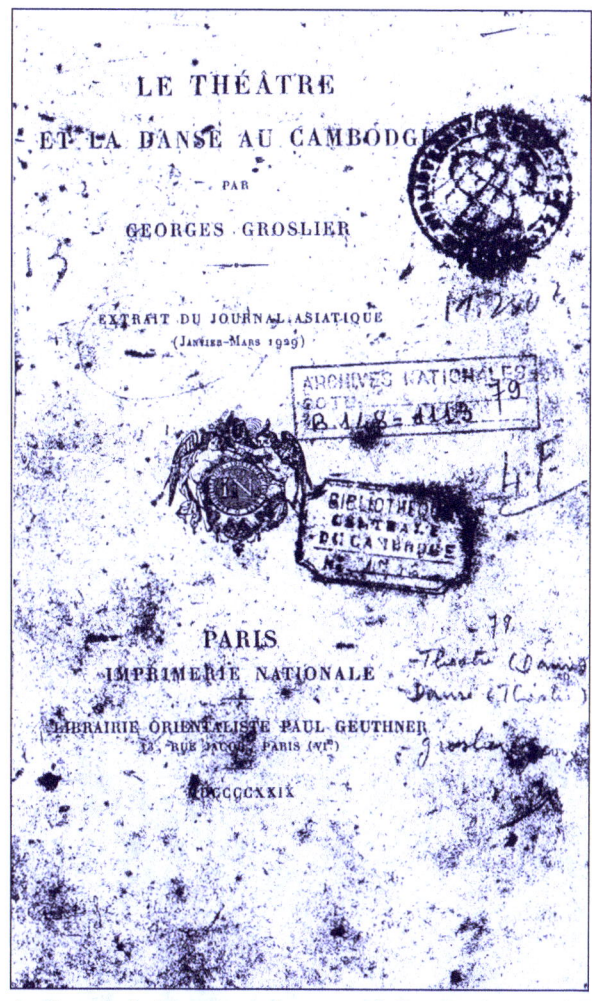

A photo of the original copy of Groslier's article, found in the archives of the Bibliothèque Nationale de Phnom Penh thanks to the help of Head Librarian Khlot Vibolla and Jade Furness.

The slides used to illustrate this conference were drawn from photographs collected by the Direction des Arts Cambodgiens. The film was shot by technicians from the Pathé company and graciously loaned by the Agence Économique de l'Indochine.

The Ouled Nail Dancers

In 1913, tales of Algeria's Ouled Nail dancers were well-known to Groslier's educated French audience. These notes will help modern readers better understand why Groslier contrasted the refined style of Cambodian dancers with the "ignoble writhing" of the Ouled Nail dancers on page 27 of his book.

Named for the Ouled Nail mountain range where they originated, Berber women from this tribe learned to dance at a very young age. At puberty, tribal customs allowed the girls to leave the hills to work independently in oasis towns as dancers. While some accounts characterize them as prostitutes this may have been a later development resulting from the degeneration of their craft under French Colonial rule.

Researcher Lawrence Morgan, who spent a year living in the oasis of Bou Saada to study them in the 1950's, wrote that they were first and foremost entertainers. Love affairs, or material gains they may have realized from such relationships, were secondary to their true profession.

Ouled Nail costumes were always magnificent. They adorned their faces with heavy jewelry and tattoos, framing them with oiled braids of hair, looped and held in place by large rings. Their eyes were heavily darkened with kohl and they went unveiled, even when most North African women covered their faces. Their costumes had a profusion of jewelry, earrings and necklaces, sometimes featuring huge bracelets with spikes and studs that they used to defend themselves.

On witnessing the Ouled Nail in the early 1900's, American dancer Ted Shawn commented:

> "It is not a suggestive dance for the simple reason that it leaves nothing to the imagination, and because of this unashamed animality, revolts the average white tourist to the point of being unable to admire the phenomenal mastery which these women have of parts of the body over which we have no voluntary control at all."

The women gathered wealth plying their trade, sewing coins into their voluminous skirts or making them into necklaces and headdresses. As their wealth grew they would one day decide to return to their homes to marry. The quality of husband one could afford depended on the dowry saved in their working years. After marriage, Ouled Nail dancers reputedly settled down to become good wives and mothers.

Appendix III

The Future of Cambodia's Royal Dance Tradition

Dr. Paul Cravath interview with Princess Buppha Devi

On January 26, 2010, Her Royal Highness Princess Buppha Devi made her first official visit to the NKFC Conservatoire Preah Ream Buppha Devi within the Angkor Heritage Park at Banteay Srey. Her visit commemorated the third anniversary of this school of traditional Cambodian dance and music, established by the Nginn Karet Foundation under her Royal Patronage. The following written queries were submitted to H.R.H. at that time. During that visit, and upon her return to Phnom Penh, Princess Buppha Devi researched and recorded her answers with the assistance of her daughter Princess Norodom Sisowath.

Photo courtesy Anders Giras

Her Royal Highness Princess Buppha Devi is the Royal Heir and Guardian of Cambodia's ancient royal dance tradition, a legacy passed from generation to generation since the dawn of the Khmer civilization in Southeast Asia.

The Princess, whose name means "Goddess of Flowers," began studying the art of Cambodian dance as a child under the guidance of her grandmother, Queen Sisowath Kossamak. By age 15, she had become a leading dancer in the Cambodian Royal Ballet. At age 18, the Princess was granted the title of *prima ballerina* and toured the world as the troupe's principal dancer.

For the Cambodian people, royal dance rituals create a spiritual link between heaven and earth. Since ancient times, the nation's classical dancers have performed to honor Khmer gods and ancestors, and to bring blessings and prosperity onto the land. Under the direction of Her Majesty Queen Kossamak, the Princess helped make these performances more visible to the people of Cambodia and the world.

Working with her brother, His Majesty King Sihamoni, the Princess secured UNESCO's recognition for the Royal Ballet of Cambodia as part of the Intangible Cultural Heritage of Humanity in 2003. The Princess has also served Cambodia as Minister of Culture and Fine Arts and as a Senator.

Dr. Paul Cravath is a scholar, actor and theatrical director with extensive Asian theater research experience. He is the tenured Professor of Theatre at the University of Hawaii-LLC in Honolulu.

In 1975, Cravath traveled to Cambodia to become one of the only Westerners in history to be given full documentary access to the teachers, dancers, archives and theater of the Royal Cambodian Ballet. Following his primary research, Cravath returned to the US for ten years of research before submitting his doctoral thesis entitled *Earth in Flower*.

In 2008, **DatAsia Press** published his thesis in book form as *Earth in Flower: The Divine Mystery of the Cambodian Dance Drama*. The book is dedicated to H.R.H. Princess Buppha Devi for her lifetime commitment to preserving and perpetuating the sacred dance tradition of Cambodia.

In 2008, *Earth in Flower* was awarded the **Kirayama Prize Award for Notable Book** and the **Nautilus Silver Award for a Multicultural Book**.

Your Highness, it is again an honor to discuss Cambodian dance with you. In the West, dance is seen as a performance art. How is the royal tradition of Cambodian dance different?

Thank you, it is again my pleasure to share our cultural heritage with you.

To best make this distinction, I will first note that Cambodian dance is divided into three broad styles of dance: Vernacular, Folk and Classical, the latter being the Royal tradition that we will speak of today.

As in the West, our most visible dances are vernacular dances that people enjoy at social occasions. These include the *ram vong*, also a popular dance in Thailand and Laos, and the *ram saravan*. One social dance, the *ram kbach*, is actually inspired by the distinctive gestures of classical royal dance.

Next are Khmer folk dances that tell stories of ancient legends and everyday life. Like performance arts in the West these are to entertain public audiences. Folk dancing gestures and movements are not strictly defined, as in Khmer classical dance, so individual dancers and troupes make their own innovations. Folk dancing preserves the traditions of hill tribes, farmers, Chams, peasants and all Cambodian ethnicities.

Finally we have the *Robam Preah Reachea Trop*, which means "Dances of Royal Wealth." This is what we term Classical Dance, a sacred art that your book, *Earth in Flower*, traces to the beginnings of the Khmer civilization. In earlier times, dancers were part of the Royal Court, performing on behalf of our kings and queens to pray to our gods, divinities and spirits of royal ancestors.

In this role, our royal dancers act as divine messengers, linking the forces of heaven and Earth for our kings and our people. This art of sacred dance preserves a spiritual legacy carefully passed down to us by generations of our ancestors in an unbroken chain reaching back to our roots in the Angkor period. It is a complex and precise art. While some say it has 4,000 gestures to express different emotions and meanings, I do not know if this number can ever be accurately counted. Sacred dance is a living tradition that evolves from generation to generation.

How is dance important to the future of Cambodia?

Our harmonizing sacred dances are as important today as they were in the past. With correct training and technique, our dance rituals bring blessings to our King, harmony to the governance of our land and prosperity to our people. The dancers accomplish this by embodying the essence of purity and strength of our Khmer race.

We believe that this art empowers them to earn these blessings. Their grace and ancient choreography actually balance the universe, bringing us into harmony with the powers of nature, ensuring fertility, health and abundance for our land and people. Royal dance contains the essence of our spiritual traditions and can truly shape a positive future for our land and people.

How did you personally become involved in the Royal dance tradition?

In the late 1950s, my August Grandmother, the late Queen Kossomak Nearireath, introduced me to dance as a child. Her dream, which she realized within her lifetime, was to share the dignity and beauty of our Royal dances with the public.

Through her efforts, royal dance became a celebrated icon of Khmer culture, now recognized throughout the world. My brother, his Majesty Norodom Sihamoni, was previously Cambodia's Ambassador to UNESCO. Together, we worked to bring Grandmother's vision of sharing our dance with the world to a new level. In 2003, UNESCO recognized the *Royal Ballet of Cambodia* as a Masterpiece of the Oral and Intangible Heritage of Humanity.

During the darkest days of Cambodian history, notably the 15th and 20th centuries, royal dance came close to extinction yet the tradition somehow survives. How is this possible?

As long as there is a Khmer race, our dance will survive. We guard our tradition with our lives and pass the knowledge directly from teacher to student. This tradition is in our blood and, I believe, it flows from the Khmer land beneath our feet. The power of dance surrounds us in nature. I believe this power can energize us. I see it today in young students here at the Conservatoire who are studying this ancient art.

Seeing this tradition blossoming here in these children born by the temples of Angkor fills me with great joy. They come from such simple backgrounds but I see the power of our ancestors and our royal tradition in them. They are living answers to your question of how our tradition continues.

Your grandmother Queen Kossamak was devoted to the royal dance tradition. How did She confer responsibility to you?

My royal bloodline made this my duty, but the responsibility was granted by divine transmission. With Grandmother's guidance, I dedicated my life to this art from a very young age. I see a young dancer here today, barely four years old, and she brings back memories of my earliest days. I did not understand the power of our dance then, but I knew I wanted to learn, and that my efforts made my August Grandmother proud.

Her Majesty was quite strict with me. I practiced for more than ten years before gaining important roles. Finally, at eighteen, she rewarded my efforts by appointing me a *Prima Ballerina* in the troupe. In that role I danced throughout the world sharing our Cambodian culture and good will.

But the true transmission of responsibility for our tradition occurred in 1962, in the royal throne room of the palace. That was the first time I performed our most sacred dance, the

Robam Tiyae Boung Soun, before the eyes of Her Majesty Queen Kossamak and the court, before the eyes of my ancestors and before the Spirit of the Dance. Your country also played an interesting role in that event.

The prior year, 1961, the United States Information Service approached My August Grandmother requesting permission to film the Royal Cambodian Ballet. In her spirit of cooperation She granted the privilege and, in fact, they filmed my sacred ritual when I assumed the role to guard this tradition.

Sadly, relations between our two countries weakened shortly after that. The film vanished into American archives for many years. But it returned to Cambodia when your new US Ambassador Carol Rodley kindly presented a copy of the film to my brother, His Majesty King Sihamoni when she took her office in January 2009.

In 2006, you granted your first Royal Patronage to this single rural school in Banteay Srey district. Why?

Because this school, here in the Angkor Heritage Site, created an opportunity to revive our Royal Dance in a way unlike any other.

For more than ten years, I had watched the school's founder, Ravynn Karet-Coxen, working to restore suitable living conditions in Banteay Srey for more than 2,500 families. She chose this area because these families were among the last released from Khmer Rouge control and are some of the poorest in Cambodia. Her dedication and commitment to them never wavered and through her efforts, they began to have adequate healthcare, hygiene, and education for their children.

Still, there was something missing. In 2005, she came to me with a dream to empower these families by giving their children a chance to learn our noble arts of dance and music. She submitted a proposal for an arts school based on traditional Khmer values. It would be built here in Angkor, the cradle of our civilization, for children born of that land. She made this vision very real to me. I was convinced that she could achieve her goal so I entrusted her with my patronage and granted my name to the Conservatoire.

In the past, royal dance was an elite art, studied in palaces. Can you please compare that tradition to this simple school?

Royal dance is still an elite art. It will always be restricted to a small group of dedicated teachers and students. That has not changed. This is a serious school in that tradition.

Understand that Cambodia has dance classes all over but they are casual. Students attend as a hobby or to learn dance to entertain the public or tourists. At the Conservatoire there is great discipline and the children study in a private place. History tells us that this art can only be taught in a controlled place. In the past, royal dancers were sequestered from the world in the palace, protected from distractions and impure influences when learning their sacred art.

How does this school's rural location compare to a city location?

This school's rural location is a true innovation. This is a peaceful, powerful place between the temple of Banteay Srey and the sacred mountain of Phnom Dei, with the mountains of Kbal Spean and Phnom Koulen on the horizon. This environment offers only beauty, heritage, and no distractions to studying the art.

The benefit is that these children are not immersed in outside media and ideas. They are pure. They trust our ancestral traditions and focus on their craft. When they practice these arts, it is so natural for this power to flow through them.

It is especially appropriate at this time but it does make the school much more difficult to operate. The facilities are very simple. There is no electricity. Teachers and staff must travel nearly an hour to reach the school. But many benefits come from this isolation.

Despite the school's remote location, King Sihamoni was aware of this troupe and actually invited them to perform for him at the Royal Palace. How was this significant?

His Majesty King Sihamoni, himself an expert in dance, had heard of this rural troupe's dedication. He invited the Conservatoire students to give him a private presentation at the Chanchhaya Hall of Dance in the Royal Palace on February 28, 2009. This was truly an historic performance.

Construction of the Chanchhaya dance pavilion began in 1913. This hall, at the front of the palace, became the primary venue for all Royal dance performances. Except for the Khmer Rouge years, it has also been used continuously for many dance rehearsals. However, I believe the last performance for a King was before 1970. So it was a splendid occasion to have these children, from such humble origins, come to privately demonstrate their skills for His Majesty. In fact, their dance was a sacred rite of blessing for the king.

How did you know they were ready for this important presentation?

I have received progress reports since the beginning but it was only after they arrived in Phnom Penh that I learned how hard the children had been working. The day before the Chanchhaya appearance, I personally reviewed the troupe. They impressed me with their poise, discipline and dignity. Most of these children had never left their villages, let alone come to Phnom Penh for such a presentation.

I worked on the choreography with them and refined their movements. Their discipline and precision seemed well beyond their age and they quickly adapted to my corrections. They were ready to dance for our king.

As I mentioned, it was a private performance and I did not attend. But soon I heard that His Majesty was also captivated by their skill, synchrony and control of the precise movements of the dance. These rural children embodied the nobility of our tradition and were so calm and professional, even on their first palace visit to perform for their king!

At that point, they only had two years of training, which even surprised the king. I believe the Spirit of the Dance guided them to deliver an extraordinary performance. His Majesty later commented that the gods of *Preah Teneang Chanchhaya* appreciated the quality of their dance and blessed the children.

What motivates children to this level of excellence?

These children are inspired by the truth of who they are: children of Angkor. They were born to walk in the footsteps of our greatest ancestors. In Cambodia we believe that the spirits of our ancestors, we call them *Boramey*, watch over us to help our people. I believe that they now protect these children and our heritage.

This idea may not fit Western logic, but I see the synchrony and power of these country children with my own eyes. The power of our land and our ancestors flows through them. This is the only way I can explain their skill to you.

My understanding is that sacred dance performers must maintain high moral standards in their personal lives. How important is this?

The Spirit of Dance will only guide a dancer who is totally immersed in the teaching. They must embody the sanctity of the dance to be filled with the power of the gods, the ancestors of our land and the spirits of our kings. To perform truly sacred rituals requires total purity and discipline.

Family strength also helps maintain this purity. The rural environment that keeps these children so close to our land also keeps them close to their families. Traditional family values in Cambodia used to be very strong in the countryside. Families system gave strength and drew strength from the purity of their children. Both personal strength and family strength make this respectable vocation possible.

This troupe dresses in an entirely unique way for ritual performances. How does this fit with a royal tradition better known for lavish costumes of luxurious fabrics?

Perhaps the time has come to reconsider modern costume ideas. The style of Cambodian dance, especially the costumes, has been greatly influenced by Thailand since the 15th century. The elaborate costumes we see today evolved in recent times. In recapturing the sacred intent of our dances, the Conservatoire dancers must be seen as entirely different from those who perform merely for entertainment.

To accomplish this, the school's founder designs distinctive costumes that are only worn when dancers perform rituals respecting our spiritual traditions. For these sacred dances, she captures the essence of our Khmer spirit with simple white gowns. These reflect the purity and dignity of our traditions without distracting from the graceful dance movements. Also honoring ancient traditions are their hairstyles and adornments, which come from natural materials like leaves, flowers, vines, nuts and banana trunk peel. The idea of these gifts of nature is to link Mother Earth to Heaven.

The inspiration for these new costumes comes directly from our sacred women, the *devata* and *apsaras*, of Angkor Wat, the Bayon and all the other great temples of the classic period of Khmer history. Now our ancient mothers and sisters who are immortalized in stone may dance again through these children, just as Mr. George Groslier wrote in his book. In truth, these children actually *are* descended from the ancient women of the temples.

How do you feel about these dancers conducting sacred performances in Khmer temples?

I think our gods and ancestors have waited many generations to be shown this respect again. These dancers have the power to re-sanctify the temples.

While tourists come to appreciate the beauty of our architecture, it is still important for Khmer people to respect these sacred places for the sake of our ancestors who built them for us.

At the dawn of our history, sacred dancers celebrated, charmed and honored our Gods, keeping the heart of each temple pure and powerful. These dancers of Banteay Srey again give us the opportunity to show gratitude and respect to our ancestors and traditions.

What do you see in the future of these children and their school?

I have offered my ongoing guidance to the school. My August Grandmother left me with a wealth of knowledge about our dance tradition, but so little could be used with the tragedy of the past few decades. Based on the progress these children have made, I know that the time has come to share that knowledge.

My hope is that these children will master unique classical and traditional repertoires of dance and music so they have the opportunity to demonstrate our Cambodian arts around the world, as I did. For example, I know the school has started training an all-female traditional orchestra, an ancient tradition that will be a first in modern Cambodia. In addition to performance arts, I hope to see other traditional arts training so children can study crafts such as making masks, costumes, shadow puppets and musical instruments.

All these goals are in addition to all students achieving a baccalaureate level of general education with functional English language skills hopefully supplemented by French.

Thank you, Your Highness, for sharing your insights about Cambodia's royal dance and the children carrying this tradition into the future.

I thank you, Dr. Cravath, for your years of dedication and research compiling "*Earth in Flower.*" You, like the eminent Mr. George Groslier, have done a great service for the Cambodian people by documenting our largely unwritten dance tradition.

May the gods and our ancestors look favorably upon our efforts to promote harmony, abundance and peace in our world by perpetuating these sacred Khmer rites.

BIBLIOGRAPHY

In 1913, French scholars led the world in documenting and analyzing the Khmer civilization. Despite being only 26 years old, George Groslier's first academic title, *Danseuses Cambodgiennes*, still stands today as a significant contribution to that great body of knowledge.

Groslier's gift was perceiving this delicate art through the eyes of an artist. By his skilled hand, we have detailed images of Cambodian dancers as they appeared in that era. In his passionate words, we have the first methodical attempt to understand the origin and meaning of the sacred dancers and their rituals that reside at the heart of Cambodia's Khmer heritage.

A formal bibliography was not included, but the author did cite a number of sources, highlighted below with **<u>bold underline</u>**. As an aid to readers, and with great regard for these early works, the editor compiled this expanded bibliography of primarily French language references *in print* when Groslier researched his topic. Physical descriptions and publication formats are provided, when available, to help scholars identify original editions.

<u>Selected Pre-1913 Books and Articles about Cambodia</u>

Source: OCLC, WorldCat

Adams, W. H. Davenport. *In the Far East: A Narrative of Exploration and Adventure in Cochin-China, Cambodia, Laos and Siam.* Book 208, [8] p.: ill.; 17 cm. London: T. Nelson and Sons, 1879.

Agostini, Jules. *Au Cambodge.* Book 32 p. illus. 22 cm. Paris: Plon, Nourrit, 1898.

<u>Aymonier, Etienne</u>. *Le Cambodge.* Book 3 vols., 818 p., front., illus. (incl. facsims.) maps, plans. 28 cm. Paris: E. Leroux, 1900.

—. *Cours de Cambodgien.* Saigon, 1875.

—. *Dictionnaire franco-cambodgien.* Saigon, 1874.

—. *Dictionnaire khmer-français.* Saigon, 1878.

—. *Excursion dans le Cambodge central.* Book 655-663 p.; 23 cm. Paris: s.n, 1880.

—. *Géographie du Cambodge*. Book, 69 p., l fold. map. 25 cm. Paris: E. Leroux, 1876.

—. *Histoire de l'ancien Cambodge*. Book [4], 198, [2] p. Strasbourg: Imprimerie du Nouveau journal de Strasbourg, date unknown.

—. *Le Cambodge et ses monuments: la province de Ba Phnom*. Paris: Imprimerie Nationale, 1897.

—. *Notice sur le Cambodge*. Book, 67 p., 1 pl. 25 cm. Paris: E. Leroux, 1875.

—. *Quelques notions sur les inscriptions en vieux Khmêr*. Book 95 p.; 22 cm. Paris: Imprimerie Nationale, 1883.

—. *Recherches et mélanges sur les Chams et les Khmers*. Saigon: Imprimerie du gouvernement, 1881.

—. *Texte khmers; Première série*. Saigon, 1878.

Aymonier, E., and George Cœdès. *Index alphabétique pour "Le Cambodge" de M. Aymonier*. 1911.

Aymonier, E., and Saveros Pou. *Notes sur les coutumes et croyances superstitieuses des combodgiens*. Bibliothèque khmère, v. 3. Paris: Centre de documentation et de recherche sur la civilisation khmère, NOTE - This collection of original papers was published in 1984.

Barth, Auguste. *Inscriptions sanscrites du Cambodge*. Paris: Imprimerie nationale, 1885.

—.. *Inscriptions sanscrites de Campā et du Cambodge: [45] planches*. Paris: Imprimerie Nationale, 1883.

—. *L'inscription sanscrite de Han Chey*. Paris: Impr. Nationale, 1883.

Barth, Auguste, and **Abel Bergaigne**. *Inscriptions sanscrites du Cambodge et de Campā*. Paris: Imprimerie nationale, 1885.

Barthélemy, Pierre François Sauvaire. *En Indo-Chine, 1894-1895; Cambodge, Cochinchine, Loas, Siam méridional*. Book ii, 248 p. plates, maps. 19 cm. Paris: E. Plon, Nourrit, 1899.

Bergaigne, Abel, and **E. Aymonier**. Book 56 p. ; 22 cm. *Les inscriptions sanscrites du Cambodge: examen sommaire d'un envoi de M. Aymonier par M. Barth, Bregaigne et Senart : rapport à M. le président de la Société asiatique*. Paris: Impr. nationale, 1882.

—. *Une nouvelle inscription du Cambodge*. Paris: Imprimerie nationale, 1882.

Beylié, Léon Marie Eugène de. *L'architecture hindoue en Extrême-Orient*. Book 416 p. illus. 28 cm. Paris: E. Leroux, 1907.

Bouillevaux, C. E. *L'Annam et le Cambodge; voyages et notices historiques*. Book 2 p. l., 544 p. map. Paris: Victor Palmé, 1874.

Bouinais, Albert Marie Aristide, and A. Paulus. *Le royaume du Cambodge*. Book 76 p.; 25 cm. Paris: Berger-Levrault, 1884.

—. *L'Indo-Chine française contemporaine; Cochinchine*. Book 2 v. fronts., plates, fold. maps, fold. tables. 25 cm. Paris: Challamel, aîné, 1885.

Bouinais, A., Claudius Madrolle, and Aegineta Paulus. *Connaissance du Cambodge*. Book 145, [34] p. : ill., map ; 21 cm. Paris: Librairie Maritime et Coloniale, 1885.

Boulangier, Edgar. *Un hiver au Cambodge; chasses au tigre, à l'éléphant et au buffle sauvage; souvenirs d'une mission officielle remplie en 1880-1881*. 400 p. illus., maps, plates. 30 cm. Tours: A. Mame et fils, 1887.

Bowring, Sir John. *The Kingdom and People of Siam: with a Narrative of the mission to that country in 1855*. Book 2 v. plates (part col.), fold. map, fold. facsim., ports. 23 cm. London: J. W. Parker, 1857.

Branda, Paul. *Ça et la: Cochinchine et Cambodge, l'ame Khmère, Ang-Kor*. See Paul Émile Marie Réveillière.

Brébion, Antoine. *Livre d'or du Cambodge, de la Cochinchine et de l'Annam: 1626-1910*. Book 79 p. ; In-8. Saïgon: Schneider, 1910.

Brossard, P. *Colonies françaises: Asie*. Paris: E. Flammarion, n.d.; ca. 1905.

Carpeaux, Charles. *Les ruines d'Angkor: de Duong-Duong et de My-Son (Cambodge et Annam)*. Book 5 leaves, 258 p. : ill., plates, port. ; 26 cm. Paris: Augustin Challamel, 1908.

Chen-la t'u chi = Mémoires sur les coutumes du Cambodge. Hanoi: Impr. F.-H Schneider, 1901.

Cœdès, George. *Documents sur la dynastie de Sukhodaya*. S.l: s.n., 1900(?).

—. *Études cambodgiennes*. [Pt.] vii-xvi. Hanoi: Imp. d'Extrême-Orient, 1913.

—. *Inventaire des inscriptions du Champa et du Cambodge*. Bulletin de l'Ecole Française d'Extrême-Orient. Hanoi [etc.]: Imprimerie d'extrême-orient, 1908.

—. *La stèle de Ta-prohm*. Hanoi: F.-H. Schneider, 1907.

—. *La stèle de Tép Praṇam (Cambodge)*. Paris: Imprimerie nationale, 1908.

—. *Les bas-reliefs d'Angkor-vat*. E. Leroux, editeur. Paris: Imprimerie national, 1911.

—. *L'inscription de Bàksĕi Čamkròn avec une note de M.A. Barth sur la date de cette inscription*. 1909,

—. *Note sur l'apothéose au Cambodge*. Paris: Ernest Leroux, 1911.

—. *Prachum silāčhāruk*. [Bangkok]: Mōm Čhao Piyarangsit, 1900(?).

—. *Tablettes votives bouddhiques du Siam*. 1911.

—. *Textes d'auteurs grecs et latins relatifs à l'Extrême Orient depuis le IVe siècle av. J.-C. jusqu'au XIVe siècle*. Paris: E. Leroux, 1910.

Croizier, Edme Casimir de. *L'art khmer. Étude historique sur les monuments de l'ancien Cambodge, avec un aperçu général su l'architecture khmer et une liste complète des monuments explorés, suivi d'un Catalogue raisonné du Musée khmer de Compiègne*. Book 142 p. front. (port.) illus., fold. map. 23 cm. Paris: E. Leroux, 1875.

—. *Les explorateurs du Cambodge*. 1878.

—. *Les monuments de l'ancien Cambodge classés par provinces*. Book [1 v.] 16 cm. 1878.

De Bellouène, ?. This source that earned Parmentier's complaint remains unidentified. WorldCat, Google, Voila.fr, Nomade.fr and Cuil failed to produce a single reference for the name, or its components.

Delaporte. Louis. *Voyage au Cambodge: L'architecture Khmer*. Book 462 p. incl. front., illus., plates (part mounted, part double) map, plans (part double) 28 cm. Paris: C. Delagrave, 1880.

Dieulefils, P. *Indo-Chine Pittoresque & Monumentale, Ruines D'Angkor Cambodge = Indo-China Picturesque and Monumental Ruins of Angkor (Cambodge) = Indo-China Malerisch Und Monumentalisch Ruinen Von Angkor Cambodge*. Book 67 plates, each with descriptive letterpress: ill. ; 28 x 36 cm. Hanoi: P. Dieulefils, Photo Publisher, 1907. *See also See also* Finot.

Donnet, Gaston. *En Indo-Chine: Cochinchine, Cambodge, Annam, Tonkin*. Book 319 p.: ill.; 33 cm. Paris: Société française d'éditions d'art, 1900s.

Dufour, Henri, **Charles Carpeaux**, and J. Cammaille. *Le Bayon d'Angkor Thom. Bas-reliefs: d'après les documents recueillis par la mission Henri Dufour*. Book 135 plates. (i.e. 234) 39 x 29 cm. Paris: E. Leroux, 1910.

Filoz, Auguste Achille Hippolyte. *Cambodge et Siam voyage et séjour aux ruines des monuments Kmers*. Book 190 p. 19 cm. Thonon: A. Dubouloz, 1876.

Filoz, Noé. *Cambodge et Siam; voyage & séjour aux ruines des monuments Kmers*. Book vi p., 1 l., 167 p. illus. 23 cm. Paris: Gedalge jeune, 1896.

Finot, Louis. *Nouvelles inscriptions du Cambodge*. S.l: s.n, 1900.

—. *Indo-Chine, Pittoresque & Monumentale: Ruines D'Angkor, Cambodge = Indo-China, Picturesque and Monumental : Ruines of Angkor, Cambodge = Indo-China, Malerisch Und Monumetalisch : Ruinen Von Angkor, Cambodge*. Hanoi: P. Dieulefils, 1909. *See also* Dieulefils.

Fournereau, Lucien. *Les ruines khmères, Cambodge et Siam: documents complémentaires d'architecture, de sculpture et de céramique*. Book [10] p., 110 plates: ill. ; 40 cm. Paris: Berthaud Frères, 1890.

—. *Le Siam ancien, archéologie - épigraphie - géographie*. Annales du Musée Guimet, t. 27, 31. Paris: E. Leroux, 1895.

Fournereau, Lucien, and Jacques Porcher. *Les ruines d'Angkor; etude artistique et historique sur les monuments khmers du Cambodge siamois*. Book viii, 206 p. illus., 100 plates, map. 40 cm. Paris: E. Leroux, 1890.

Feer, Léon (1830-1902). *Avadāna-Çataka : cent légendes (bouddhiques)*. Translated from Sanskrit. Paris: Leroux, 1891. Book, XXXVIII, 496 p., (Annales du Musée Guimet; 18).

Gallois, Eugène. *La France d'Asie. Un Français en Indo-Chine. Siam - Cochinchine - Cambodge - Laos - Tonkin - Annam*. Book [269] p. 19 cm. Paris: J. André, 1900.

Garnier, Francis. *Note sur l'exploration du cours du Cambodge par une commission scientifique Française*. Paris: E. Martinet, 1869.

—. *Chronique royale du Cambodge*. Book 336-386, 112-144 p. map. 23 cm. Paris: Impr. nationale, 1871.

Gervais-Courtellement, Jules, and Augustin Challamel. *Empire colonial de la France: l'Indo-Chine: Cochinchine, Cambodge, Laos, Annam, Tonkin*. Collection Courtellemont. Book xv, 195 p.: ill., col. map; 33 cm. Paris: Firmin-Didot, 1901.

Hamy, E. T. *Coup d'oeil sur l'anthropologie du Cambodge rapport présenté da la Société d'anthropologie dans la séance du 7 septembre 1871*. 26 p. 22 cm. Paris: A. Hennuyer, 1871.

Harry, Myriam. *L'Indo-Chine*. Vincennes: Les Arts graphiques, 1912.

Henrique, Louis. *Les colonies françaises; notices illustrées*. Vol. III. *Colonies et protectorats d'Indo-Chine: Cochinchine. Cambodge. Annam. Tonkin*. 19 cm. Paris: Quantin, 1889.

Henry, Lucien. *Promenade au Cambodge et au Laos*. Paris: P. Ollendorf, 1894.

Herz, Martin Florian. *A Short History of Cambodia from the Days of Angkor to the Present*. Book 141 p. illus. 22 cm. New York: F.A. Praeger, 1900.

Intronisation de S. M. L'Obbarach, Roi du Cambodge, successeur de S. M. Norodom 1er: allocutions et documents officiels. Phnom-Penh: Imprimerie du protectorat, République française, Protectorat du Cambodge, 1904.

Julien, Félix. *Doudart de Lagrée au Cambodge et en Indo-Chine*. Book 221 p.: port., folded map; 19 cm. Paris: Challamel Aîné, 1886 (2nd edition).

Lagrillière-Beauclerc, Eugène. *Au Cambodge et en Annam: voyage pittoresque*. Book 153 p.: ill.; 26 cm. Paris: Albin Michel, 1900s.

Leclère, Adhémard. *Cambodge; contes, légendes & jatakas*. Book : Fiction 106 p. 25 cm. Niort: Impr. G. Clouzot, 1912.

—. *Cambodge. La crémation et les rites funéraires*. Book 2 p. l., iv, 154 p., 1 l. 10 pl., 2 plans. 4to. Hanoi: F.-H. Schneider, 1908.

—. *Cambodge; le roi, la famille royale et les femmes du palais*. Book 26 p., 1 l. 26 cm. Saigon: Imprimerie-Librairie Claude & Cie, 1905.

—. *Le buddhisme au Cambodge*. Book xxxi, 535 p. front., illus., plates. 26 cm. Paris: E. Leroux, 1899.

—. *Les livres sacrés du Cambodge. Première partie*. Book 340 p. 25 cm. Paris: Ernest Leroux, 1906.

—. *Le théâtre cambodgien*. Book [1], 26 p. illus., 4 pl. 28.5 cm. Paris: Ernest Leroux, 1911.

Leclère, Adhémard, and **Léon Feer**. *Cambodge. Contes et légendes*. Book xxii, 308 p. 22 cm. Paris: Librairie Émile Bouillon, 1895.

Lemire, Marie Charles Désiré. *Cochinchine française, royaume de Cambodge, royaume d'Annam, et Tonkin*. Book, 3rd edition, 414, viii, p., [2] leaves of plates : ill., maps (2 folded) ; 25 cm. Paris: Challamel ainé, 1884.

Loti, Pierre. *Siam*. Book xi, 182 p. : ill. ; 23 cm. London: T.W. Laurie, 1900.

—. *Un pèlerin d'Angkor*. Paris: Calmann-Levy, 1912.

Louvet, Simone Lévêque. *Le royaume de Cambodge*. Book 2 v. illus., map. Paris: E. Leroux, 1883.

Lunet de Lajonquière, E. *Atlas archéologique de l'Indo-Chine. Monuments du Champa et du Cambodge*. Book 24 p. incl. tables. 5 double maps. 67 x 38 cm. Paris: Imprimerie nationale, E. Leroux, éditeur, 1901.

—. *Inventaire descriptif des monuments du Cambodge*. Book 3 v. illus., fold. plates, plans (part fold.) and atlas of 2 fold. maps. 28 cm. Paris: E. Leroux, 1902.

Maître, Henri. *Les jungles moï; exploration et histoire des hinterlands moï du Cambodge, de la Cochinchine, de l'Annam et du bas Laos*. Book iv, 578 p. 197 illus. 28 cm. Paris: E. Larose, 1912.

Marchal, Henri. *Angkor. La résurrection de l'art khmer et l'œuvre de l'École française d'Extrême-Orient*. Book 32 p. illus. 21 cm. Paris: Office Français d'Édition, 1900.

Maspero, Georges. *L'empire Khmèr: histoire et documents*. Book 115, [29] p.; 33 cm. Phnom-Penh: Imprimerie du Protectorat, 1904.

—. *Tableau chronologique des souverains de l'Annam*. Leide: E.J. Brill, 1894.

Meyer, Roland. *Cours de cambodgien*. Phnom-Penh: Impr. nouvelle Albert Portail, 1912.

Meyniard, Charles. *Le second empire en Indo-Chine (Siam-Cambodge-Annam)*. Book xviii, 508 p. illus., port., maps, facsims. 25 cm. Paris: Société d'éditions scientifiques, 1891.

Monod, G.H. *Légendes cambodgiennes: que m'a contées le Gouverneur Khieu*. Manuscript, 352 p. 1906.

Morand, Charles. *Notes et images pour mieux faire connaître les monuments et les arts des anciennes civilizations du Cambodge et du Laos: villa de la Valérane, Carqueiranne (Var)*. S.l: s.n.], 1907.

Mouhot, Henri. *Travels in the Central Parts of Indo-China (Siam), Cambodia, and Laos, During the Years 1858, 1859 and 1860*. Book 2 vol. (303, 301 s.): ill., kartor. London: John Murray, 1864.

—. *Voyage dans les royaumes de Siam, de Cambodge, de Laos et autres parties centrales de L'Indo-Chine*. Book, viii, 335 p., [28] leaves of plates: ill., map (fold.), ports ; 23 cm. Paris: Librairie Hachette, 1868.

Moura, J. *Le royaume du Cambodge*. [Author's true name was Simone Lévêque Louvet] Book 2 v. illus. (incl. ports., facsim.) 2 pl. (1 double) fold. map, 3 fold. plans. 29 cm. Paris: Ernest Leroux, 1883.

Nicolas, Pierre. *Notices sur l'Indo-Chine, Cochinchine, Cambodge, Annam, Tonkin, Laos, Kouang-Tchéon-Quan, publiées à l'occasion de l'Exposition universelle de 1900. Exposition universelle de 1900*. Book 2 p.l., [13]-25, [3]-320 p. incl. illus.,ports., col. plates, fold. map. 23 cm. Paris: Colonies et pays de protectorats, 1900.

Noir, Louis. *Les Français au Siam et au Cambodge: le conflit anglo-français à Bang-Kok*. Paris: A. Fayard et fils, 1894.

Noulet, Jean Baptiste. *L'âge de la pierre polie & du bronze au Cambodge, d'après les découvertes de M.J. Moura*. Book 33 p. pl. h.t. 32 cm. Toulouse: E. Privat, 1879.

Pavie, Auguste. *Recherches sur la littérature du Cambodge, du Laos et du Siam*. Book 2 p. l. xlvi p., 367 p., 1 l. illus., pl., maps. 29 cm. Paris: E. Leroux, 1898.

—. *Exposé des travaux de la mission*. Book 2 v. illus. (incl. ports., maps) XIV maps (part double) 28 cm. Paris: E. Leroux, 1901.

—. *Mission Pavie Indo-Chine: 1879-1895. Geographie et voyages*. Book v. : ill. ; 28 cm. Paris: E. Leroux, 1901.

Pavie, Auguste, and M. Schmitt. *Recherches sur l'histoire du Cambodge, du Laos et du Siam*. Book [V], XLV, 494 p. : ill. ; in-8. Paris: Leroux, 1898.

—. *Contes populaires du Cambodge, du Laos et du Siam*. Paris: E. Leroux, 1903.

—. *Recherches sur la littérature du Cambodge, du Laos et du Siam*. Book 2 p. l. xlvi p., 367 p., 1 l. illus., pl., maps. 29 cm. Paris: E. Leroux, 1898.

Petit, Maxime. *Les colonies francaises; petite encyclopédie coloniale publiée sous la direction de M. Maxime Petit*. Paris: Librairie Larousse, 1902.

Programme des fêtes du couronnement de S.M. Prèa Bat Samdach Prèa Sisowath roi du Cambodge. Paris: Imprimerie Nationale, 1906.

Réveillière, Paul Émile Marie. *Ça et la Cochinchine et Cambodge; L'ame khmère; Ang-Kor*. Book 451 p. 19 cm. Paris: Fischbacher, 1886.

Salaun, Louis. *Indochine*. Paris: Imprimerie National, 1903.

Testoin, Édouard. *Le Cambodge, passé, présent, avenir*. Book 191 p. fold. map. 26 cm. Tours: Impr. E. Mazereau, 1886.

Thalasso, Adolphe. *Anthologie de l'amour asiatique*. Book 377 p. ; 18 cm. Paris: Société du Mercure de France, 1907.

Thiounn, S. E. *Les fêtes anniversaires de la naissance de sa majesté le roi du Cambodge*. Paris: Augustin Challamel, 1906.

Thouvenot, Maurice. *Une idylle au pays Khmer; roman de moeurs cambodgiennes*. Book 273 p. 19 cm. Paris: Jouve & Cie, 1913.

Tissandier, Albert. *Cambodge et Java: ruines khmères et javanaises 1893-1894*. Book vi, 160 p., [25] leaves of plates: ill., map, plans; 31 cm. Paris: G. Masson, 1896.

Vincent, Frank. *The Land of the White Elephant: Sights and Scenes in Southeastern Asia. A Personal Narrative of Travel and Adventure in Farther India, Embracing the Countries of Burma, Siam, Cambodia, and Cochin-China. (1871-2)*. New York: Harper & Bros, 1874.

Zhou, Daguan, and Paul Pelliot. *Mémoire sur les coutumes du Cambodge*. Book 1 v. (unpaged) 27 cm. 1902.

INDEX

Angkor Thom:
   garuda, 57, 153;
   accessories depicted, 128, 139, 142, 146;
   inscriptions, 124;
   women depicted, 130

Angkor Wat:
   accessories depicted, 139, 140, 142, 146, 150;
   bird-woman, 147;
   built in the image of Indra's heaven, 148-149;
   celestial dancers (*Apsara, Devata*), 118, 151;
   women depicted, 122, 123, 132

Anjali, 151. *See also* grand salute

Apsaras, 11, 116-118, 143, 146, 151. *See also Devata*

arm bending. *See* dancers

Asuras, 117

Aymonier, Étienne François, (1844-1929):
   analysis, 141, 146;
   translations, 120, 124, 139, 152

Bakou, 120, 146, 152

Barth, Auguste, (1834-1916). 124, 153

Bergaigne, Abel (1838-1888). 124, 144, 154

Bassac, 101, 124

Bayon:
   accessories depicted, 128, 135, 153, 154;
   women depicted, 143;
   worship depicted, 151, 152, 154

betel use, 12, 17, 36, 49, 76, 87, 98

bird-woman. *See* characters

Bosseba. *See* characters

Buddha, Buddhism, 21, 114, 125, 133, 150;
   offerings, 69

Butsomali. *See* characters

celestial dancers. *See Apsara* and *Devata*

Carpeaux, Charles, (1870-1904). 152

Cambodian:
   attitudes toward nudity, 127, 134, 145;
   clothing, 92;
   dance audiences, 11-12, 15-16;
   definition of beauty, 121;
   origin of dance, 130;
   songs, 100-101;
   understanding of traditions, 110

Ceylon. *See* Sri Lanka

Champa, 143, 144

characters:
   bird-woman, 7, 60, 66, 142, 147;
   Bosseba, 31, 36, 40, 43, 45, 52, 54;
   Butsomali, 45, 47;
   clowns, 60, 62, 136;
   Garuda, 45, 48, 57, 153;
   Hanuman, 57;
   King of the Giants, 45, 47;
   King of the Nagas, 125;

mermaid, 15, 60;
Ngo, 57;
prince, 52, 56, 60, 66, 117, 129;
princess, 10, 31, 36, 38, 44, 45, 52, 56, 66, 117;
white monkey, 7, 57

color use:
    by the day of the week, 86;
    clothing, 12, 37, 92. *See also* white

Colombo Museum. *See* Sri Lanka

commin. *See* scarf

costumes, 56, 58, 64, 66;
    ancient style, 116, 117, 121, 122, 125, 126, 129, 131, 134-6, 138, 145;
    color, 86;
    cost, 64, 69;
    European influence, 135, 138;
    Malayan influence, 60;
    male roles, 77;
    manufacture, 64;
    reuse and destruction of, 64;
    sewn closed, 18, 54;
    storage, 63. *See also* jewelry, crowns, make up, *sampot*, scarf

crowns, 60, 68, 81, 140;
    ancient, 118, 122, 135, 139, 140;
    cost, 69;
    male character tiara, 68;
    mokot, 68, 74, 135, 139;
    panntiereth, 69, 141;
    symbolizing Mt. Meru, 81;
    weight, 74. *See also* jewelry, costumes, make up

dance gestures: absolute principles, 32-33;
    ancient origins and representations of, 111, 154, 156, 157, 158;
    emotion expressed by, 41;
    flying (through aerial suspension), 10, 11, 44-45, 62, 151;
    grand salute, 38, 111, 114, 151, 156, 158;
    horseback riding, 47;
    improvisation, 40;
    offering (a flower), 112, 114, 118, 154, 156-157;
    precision of, 32, 33, 41;
    promenades, 40, 116;
    ritual poses, 10, 24, 31, 51, 107, 118, 134, 153;
    rowing a boat, 46;
    saluting the tiara, 81
    toes, 33, 151.

dancers (*lokhon*): ancient, 111, 114-115, 122, 127, 134, 138, 141, 152;
    apartment, 92-93;
    arm bending (*See* hyperextension);
    as actress or mime, 31, 41, 45, 50, 125;
    bathing, 95;
    chastity, 24, 44, 54, 110;
    daily life, 23, 98;
    decline of the, 106-107;
    early training, 21, 25, 110;
    hairstyles (ancient and modern), 141;
    hyperextension, 26-27, 150;
    marriage, 99;
    meals, 93;
    personality, 99, 110;
    practice and rehearsal, 25, 26, 33, 34, 80, 84, 96;
    punishment, 34, 63;
    retirement, 90, 103-104;
    salary, 33-34, 84, 89, 93;
    seclusion, 24;
    service to the king, 86, 87-88, 120;
    superstitions, 69;
    troupes, 24, 84

De Bellouène, 124

devadasi, 122, 124, 126-128, 132, 138, 145, 148;
    defloration ceremony, 124

Devas, 117

Dufour, Henri. 152

Enao. *See* Inao

European influence, 11, 106, 107

Feer, Léon, (1830-1902), 125, 143, 151

Finot, Louis (1864-1935), 108

flowers, 37, 95, 128, 129, 148-149, 154;
    bracelets, 17, 37, 73, 80, 122, 146;
    champa, 36, 80, 87, 98;
    lotus, 115, 116, 141, 149;
    offering, 44, 111, 112, 132, 136, 156;
    pattern, 7, 37, 64, 66, 86, 89, 113, 115, 122, 140

Fournereau, Lucien, (1846-1906). 147

Funan, 123

Garuda. *See* characters

gold. *See* jewelry

grand salute, 38, 111;
    ancient salute, 114, 151, 156;
    saluting the mokot, 81. *See also* Anjali

Hall of Dance, 10, 12, 14-15, 17-18, 58

Hanuman. *See* characters

harem, 21, 120, 125, 131, 136; eunuchs, 24

Hindu, 123-124, 127-129, 132, 136

Inao, 45, 60, 99

Indra, 106, 117, 127, 148

Indravarman, 120

Jayavarman, 120, 124

Java, 45, 60

jewelry: anklets, 73, 149;
    belts, 70, 116, 142, 143, 145-146, 149;
    bird decoration for favorite dancers, 69;
    bracelets, 37, 53, 73, 129, 80, 116, 128-129, 141, 143, 149;
    cost, 69, 74; diamonds, 17, 37, 38, 53, 68, 69-74, 139, 141;
    gold, 24, 36, 37, 38, 53, 60, 64, 66, 68-70, 73-74, 123, 133, 139, 142-143, 153-154;
    omen of gem detaching from, 69;
    pearls, 12, 66, 69, 73, 128, 129, 138, 140, 141, 142, 143;
    rings, 72, 141;
    sautoir, 37, 116, 122, 128;
    weight, 74

Kambuja, 123

King of Cambodia:
    Norodom, H.M., 11, 23, 34, 64, 84, 93, 136;
    royal box, 17;
    Sisowath, H.M., 23, 84, 93, 95, 139;
    personal items at dance, 17. *See also* Varmans

King of the Giants. *See* characters

King of the Nagas, *See* characters

Kiao-Tchin-Jou, 139

Khoun Tanh, Princess, 84

Khoun Prea Nieth, Princess, 84

Koh Ker, 120

Laos, 133

Lolei, 120, 152

lokhon. *See* dancers

Maignan, Albert, (1845-1908), 6

make-up, 76-77;
    ancient use of, 144;
    danger in using, 77;
    white paste, 51, 77-78, 81, 92, 144

Malaysia, 12, 135, 146

Man Soun, Princess, 84

masks, 56-57;
    difficulty wearing, 84, 102;
    occult powers of, 69

Maspero, Georges (1872-1942), 133

mermaid. *See* characters

moon, 11, 17-18, 51, 121, 123, 144

Mount Meru, 81

music, 14, 18, 32

musical instruments, 14;

ancient, 152;
harp, 152;
time-keeping sticks, 18, 32, 36, 80;
tom-tom, 14, 33, 123;
xylophone, 14, 152

musicians, 10, 84, 86, 87;
ancient, 117, 120, 124;
chorus, 10, 18, 31, 32, 84, 87, 110;
Khmer orchestra, 14, 18, 34, 152;
time-keepers, 32, 36, 80

Naga, *nagas*, 125, 152

nautchny, 126-128

Ngo. *See* characters

nymph. *See Apsara* and *Devata*

Préah Khan, 130

Préa Khet Méaléa, Prince, 148

Préah-Net-Préah, 120

premières danseuses, 24, 34, 84, 93

Ramayana, 7, 56, 60, 125, 138

Rmman, 120. *See also* dancers

Royal Palace, 21, 23-24, 34, 98, 104;
Hall of Dance, 10-12, 14, 15, 18, 31, 58;
King's bedroom, 86-88;
swimming pools, 84, 95;
women's quarters, 84, 92-93

Rulachak. *See* King of the Giants

salute. *See* grand salute

sampot, 11, 17, 34, 38, 53, 66, 78, 92, 107;
ancient, 117, 126, 135;
color choice, 86;
cost, 64;
manufacture, 64

sarong. See sampot

Sarraut, Albert Pierre (1872-1962). 8, 134

scarf, 37, 40, 45, 52, 60, 64, 66, 76, 78-79, 89, 90, 135, 138;
loaned for weddings, 107. See also *sampot*

Sea of Milk, 25, 51, 117

Séla, 45, 46

Siamese:
attitudes toward nudity, 134;
bird-woman, 147;
clothing and jewelry styles, 34, 92, 135, 139, 140;
dancers and instructors, 8, 136;
hairstyle (modern), 141;
invasion, 133;
musical influence, 14, 152;
preserving Khmer traditions, 134;
sampot, 11

Siva, Saivites, 120, 124, 128, 133, 141, 153

songs. *See* Cambodian songs

Sri Lanka, 130, 150;
Colombo Museum. 128, 129, 140, 145

stupa, 135

Suvarna Bhumi, 133

Ta Phrom, 141

Devata, 116, 118;
origin of, 108, 117, 126

Varmans, 127, 130, 153

Vishnu, 57, 115, 126, 127, 128, 141, 151

Wat Nokor, 130

white (significance of):
associated with the King, 17, 51;
clothing, 11, 12, 16, 64, 90, 135;
dancer's make-up, 51, 58, 77-78, 81, 92, 144;
as a desirable skin color, 21, 24, 36, 38, 40, 50, 51, 127, 144, 148. *See also* color use

Yasovarman, 124

Earth in Flower
The Divine Mystery of the Cambodian Dance Drama
by Paul Cravath
ISBN 978-1-934431-28-3

    The most comprehensive academic analysis of Southeast Asia's esoteric female performing art: the ancient Cambodian ballet.

    Since the dawn of recorded history, Khmer royalty nurtured a dance style unique to their Asian kingdom, yet instantly recognizable throughout the world. Spiritually, their graceful dancers embody the essence and strength of the Khmer race.

    Earth in Flower examines the art, culture, origin and spiritual relevance of this sacred dance tradition. A wartime twist of fate made Dr. Paul Cravath one of the only Westerners in history to gain full access to this formerly sequestered troupe of royal dancers, their archives, theater and teachers. In *Earth in Flower* he gives new insights into this beautiful art, its long-hidden mysteries, the dancers themselves, and how they balance the Khmer relationship between heaven and earth.

www.EarthInFlower.com

DatAsia

Daughters of Angkor Wat
Unlocking the Secrets of Asia's Ancient Khmer Goddesses
Edited by Kent Davis

ISBN 978-1-934431-17-7

Lost in the jungles of Southeast Asia for centuries, the Khmer temple of Angkor Wat is the largest religious structure ever built by humankind. Inside, it protects an extraordinary treasure unlike any on Earth: detailed portrait carvings of nearly 2,000 ancient women immortalized in stone.

Today, their identity and purpose remain a mystery. Were they wives of the king? Servants and dancers? Imaginary angels rendered by skilled sculptors? Or do these women represent a storehouse of knowledge beyond anything previously imagined?

Daughters of Angkor Wat begins unlocking their secrets with surprising theories, hundreds of original photos and insights from leading experts including: Paul Cravath, Kent Davis, Madeleine Giteau, George Groslier, Trudy Jacobsen, Julie Mehta, Peter Sharrock, Krishna Srivastava...and other enlightened observers.

www.Devata.org

DatAsia

In The Shadow of Angkor
Unknown Temples of Ancient Cambodia

ISBN 978-1-934431-90-0

On Friday June 6, 1913, the twenty-six year old French explorer George Groslier set out on a six-month journey through the jungles of Cambodia. Accompanied by only a handful of native helpers, his mission was to document remote temples built by the mysterious Khmer civilization that ruled Southeast Asia from the 9th to the 13th centuries.

Opening with a Foreword by historian Milton Osborne, this revised edition presents the first English translation of the dangers, discoveries and people the young man encountered on his adventure. Today, nearly a century later, many temples on his route — Preah Vihear, Wat Phu, Beng Melea and Banteay Chhmar — are still remote sites that are rarely visited. George's impressions, insights and experiences presented with classic and modern photographs of the sites will fascinate modern readers who, even today, seek answers in the ancient shrines of Cambodia.

www.DatAsia.us

DatAsia

Water and Light
Personal Glimpses of the Cambodian Mekong

ISBN 978-1-934431-87-0

"Phnom Penh, stretching out in the rising sun, appeared to me nearly submerged, like a narrow scarf gently wavering at my departure, the roofs of the Royal Palace and the spire of the Silver Pagoda, with their yellow and green tiles, glistening like sequins. And then, from hour to hour, the weather changed and each bend of the river was overcast by a different sky."

With an eye for detail, a rich understanding of Khmer culture and a deep love for Cambodia and her people, George Groslier penned this vibrant travel diary of rural life along the Mekong River in 1929.

In 1887, George became the first French child born in Cambodia. He went to Paris to train as a fine artist before returning to his birthplace to devote the rest of his life to reviving Cambodian art and culture. This new edition, with a Foreword by historian Milton Osborne, presents the first English translation of his rustic journey with all his original photographs.

www.DatAsia.us

DatAsia

Angkor The Magnificent
by Helen Churchill Candee
ISBN 978-1-934431-00-9

"Hidden in the jungles of Indochina, the vast city of Angkor lay in ruins for centuries, undreamed of. Now Angkor is becoming one of the talked of wonders of the world."

"All the fascination of discovering a lost city is in this delightful travel story; all the wonder, mystery and romance. The pages are steeped in the glowing beauty of the Orient. Author Helen Candee is an artist at heart, omitting nothing of the glamour and colorful beauty of Angkor."

"A novelty of lost civilization, for those who travel by steamer or from a comfortable chair by their hearth-fire."

1924 Edition Cover Description

This new volume presents Helen Candee's complete classic work, with 79 original photos and map, supplemented with the first biography of Ms. Candee by historian Randy Bryan Bigham, the author's original account of surviving the sinking of the RMS Titanic, personal photos, a bibliography and index.

www.AngkorSecrets.com

DatAsia

Song of Peace
A Poem to the Khmer People
By Makhali-Phal

ISBN 978-1-934431-77-1

A timeless poem of the mythical years…inspired by an ancient era of conquest and meditation, yet still capable of touching the great grandchildren of today's children. To be understood by them, and retained, and recited.

EDMOND JALOUX ❈ **The French Academy**

In 1898, Makhali-Phāl was born a Franco-Khmer child in Cambodia, with her very blood blending the wisdom of two diverse cultures. As an author and poet, she devoted her life to expressing the conflict, harmony and hope inherent in the powerful forces of East and West that lived within her body and mind.

Song of Peace is the author's ultimate literary bequest to her people with a clear message of purpose and enlightenment for our materialistic modern world. Her Majesty The Queen Mother Norodom Monineath Sihanouk introduces this special first edition presenting this monumental poem in French and English. Khmer and Thai language editions are now in preparation.

www.Makhali-Phal.org

DatAsia

In 2009, the Nginn-Karet Foundation established a unique school in Banteay Srey district to perpetuate the sacred Cambodian traditions of dance and music. In the heart of Angkor, the strength, discipline and dignity of Khmer heritage still enrich each child's life while maintaining this precious legacy.

Rural children who commit to the rigorous training participate at no cost to their families, thanks to generous sponsors who cover the modest costs for each student. A portion of the proceeds from every copy of *Cambodian Dancers* support this effort. We invite you to participate in this historic revival of ancient arts by sponsoring a young dancer or musician.

www.NKFC.org

NKFC CONSERVATOIRE
Preah Ream Buppha Devi
Chhouk Sar — Banteay Srey

www.ingramcontent.com/pod-product-compliance
Lightning Source LLC
Chambersburg PA
CBHW051359070526
44584CB00023B/3213